Balanced Literacy

Through Cooperative Learning & Active Engagement

by Sharon Skidmore
& Jill Graber

In consultation with Dr. Jacqueline Minor

Kagan

Kagan Publishing
981 Calle Amanecer
San Clemente, CA 92673
1 (800) 933-2667
www.KaganOnline.com

ISBN: 978-1-933445-08-3

Balanced Literacy
Kindergarten
Introduction

Do you remember when you learned to ride a bike? You watched the neighborhood kids zooming down the street on their bikes. You knew you wanted to join them. You watched and listened carefully as your parents demonstrated and explained how to start and stop. Getting on the bike was a little scary at first. However, training wheels, the reassurance of supporting hands, and encouraging words gave you the confidence needed to successfully practice your new skill. With each practice, your ability grew and parental support was gradually withdrawn. Your new skills soon allowed you to ride your bike independently and successfully as you zoomed down the street with your neighborhood friends.

Just as learning to ride a bike requires a series of supported steps, literacy requires guiding the learner through scaffolded instruction. The balanced literacy components provide the framework for developing deep thinkers and strategic readers. Balanced literacy increases teachers' effectiveness as they explicitly instruct through varying degrees of demonstration and practice, teacher feedback, and ongoing assessment.

[Effective teachers provide] just the right amount of support that allows the learner to assume increasing control of the task. It's a gentle dance that requires careful leading, following, and occasionally sidestepping. Gradually, as students become competent, we reduce the amount of support we offer. Intrinsic to this belief is allowing enough time, support, and feedback.

Regie Routman

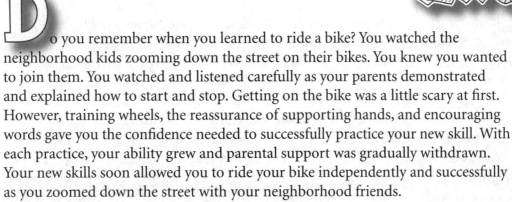

Kindergarten Book Organization

In this book we have provided lessons and activities to support the balanced literacy components of aloud, shared, guided, and independent practice to strengthen national standards in comprehension, word study (phonemic awareness and phonics), vocabulary, fluency, and writing. Research emphasizes that learners need to acquire skills in these areas to be proficient readers and writers. Activities appropriate for kindergarten students have been developed for each of the four sections in this book, incorporating Kagan Cooperative Learning Structures.

As educators ourselves, we understand the limited time teachers have to develop student materials to support the literacy outcomes for their particular grade level. One of our goals for this book was to develop teacher-friendly materials. Therefore, you will find blackline masters (cards, spinners, cubes, and mats) designed to support the activities in each section. These are located directly behind the direction page for each cooperative learning structure. You may want to consider copying these pages onto cardstock for durability. Blank templates have been included for some of the activities, giving you the flexibility to tailor activities to closely match specific literature or skills for your individual class.

The five national literacy standards of comprehension, word study (phonemic awareness and phonics), vocabulary, fluency, and writing are addressed in separate sections of this book, with the exception of vocabulary, which is included in both the Comprehension and Word Study sections.

Section 1: Comprehension

Section 2: Word Study (Phonemic Awareness and Phonics)

Section 3: Fluency

Section 4: Writing

Kindergarten
A Note to the Reader

T he ideas for this book are drawn from our combined experiences in the elementary classroom and as literacy coaches. As educators we are always striving to maximize learning and make every moment count as we endeavor to educate our students. It is our intention that this book will be a resource for you as you systematically think about literacy: What are the needs of my students? How can I best deliver instruction? What is the most effective use of instructional time?

When we combine balanced literacy and Kagan Cooperative Learning, our classroom practices become more purposeful and connected resulting in increased student performance. We hope that this book will be a guide as you strive to improve instruction and enhance student learning.

A special thanks to Dr. Jacqueline Minor, our former Assistant Superintendent of Curriculum and Instruction and the present Director of Curriculum and Instruction for Kagan Professional Development, whose vision and knowledge continues to challenge us professionally. It has been with her involved guidance and encouragement that the ideas for the lessons and activities were organized for this book. Because of Jackie, this book has now become a reality.

Appreciations:

- **Illustrations:** Erin Kant
- **Graphic Designers and Layout Artists:**
  Heather Malk
  Alex Core
  Becky Herrington
- **Copyeditor:** Kim Fields
- **Publications Director:** Miguel Kagan

Kindergarten
Table of Contents

Section 1
Comprehension

Comprehension Resources

Comprehension Activities and Lessons

Section 2
Word Study

Word Study Resources

Word Study Activities and Lessons

Kindergarten
Table of Contents Continued

Section 3
Fluency

Fluency Resources

Fluency Activities

Section 4
Writing

Writing Resources

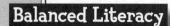

Balanced Literacy

Comprehension

Word Study

Fluency

Writing

Comprehension

Comprehension Overview

Comprehension research as reviewed by the National Reading Panel (NICHD, 2000) suggests that students learn best when teachers are explicit in their instruction. This is most effectively accomplished when teachers tell students what they are expected to do and model their own thinking processes for the students (aloud). As students are encouraged to ask questions, discuss possible answers, and apply other comprehension strategies, active engagement increases (shared, guided, and independent).

Comprehension provides the purpose for all reading and listening. Proficient readers are aware of their own thinking processes, making conscious decisions to apply different comprehension strategies as they read and listen.

Table of Comprehension Resources

Page(s)	Resources	Balanced Literacy				
		Aloud	Shared	Guided	Independent	Literature Circles
	Metacognitive Awareness					
8	Metacognitive Awareness Descriptions					
10	Metacognitive Awareness Thinking Strategies Posters	●	●	●	●	●
12	Metacognitive Awareness Poster Cards	●	●	●	●	●
17	Metacognitive Awareness Poster Strips	●	●	●	●	●
22	Metacognitive Awareness Lesson Planning Form	●	●			
23	Book List for Metacognitive Awareness Shared Read Alouds	●	●			

Table of Comprehension Activities and Lessons

Page(s)	Activities/Lessons	Blacklines	Balanced Literacy				
			Aloud	Shared	Guided	Independent	Literature Circles
26	**Timed Pair Share Activity**						
26	Metacognitive Awareness Shared Read Aloud Comprehension Lesson	• Comprehension Lesson	●	●			
28	**Listen-Sketch-Draft Activity**						
29	Listen-Sketch-Retell	• Listen-Sketch-Retell Forms	●	●	●		
31	**Showdown Activities**						
32	Comprehension Questions	• Teacher Set • Student Set • Blank Form	●	●	●		
35	Sequencing Events	• Teacher Set • Student Set	●	●	●		
39	**Quiz-Quiz-Trade Activity**						
40	Understanding Action Words	• 9 pages of question/ answer cards			●		
49	**Timed Pair Share Activities**						
50	Prediction Mat	• Prediction Mat • Blank Story Element Cards • Story Element Example Cards	●	●	●	●	
55	Drawing Word Meanings	• Worksheet • Blank Form	●	●	●	●	

Balanced Literacy • Kindergarten • Skidmore & Graber
Kagan Publishing • 1 (800) 933-2667 • www.KaganOnline.com

Table of Comprehension Activities and Lessons (continued)

Page(s)	Activities/Lessons	Blacklines	Balanced Literacy				
			Aloud	Shared	Guided	Independent	Literature Circles
57	**RallyCoach Activities**						
58	Sorting Mat	• Sorting Mat • 4 pages of cards		●	●		
64	Retelling	• Retelling Mat • Cards		●	●		
66	**Team Line-Ups Activity**						
67	Jumbled Sentences	• Word Cards		●	●		

Comprehension Resources

Metacognitive Awareness Comprehension

Resources/Materials Descriptions

How do we, as teachers, help our struggling readers improve their comprehension? We can show them how to build up their sight words, build their book list, and build time to practice reading. All of these activities are valuable but won't improve comprehension until we help students build a bridge . . . a bridge between their brains and the text.

Years of research have provided teachers with a list of comprehension strategies that good readers use while reading. Good readers are actively thinking while they read. They are aware when meaning has broken down, and they stop to fix the confusion. These strategies (Clarifying, Connecting, Identifying Important Ideas, Inferring, Predicting, Prior Knowledge, Questioning, Responding Emotionally, Retelling, and Visualizing) become the thinking tools needed for bridge building.

Metacognitive awareness means the reader is aware of his or her thinking during reading and listening to texts. Through metacognitive awareness lessons, students learn to apply self-monitoring comprehension strategies. The components of balanced literacy become the avenue for the teaching and strengthening of these metacognitive comprehension strategies. Students are supported as they hear the teacher explain and use the strategies (aloud); observe the teacher use the strategies with text and participate at specific points (shared); practice the strategies with direct support and feedback (guided); and own the strategies through additional practice opportunities (independent).

Metacognitive Awareness (Thinking Strategies) Posters (p. 10)

- This two-page poster identifies ten comprehension strategies for the teacher to use as a visual with modeling.
- It may be enlarged to use as a classroom poster or individually copied for students to keep in reading notebooks or journals for reference while reading.
- Now that students are aware that good readers think while reading, the teacher should model these strategies by stopping at various points during read aloud and explaining what she or he is thinking.
- Modeling of the use of these thinking strategies should be applied during the reading of various text types (narrative, expository, persuasive, and technical).

Metacognitive Awareness Poster Cards and Metacognitive Awareness Poster Strips (p. 12)

- As the teacher reads aloud, one strategy poster card or poster strip can be held up or referred to at a time, helping to focus the students' attention on the one strategy being modeled and explained.
- These cards or strips may be made into overhead transparencies to be used during shared read alouds.
- The cards may also be attached to a big book page with paper clips at the point in the text where the teacher stops to verbalize her thinking or when the students are sharing during **Timed Pair Share**.

Metacognitive Awareness Lesson Planning Form (Shared Read Aloud) (p. 22)

As the teacher continues to model the metacognitive awareness strategies, the Metacognitive Awareness Lesson Planning Form can be used to preplan specific, targeted comprehension strategies.

Book List for Metacognitive Awareness Shared Read Alouds (p. 23)

The book list is a resource for teacher read aloud or shared read aloud that focuses on metacognitive awareness (thinking) strategies.

Metacognitive Awareness
Thinking Strategies Posters

Instructions: Enlarge for use as a classroom poster or make individual copies for students to keep as a reference in reading notebooks or journals.

What do I know about it?
(Prior Knowledge)

What might happen next?
(Predicting)

What do I wonder about?
(Questioning)

What is the picture in my mind?
(Visualizing)

Why do things happen?
(Inferring)

 # Metacognitive Awareness Thinking Strategies Posters

Instructions: Enlarge for use as a classroom poster or make individual copies for students to keep as a reference in reading notebooks or journals.

 ## How does the character feel?
(Responding Emotionally)

 ## What words or ideas don't I understand?
(Clarifying)

 ## What is important in the text?
(Identifying Important Ideas)

 ## How is it like something else?
(Making Connections)

- Text to self
- Text to text
- Text to world

 ## What was the text about?
(Retelling)

Metacognitive Awareness
Poster Cards

Instructions: These cards may be copied on paper or made into overhead transparencies and cut apart to be used during teacher modeling or Timed Pair Share during shared read alouds.

Metacognitive Awareness Poster Cards

What might happen next? (Predicting)

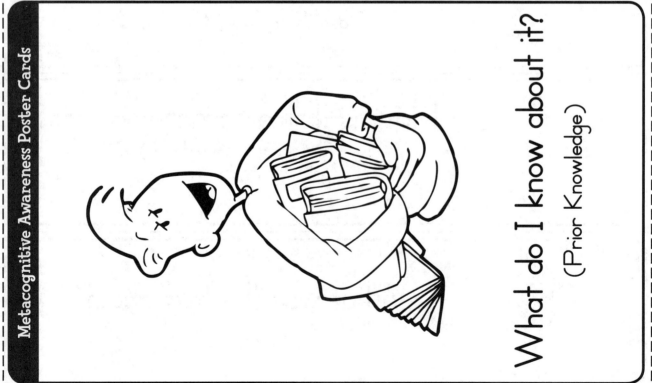

Metacognitive Awareness Poster Cards

What do I know about it? (Prior Knowledge)

Metacognitive Awareness
Poster Cards

Instructions: These cards may be copied on paper or made into overhead transparencies and cut apart to be used during teacher modeling or Timed Pair Share during shared read alouds.

Metacognitive Awareness Poster Cards

Instructions: These cards may be copied on paper or made into overhead transparencies and cut apart to be used during teacher modeling or Timed Pair Share during shared read alouds.

Metacognitive Awareness Poster Cards

How does the character feel?
(Responding Emotionally)

Metacognitive Awareness Poster Cards

Why do things happen?
(Inferring)

Kagan Publishing • 1 (800) 933-2667 • www.KaganOnline.com

Metacognitive Awareness Poster Cards

Instructions: These cards may be copied on paper or made into overhead transparencies and cut apart to be used during teacher modeling or Timed Pair Share during shared read alouds.

Metacognitive Awareness Poster Cards

What is important in the text?
(Identifying Important Ideas)

Metacognitive Awareness Poster Cards

explanation

What words or ideas don't I understand?
(Clarifying)

Metacognitive Awareness
Poster Cards

Instructions: These cards may be copied on paper or made into overhead transparencies and cut apart to be used during teacher modeling or Timed Pair Share during shared read alouds.

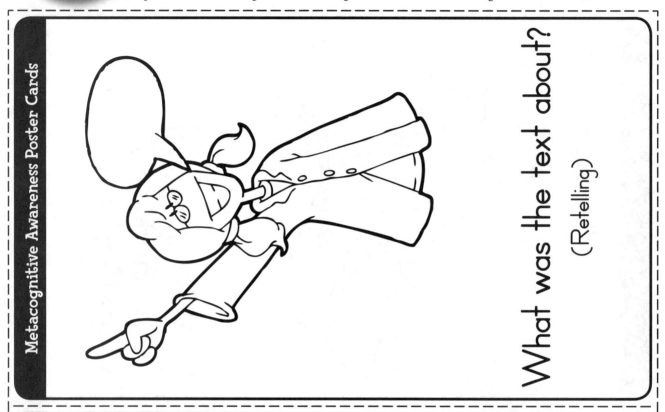

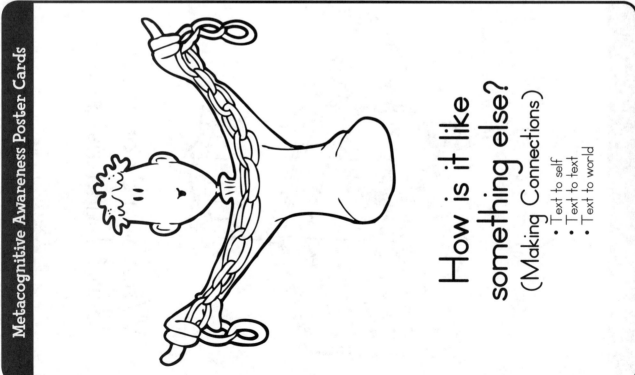

Metacognitive Awareness
Poster Strips

Instructions: These strips may be copied on paper or made into overhead transparencies and cut apart to be used during teacher modeling or Timed Pair Share during shared read alouds.

Metacognitive Awareness Poster Strips

What do I know about it?
(Prior Knowledge)

Metacognitive Awareness Poster Strips

What might happen next?
(Predicting)

Metacognitive Awareness Poster Strips

Instructions: These strips may be copied on paper or made into overhead transparencies and cut apart to be used during teacher modeling or Timed Pair Share during shared read alouds.

Metacognitive Awareness
Poster Strips

Instructions: These strips may be copied on paper or made into overhead transparencies and cut apart to be used during teacher modeling or Timed Pair Share during shared read alouds.

Metacognitive Awareness Poster Strips

Why do things happen?
(Inferring)

Metacognitive Awareness Poster Strips

How does the character feel?
(Responding Emotionally)

Metacognitive Awareness
Poster Strips

Instructions: These strips may be copied on paper or made into overhead transparencies and cut apart to be used during teacher modeling or Timed Pair Share during shared read alouds.

Metacognitive Awareness Poster Strips

What words or ideas don't I understand?

(Clarifying)

Metacognitive Awareness Poster Strips

What is important in the text?

(Identifying Important Ideas)

Metacognitive Awareness
Poster Strips

Instructions: These strips may be copied on paper or made into overhead transparencies and cut apart to be used during teacher modeling or Timed Pair Share during shared read alouds.

Metacognitive Awareness Poster Strips

How is it like something else?
(Making Connections)

• Text to self
• Text to text
• Text to world

Metacognitive Awareness Poster Strips

What was the text about?
(Retelling)

Metacognitive Awareness Lesson Planning Form
Shared Read Aloud

The teacher thinks aloud as she reads to the students. Big books or overhead transparencies of specific pages from the book are used several times. Students participate by reading or following along on the transparencies and then discussing the use of metacognitive strategies in teams.

Directions: Use this page to plan your lesson.

_____

by: _____

Page	Reading Materials	Metacognitive Strategies (Teacher Think Aloud)

Metacognitive Awareness Shared Read Alouds

In addition to the following list of trade books, Big Books (both informational and literacy text) are ideal for Shared Read Alouds. Some of the books on the list may also be available in a Big Book format.

Book Title	Author
Cuddly Duddly	Alborough, Jez
Sunflower Sal	Anderson, Janet S.
Little Nino's Pizzeria	Barbour, Karen
Animals Should Definitely Not Wear Clothing	Barrett, Judi
The Terrible Thing That Happened at Our House	Blaine, Marge
The Mitten	Brett, Jan
Flower Garden	Bunting, Eve
The Very Busy Spider	Carle, Eric
Now One Foot, Now the Other	De Paola, Tomie
Mushroom in the Rain	Ginsburg, Mirra
Chrysanthemum	Henkes, Kevin
Lilly's Purple Plastic Purse	Henkes, Kevin
Leo, the Late Bloomer	Kraus, Robert
No Dragon on My Quilt	Laury, Jean Ray
Bizzy Bones and the Lost Quilt	Martin, Jacqueline Briggs
If the Dinosaurs Came Back	Most, Bernard
The Kissing Hand	Penn, Audrey
Babushka's Doll	Polacco, Patricia
Gregory, the Terrible Eater	Sharmat, Mitchell
Caps for Sale	Slobodkina, Esphyr
The Popcorn Dragon	Thayer, Jane
Ira Sleeps Over	Waber, Bernard
The Big Boasting Battle	Wilhelm, Hans
The Napping House	Wood, Audrey
Quick as a Cricket	Wood, Audrey
William's Doll	Zolotow, Charlotte

Comprehension Activities and Lessons

Metacognitive Awareness Shared Read Aloud

Chrysanthemum
by Kevin Henkes

Materials:
- *Chrysanthemum* by Kevin Henkes
- **Metacognitive Awareness Poster Cards:** Display and refer to the appropriate cards during the shared read aloud.

Metacognitive Awareness Comprehension Lessons may be used during interactive read alouds (trade books) or shared reading (Big Books, overhead transparencies, or enlarged texts).

Text Page	Structure	Metacognitive Strategies Teacher Think Aloud
Cover		**Prior Knowledge:** What Do I Already Know? Has anyone ever heard of the word, *Chrysanthemum*? Why do you think the author put a picture of a flower and a girl on the cover of this book and on the title page?
1	Timed Pair Share	**Connecting:** Text to Self What do you think your parents said about you?
2		Confirm prediction about the word, *Chrysanthemum*.
3–4		Read.
5	Timed Pair Share	**Connecting:** Text to Self Share with your partner what you think of your name and why.
6		Read.
7		**Predicting:** (after reading sentences and names of students) Why do you think everyone giggled?
8		**Clarifying:** What Words Don't I Understand? *Teacher Think Aloud:* I like the word *wilted* because . . . Have students show what "wilted" looks like.
9		Read.
10	Timed Pair Share	**How Does the Character Feel?** Responding Emotionally How would you feel if your friends made the same comments about your name? How do you think Chrysanthemum is feeling right now?

Metacognitive Awareness Shared Read Aloud (continued)

Chrysanthemum

Text Page	Structure	Metacognitive Strategies Teacher Think Aloud
11–12		Read.
13	Timed Pair Share	**How Does the Character Feel?** Responding Emotionally Why do you think the name Jane helped Chrysanthemum have a pleasant dream? (short, simple, common)
14–16		Read.
17		**How Does the Character Feel?** Responding Emotionally What do you think of Victoria's behavior/words? How do Victoria's words make Chrysanthemum feel?
18–20		Read.
21		*Teacher Think Aloud:* I'm thinking that Chrysanthemum loaded her pockets with her most prized possessions and good luck charms because she wanted to have a good day.
22		**Questioning:** What Do I Wonder About? Why do the students want to impress Mrs. Twinkle?
23–25		Read.
26	Timed Pair Share	**Predicting:** What Might Happen Next? How do you think Chrysanthemum feels now?
27		Show the pictures—what do the pictures tell us? Read the sentences to confirm/adjust predictions from page 26.
28		What are Marigolds, Carnations, and Lily of the Valley? (flowers) Why do the students want to be called these names?
29–30		Read.

Listen-Sketch-Retell

Students sketch content chunk by chunk and then use their sketches to orally retell.

Activity Steps

1   Students listen while teacher presents the first chunk of information.

2   Teacher stops presenting and calls for each student to sketch the most important details in one of the Retell Form boxes (Form #1 or Form #2).

3   Students share sketches using either:
    • **RoundRobin**
    • **Timed Pair Share**

4   The process is repeated for the next chunk of information.

5   When all chunks have been presented, students each use their completed sketches to orally retell the entire text.

STRUCTURE

Listen-Sketch-Draft

Note:
If students use Listen-Sketch-Retell Form #2, they will put checks in the boxes next to their sketches as they proceed through the oral retelling in sequence.

Blacklines

Listen-Sketch-Retell Form #1

Listen-Sketch-Draft

Instructions: Copy for each student. Retell orally using your sketches.

2.

4.

1.

3.

Listen-Sketch-Retell Form #2

Listen-Sketch-Draft

Instructions: Copy for each student. Retell orally using your sketches. Put a check in each box as you tell about the sketch.

1.	☐
2.	☐
3.	☐
4.	☐

Comprehension Showdown

Teams play Showdown to answer comprehension questions.

Activity Steps

1 Each student holds Student Card Set in his or her hand.

2 Teacher is the Showdown Captain.

3 Showdown Captain (teacher) reads the first question.

4 Working alone, students individually identify the answer using the cards in their hands.

5 When finished, teammates signal they are ready.

6 Showdown Captain (teacher) calls, "Showdown!"

7 Teammates show their answers at the same time.

8 Showdown Captain (teacher) leads checking.

9 If correct, the team celebrates. If not, the teammates coach, then celebrate.

10 The teacher is the Showdown Captain for the remaining rounds.

STRUCTURE

Showdown

Note:
For Kindergarteners, the teacher is the Showdown Captain, rather than rotating the responsibility among the team.

Blacklines

Comprehension Questions
Showdown (Teacher Set)
Chrysanthemum by Kevin Henkes

Instructions: Teacher uses cards to orally ask comprehension questions.

Comprehension Questions
Question: Chrysanthemum's parents thought she was absolutely perfect. Answer: **Yes**

Comprehension Questions
Question: Chrysanthemum liked her name at the beginning of the story. Answer: **Yes**

Comprehension Questions
Question: Chrysanthemum's first day of school was absolutely perfect. Answer: **No**

Comprehension Questions
Question: Everyone loved Chrysanthemum's name. Answer: **No**

Comprehension Questions
Question: Everyone clapped when Mrs. Chud called Chrysanthemum's name during roll call. Answer: **No**

Comprehension Questions
Question: The students made fun of Chrysanthemum's name because it was so long. Answer: **Yes**

Comprehension Questions
Question: A chrysanthemum is a kind of tree. Answer: **No**

Comprehension Questions
Question: The students made fun of Chrysanthemum's name because it was the name of a flower. Answer: **Yes**

Comprehension Questions
Question: Chrysanthemum started to <u>not</u> like her name. Answer: **Yes**

Comprehension Questions
Question: Chrysanthemum's parents said that she could change her name. Answer: **No**

Comprehension Questions-
Question: Mrs. Twinkle, the music teacher, made Chrysanthemum feel better because her name was also long and was the name of a flower. Answer: **Yes**

Comprehension Questions
Question: Mrs. Twinkle said that she might name her baby Daisy. Answer: **No**

Comprehension Questions
Question: The children started wishing their names were names of flowers. Answer: **Yes**

Comprehension Questions
Question: Mrs. Twinkle named her new baby Chrysanthemum. Answer: **Yes**

Comprehension Questions
Showdown (Student Set)

Note: This page has cards for four students (one team). Copy, cut apart, and give each student one "yes" and one "no" card.

Comprehension Questions

Comprehension Questions

Comprehension Questions

Comprehension Questions

Comprehension Questions

Comprehension Questions

Comprehension Questions

Comprehension Questions

Blank Comprehension Questions Form
Showdown

Book/Story/Article: _____ **Author:** _____

Instructions: After formulating questions for a specific text, read questions as students respond on marker boards or by using student cards.

Comprehension Questions Form	Comprehension Questions Form
Question: Answer:	Question: Answer:
Question: Answer:	Question: Answer:
Question: Answer:	Question: Answer:
Question: Answer:	Question: Answer:
Question: Answer:	Question: Answer:
Question: Answer:	Question: Answer:
Question: Answer:	Question: Answer:

Sequencing Events
Showdown (Teacher Set)

Instructions: Teacher uses cards to orally ask comprehension questions.

Sequencing Events

Question: Does this order make sense?

- I poured milk on my cereal.
- I got my bowl out of the cupboard.

Answer: **No**

Sequencing Events

Question: Does this order make sense?

- I picked the yellow and blue flowers.
- I put the flowers in a vase.

Answer: **Yes**

Sequencing Events

Question: Does this order make sense?

- I brushed my teeth.
- I ate a treat.

Answer: **No**

Sequencing Events

Question: Does this order make sense?

- I bought new crayons at the store.
- I brought my new crayons to school.

Answer: **Yes**

Sequencing Events

Question: Does this order make sense?

- I ate breakfast.
- I put the dishes in the dishwasher.

Answer: **Yes**

Sequencing Events

Question: Does this order make sense?

- I tied my shoes.
- I put on my socks.

Answer: **No**

Sequencing Events

Question: Does this order make sense?

- I ate a piece of my birthday cake.
- I blew out the candles on my birthday cake.

Answer: **No**

Sequencing Events

Question: Does this order make sense?

- I practiced playing the song on the piano.
- I played the song in a recital.

Answer: **Yes**

Sequencing Events

Question: Does this order make sense?

- I put my math paper in the basket.
- I put my name on my math paper.

Answer: **No**

Sequencing Events

Question: Does this order make sense?

- My dad read a book to me.
- I went to sleep.

Answer: **Yes**

Sequencing Events
Showdown (Teacher Set)

Instructions: Teacher uses cards to orally ask comprehension questions.

Sequencing Events

Question: Does this order make sense?

• Ted ran two miles.
• Ted was very tired.

Answer: **Yes**

Sequencing Events

Question: Does this order make sense?

• There was a windstorm.
• Tree branches were on the street.

Answer: **Yes**

Sequencing Events

Question: Does this order make sense?

• Sid took a shower.
• Sid played in the mud puddle.

Answer: **No**

Sequencing Events

Question: Does this order make sense?

• Dad backed out of the garage.
• Dad opened the garage door.

Answer: **No**

Sequencing Events

Question: Does this order make sense?

• The crowd cheered.
• Bill made a goal.

Answer: **No**

Sequencing Events

Question: Does this order make sense?

• The children were cold.
• Mom lit a fire in the fireplace.

Answer: **Yes**

Sequencing Events

Question: Does this order make sense?

• Polly frosted the cake.
• Polly baked a chocolate cake.

Answer: **No**

Sequencing Events

Question: Does this order make sense?

• Max put a worm on the hook at the end of his fishing pole.
• Max caught a big fish.

Answer: **Yes**

Sequencing Events

Question: Does this order make sense?

• Natalie and Andrew were hungry.
• Natalie and Andrew's mom made pizza for lunch.

Answer: **Yes**

Sequencing Events

Question: Does this order make sense?

• Shawn crossed the finish line first.
• Shawn started the race when the whistle blew.

Answer: **No**

Sequencing Events
Showdown (Teacher Set)

Instructions: Teacher uses cards to orally ask comprehension questions.

Sequencing Events

Question: Does this order make sense?

• Katie put the book on the shelf.
• Katie read the book.

Answer: **No**

Sequencing Events

Question: Does this order make sense?

• Keith put up his umbrella.
• Keith ran to his truck in the rain.

Answer: **Yes**

Sequencing Events

Question: Does this order make sense?

• Sharon bought milk and bread at the store.
• Sharon drove her car to the store.

Answer: **No**

Sequencing Events

Question: Does this order make sense?

• Hannah gave her cat, Sophie, a bowl of cat food.
• Sophie ate the cat food.

Answer: **Yes**

Sequencing Events

Question: Does this order make sense?

• Chloe organized her books on her new bookshelf.
• Chloe's dad built her a new bookshelf.

Answer: **No**

Sequencing Events

Question: Does this order make sense?

• The puppy, Buddy, chased the tennis ball.
• Micah threw the tennis ball.

Answer: **No**

Sequencing Events

Question: Does this order make sense?

• Danny took a sheet of paper from the drawer.
• Danny drew a picture with his new markers.

Answer: **Yes**

Sequencing Events

Question: Does this order make sense?

• Ashley kicked the soccer ball toward the goal.
• Ashley made a goal.

Answer: **Yes**

Sequencing Events

Question: Does this order make sense?

• Christa wrote a story about a silly hamster.
• Christa read her story to the class.

Answer: **Yes**

Sequencing Events

Question: Does this order make sense?

• Jessie drank two tall glasses of water.
• Jessie was thirsty.

Answer: **No**

Sequencing Events
Showdown (Student Set)

Note: This page has cards for four students (one team). Copy, cut apart, and give each student one "yes" and one "no" card.

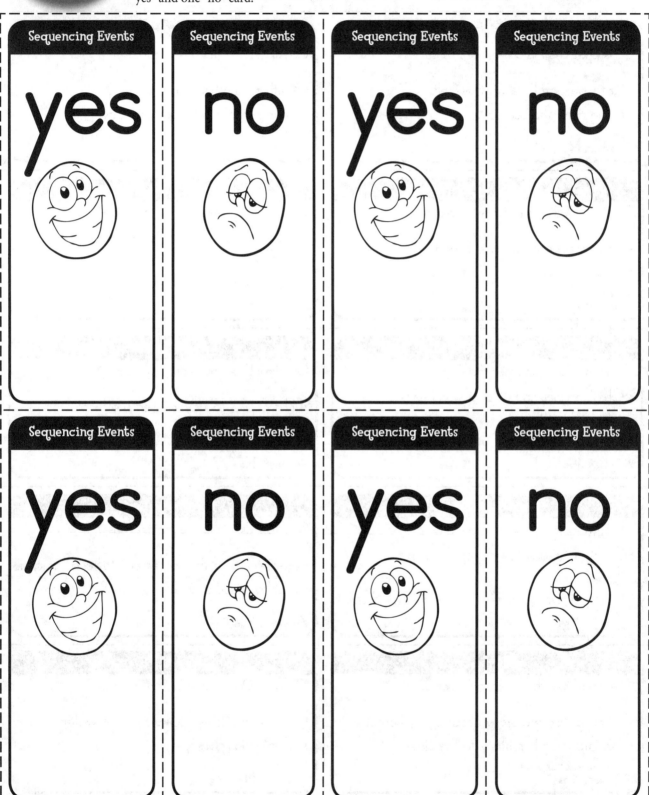

Understanding Action Words

Teams play Quiz-Quiz-Trade for comprehension of action words.

STRUCTURE

Quiz-Quiz-Trade

Activity Steps

1. Each student receives a card with a picture (question) on the front and an answer on the back.

2. Students stand up, put a hand up, and pair up with another student.

3. Partner A quizzes (shows picture) Partner B using the card.

4. Partner B answers the question (names the action in the picture).

5. Partner A praises or coaches.

6. Partner B now quizzes Partner A, Partner A answers, and Partner B praises or coaches.

7. Partners trade cards and find a new partner to quiz. The activity continues for multiple rounds, allowing students to quiz and get quizzed multiple times.

Question (Front)

Understanding Action Words
Question: What is the action in the picture?

Answer (Back)

Understanding Action Words
Answer: cook

Variation

Students state the action word <u>and</u> uses the action word in a complete sentence.

Blacklines

Understanding Action Words
Quiz-Quiz-Trade

Instructions: Copy enough cards so each student has one card. Cut on dotted lines and fold in half.

Understanding Action Words Question: What is the action in the picture? 	**Understanding Action Words** Answer: **saw** 
Understanding Action Words Question: What is the action in the picture? 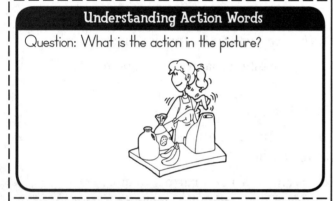	**Understanding Action Words** Answer: **sell** 
Understanding Action Words Question: What is the action in the picture? 	**Understanding Action Words** Answer: **sew** 
Understanding Action Words Question: What is the action in the picture? 	**Understanding Action Words** Answer: **fly** 

Understanding Action Words
Quiz-Quiz-Trade

Instructions: Copy enough cards so each student has one card. Cut on dotted lines and fold in half.

Understanding Action Words

Question: What is the action in the picture?

Understanding Action Words

Answer:
talk

Understanding Action Words

Question: What is the action in the picture?

Understanding Action Words

Answer:
paint

Understanding Action Words

Question: What is the action in the picture?

Understanding Action Words

Answer:
dig

Understanding Action Words

Question: What is the action in the picture?

Understanding Action Words

Answer:
weigh

Understanding Action Words
Quiz-Quiz-Trade

Instructions: Copy enough cards so each student has one card. Cut on dotted lines and fold in half.

Understanding Action Words	Understanding Action Words
Question: What is the action in the picture? 	Answer: **mow** 
Understanding Action Words	Understanding Action Words
Question: What is the action in the picture? 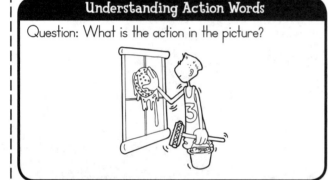	Answer: **wash** 
Understanding Action Words	Understanding Action Words
Question: What is the action in the picture? 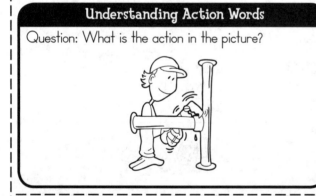	Answer: **fix** 
Understanding Action Words	Understanding Action Words
Question: What is the action in the picture? 	Answer: **unroll** 

Understanding Action Words
Quiz-Quiz-Trade

Instructions: Copy enough cards so each student has one card. Cut on dotted lines and fold in half.

Understanding Action Words Question: What is the action in the picture? 	**Understanding Action Words** Answer: **carry** 
Understanding Action Words Question: What is the action in the picture? 	**Understanding Action Words** Answer: **push** 
Understanding Action Words Question: What is the action in the picture? 	**Understanding Action Words** Answer: **cook** 
Understanding Action Words Question: What is the action in the picture? 	**Understanding Action Words** Answer: **skate** 

Understanding Action Words
Quiz-Quiz-Trade

Instructions: Copy enough cards so each student has one card. Cut on dotted lines and fold in half.

Understanding Action Words
Question: What is the action in the picture?

Understanding Action Words
Answer:
play

Understanding Action Words
Question: What is the action in the picture?

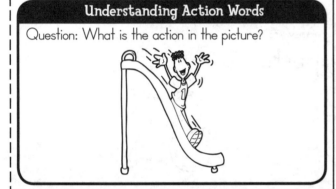

Understanding Action Words
Answer:
slide

Understanding Action Words
Question: What is the action in the picture?

Understanding Action Words
Answer:
kick

Understanding Action Words
Question: What is the action in the picture?

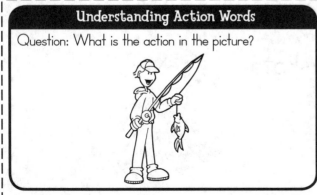

Understanding Action Words
Answer:
fish

Understanding Action Words
Quiz-Quiz-Trade

Instructions: Copy enough cards so each student has one card. Cut on dotted lines and fold in half.

Understanding Action Words Question: What is the action in the picture? 	**Understanding Action Words** Answer: **swim** 
Understanding Action Words Question: What is the action in the picture? 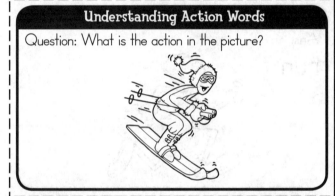	**Understanding Action Words** Answer: **ski** 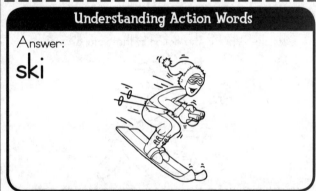
Understanding Action Words Question: What is the action in the picture? 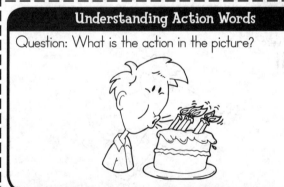	**Understanding Action Words** Answer: **blow** 
Understanding Action Words Question: What is the action in the picture? 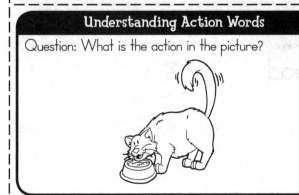	**Understanding Action Words** Answer: **eat** 

Understanding Action Words
Quiz-Quiz-Trade

Instructions: Copy enough cards so each student has one card. Cut on dotted lines and fold in half.

Understanding Action Words

Question: What is the action in the picture?

Understanding Action Words

Answer:

hop

Understanding Action Words

Question: What is the action in the picture?

Understanding Action Words

Answer:

run

Understanding Action Words

Question: What is the action in the picture?

Understanding Action Words

Answer:

fall

Understanding Action Words

Question: What is the action in the picture?

Understanding Action Words

Answer:

read

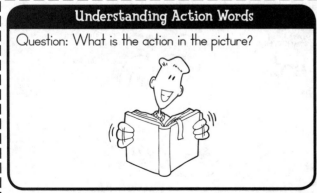

Understanding Action Words
Quiz-Quiz-Trade

Instructions: Copy enough cards so each student has one card. Cut on dotted lines and fold in half.

Understanding Action Words	Understanding Action Words
Question: What is the action in the picture? 	Answer: **sleep** 
Understanding Action Words	Understanding Action Words
Question: What is the action in the picture? 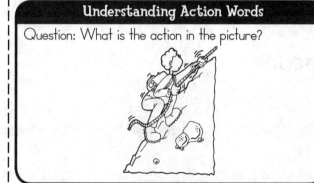	Answer: **climb** 
Understanding Action Words	Understanding Action Words
Question: What is the action in the picture? 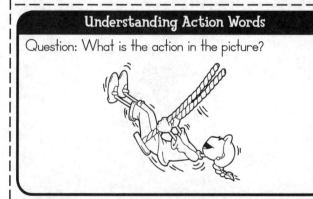	Answer: **swing** 
Understanding Action Words	Understanding Action Words
Question: What is the action in the picture? 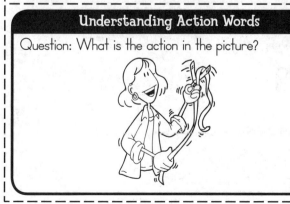	Answer: **cut** 

Understanding Action Words
Quiz-Quiz-Trade

Instructions: Copy enough cards so each student has one card. Cut on dotted lines and fold in half.

Understanding Action Words	Understanding Action Words
Question: What is the action in the picture? 	Answer: **shave** 
Understanding Action Words	Understanding Action Words
Question: What is the action in the picture? 	Answer: **pour** 
Understanding Action Words	Understanding Action Words
Question: What is the action in the picture? 	Answer: **hit** 
Understanding Action Words	Understanding Action Words
Question: What is the action in the picture? 	Answer: **hug** 

Balanced Literacy • Kindergarten • Skidmore & Graber
Kagan Publishing • 1 (800) 933-2667 • www.KaganOnline.com

Story Predictions

Students manipulate cards with possible characters, settings, problems, and solutions to the text on the prediction mat. They confirm or adjust their predictions during reading and after reading the selection. Partners take timed turns listening and sharing about their Prediction Mats.

Activity Steps

STRUCTURE
Timed Pair Share

1. The teacher creates Story Element Cards corresponding to the story the class will read. (Two sample sets are provided.)

2. Each student receives a Prediction Mat and a set of story cards.

3. As the story is read, students are stopped periodically and given time to make story predictions by manipulating their Story Cards on their Prediction Mats. Stories can be read using:
   - Teacher read aloud
   - RallyRobin reading (partners take turns)
   - Independent reading

4. After each prediction adjustment, students are each given one minute to share their prediction with a partner.

Blacklines

Prediction Mat
Timed Pair Share

Instructions: Copy for each student.

Characters	Setting

Problem	Solution

Important Words

Blank Story Element
Cards for Prediction Mat
Timed Pair Share

Instructions: Teacher writes possible story elements in these boxes and makes copies for each student.

Blank Story Element Cards	Blank Story Element Cards	Blank Story Element Cards	Blank Story Element Cards
Blank Story Element Cards	Blank Story Element Cards	Blank Story Element Cards	Blank Story Element Cards
Blank Story Element Cards	Blank Story Element Cards	Blank Story Element Cards	Blank Story Element Cards
Blank Story Element Cards	Blank Story Element Cards	Blank Story Element Cards	Blank Story Element Cards

Story Element Cards for Prediction Mat
Timed Pair Share
Chrysanthemum by Kevin Henkes

Instructions: Copy for each student. Cut apart.

Story Element Cards	Story Element Cards	Story Element Cards	Story Element Cards
Chrysanthemum	school	giggles	flower
home	Victoria	name	miserable
wilted	musical	Mrs. Twinkle	13 letters
absolutely perfect	teasing	baby girl	mom and dad

Story Element Cards for Prediction Mat
Timed Pair Share
The Kissing Hand by Audrey Penn (Scholastic)

Instructions: Copy for each student. Cut apart.

Story Element Cards	Story Element Cards	Story Element Cards	Story Element Cards
Chester	forest	secret	hand
Mrs. Raccoon	lonely	school	tree
night	home	warm thoughts	I Love You
scared	kiss	*Blank Story Element Cards*	*Blank Story Element Cards*

Activity

Word Meanings

Students draw pictures representing word meanings for vocabulary words chosen by the teacher from a previously read aloud book.

Activity Steps

1. Teacher announces a vocabulary word to the class and sets the time for 30 seconds.

2. Students individually draw a quick sketch showing the meaning of the word. (This is their think time.)

3. Teacher states how long each student will have to share about their drawing and the meaning of the word with partners.

4. In pairs, Partner A shares; Partner B listens.

5. Partner B responds.

6. Partners switch roles.

7. Repeat from Step 1 with a new word.

STRUCTURE
Timed
Pair Share

BlackLines

Drawing Word Meanings
Timed Pair Share

Title: Cuddly Duddly   **Author:** Jez Alborough

Instructions: Copy for each student.

1. diving	2. splashing
3. cuddle	4. following

Drawing Word Meanings Blank Form

Timed Pair Share

Title: _____ Author: _____

Instructions: Copy for each student.

1. _____	2. _____
3. _____	4. _____

Categories

Partners take turns sorting Picture Word Cards on a category sorting mat.

STRUCTURE
RallyCoach

Activity Steps

1 Partner A puts a Picture Word Card in the correct column on the sorting mat.

2 Partner B watches and listens, checks, and praises.

3 Partner B puts a Picture Word Card in the correct column on the sorting mat.

4 Partner A watches and listens, checks, and praises.

5 Repeat starting at Step 1.

Blacklines

Sorting Mat
RallyCoach

Instructions: Copy for each pair of students.

Clothes	
Food	
People	
Animals	
Toys	

Picture Word Cards
RallyCoach

Instructions: Copy for each pair of students. Cut apart.

Picture Word Cards	Picture Word Cards	Picture Word Cards	Picture Word Cards
rabbit	pizza	grandma	soup
singer	cow	tacos	mittens
sandals	shoes	boy	carrot
turtle	family	squirrel	drummer

Picture Word Cards
RallyCoach

Instructions: Copy for each pair of students. Cut apart.

Picture Word Cards	Picture Word Cards	Picture Word Cards	Picture Word Cards
goat	cap	wagon	pants
top	necklace	bear	sweater
cheese	grandpa	hamburger	girl
baby	shorts	blocks	dress

 Balanced Literacy • Kindergarten • Skidmore & Graber
Kagan Publishing • 1 (800) 933-2667 • www.KaganOnline.com

Picture Word Cards
RallyCoach

Instructions: Copy for each pair of students. Cut apart.

Picture Word Cards	Picture Word Cards	Picture Word Cards	Picture Word Cards
belt	bat	doll	frog
pilot	skirt	corn	tie
panda	farmer	kangaroo	popcorn
man	artist	kite	seal

Picture Word Cards
RallyCoach

Instructions: Copy for each pair of students. Cut apart.

Picture Word Cards	Picture Word Cards	Picture Word Cards	Picture Word Cards
painter	whale	socks	orange
butterfly	gloves	eagle	shirt
grapes	watermelon	dentist	apple
ball	giraffe	jump rope	walrus

 Balanced Literacy • Kindergarten • Skidmore & Graber
Kagan Publishing • 1 (800) 933-2667 • www.KaganOnline.com

Retelling Meanings

Partners take turns placing Picture Cards on the mat as they retell a fiction book or story.

STRUCTURE
RallyCoach

Activity Steps

1. Each pair receives a Retelling Mat and a set of Picture Cards.

2. Partner A picks up card #1 and retells the correct information as he or she places it on the mat.

3. Partner B watches, listens, checks, and praises.

4. Partner B picks up card #2 and retells the correct information as he or she places it on the mat.

5. Partner A watches, listens, checks, and praises.

6. The process is continued until the pair completes the Retelling Mat.

Blacklines

Retelling Mat
RallyCoach

Instructions: Make a copy of the Retelling Mat for each pair of students.

1. Title

2. Who? (characters)

3. Where? (setting)

4. Beginning

5. Middle

6. End

Balanced Literacy • Kindergarten • Skidmore & Graber
Kagan Publishing • 1 (800) 933-2667 • www.KaganOnline.com

Retelling Mat Picture Cards

RallyCoach

Instructions: Make a copy of the retelling picture cards for each pair of students. Cut apart. Partners place the picture cards on the retelling mat as they retell a fiction book or story.

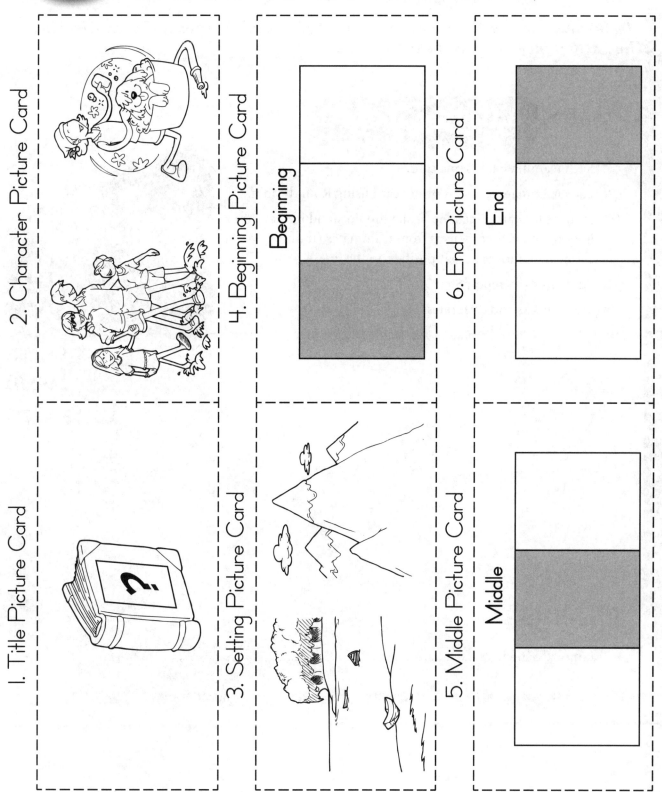

2. Character Picture Card

4. Beginning Picture Card

Beginning

6. End Picture Card

End

1. Title Picture Card

3. Setting Picture Card

5. Middle Picture Card

Middle

Activity

Jumbled Sentences

Teammates each receive a card with a word on it, and they position themselves in a line so that they correctly make a sentence.

Activity Steps

1 Each teammate takes one card.

2 Each teammate reads his or her card using RoundRobin.

3 Student #1 states where he or she should stand in the team line-up and gets consensus from teammates (thumbs up). He or she then moves to that position in the line.

4 Students #2–4 repeat Step 3.

5 Team checks and celebrates.

STRUCTURE
Team Line-Ups

Blacklines

Jumbled Sentences
Team Line-Ups

Instructions: Copy one card set for each team. The numbers in the corners of the cards indicate which cards belong to each sentence.

Jumbled Sentences Cards	Jumbled Sentences Cards	Jumbled Sentences Cards	Jumbled Sentences Cards
A 1	cat 1	can 1	run 1
I 2	can 2	see 2	you 2
The 3	dog 3	is 3	big 3
Mom 4	is 4	so 4	mad 4
Can 5	I 5	go 5	too 5
Look 6	at 6	me 6	run 6
Can 7	you 7	see 7	me 7

Jumbled Sentences
Team Line-Ups

Instructions: Copy one card set for each team. The numbers in the corners of the cards indicate which cards belong to each sentence.

Jumbled Sentences Cards **The** 8	Jumbled Sentences Cards **cat** 8	Jumbled Sentences Cards **is** 8	Jumbled Sentences Cards **fat** 8
Jumbled Sentences Cards **Look** 9	Jumbled Sentences Cards **at** 9	Jumbled Sentences Cards **me** 9	Jumbled Sentences Cards **jump** 9
Jumbled Sentences Cards **I** 10	Jumbled Sentences Cards **like** 10	Jumbled Sentences Cards **the** 10	Jumbled Sentences Cards **cat** 10
Jumbled Sentences Cards **I** 11	Jumbled Sentences Cards **ran** 11	Jumbled Sentences Cards **to** 11	Jumbled Sentences Cards **you** 11
Jumbled Sentences Cards **My** 12	Jumbled Sentences Cards **dad** 12	Jumbled Sentences Cards **is** 12	Jumbled Sentences Cards **big** 12
Jumbled Sentences Cards **He** 13	Jumbled Sentences Cards **is** 13	Jumbled Sentences Cards **my** 13	Jumbled Sentences Cards **dad** 13
Jumbled Sentences Cards **She** 14	Jumbled Sentences Cards **is** 14	Jumbled Sentences Cards **my** 14	Jumbled Sentences Cards **mom** 14

Balanced Literacy

Comprehension

Word Study

Fluency

Writing

Word Study

Word Study Overview

Effective word study instruction at the kindergarten level includes phonemic awareness (hearing and manipulating sounds), phonics (connecting sounds with letters and decoding words), and vocabulary (deriving meaning from words). Phonemic awareness is a prerequisite skill to reading and writing. It is the ability to hear units of sound and manipulate those sounds in spoken words. Phonics allows student to take words apart while reading and put words together while writing. As students participate in word study activities, they become aware of relationships between sounds, letters, letter combinations, and word parts. Various cooperative activities in this book provide opportunities for students to practice application of phonemic awareness and phonics skills as a foundation for reading and writing.

"Researchers have found that phonemic awareness and letter knowledge are the two best school-entry predictors of how well students will learn to read during the first two years of instruction." (Share, Jorm, Maclean & Matthews, 1984. Sources of individual differences in reading achievement. *Journal of Education Psychology*, 76, 1309–1324.)

Following the framework of balanced literacy allows the teacher to scaffold instruction through use of explicit teaching during read/write alouds and shared reading/writing to explain strategies used to decode words and understand their meanings. Scaffolding continues during guided reading/writing as the teacher monitors and provides feedback to students applying word-solving skills and strategies. Support is withdrawn as students independently apply these skills and strategies successfully.

Table of Word Study Resources

Page(s)	Resources	Balanced Literacy				
		Aloud	Shared	Guided	Independent	Literature Circles
Word Study Descriptions and Lists						
80	Levels of Phonemic Awareness	●	●	●	●	
81	Structures and Phonemic Awareness Activities	●	●	●	●	

Table of Word Study Activities and Lessons

Page(s)	Activities/Lessons	Blacklines	Balanced Literacy				
			Aloud	Shared	Guided	Independent	Literature Circles
84	Partner Word Study Activities		●	●	●	●	●
88	Team Word Study Activities		●	●	●	●	●
92	Class Word Study Activities		●	●	●	●	●
93	**Making Words Lesson Plans**						
94	**Lesson 1:** *Plant*						
94	**RallyCoach Activity**						
94	Activity 1: Making Words	• Teacher Transparency Form • Student Form	●	●	●	●	
96	**Find My Rule Activity**						
96	Activity 2: Sorting	• Teacher Transparency Form • Find My Rule Mat	●	●	●	●	
97	**RallyCoach Activity**						
97	Activity 3: Transfer		●	●	●	●	
100	**Lesson 2:** *Plays*						
100	**RallyCoach Activity**						
100	Activity 1: Making Words	• Teacher Transparency Form • Student Form	●	●	●	●	
101	**Find My Rule Activity**						
101	Activity 2: Sorting	• Teacher Transparency Form • Find My Rule Mat	●	●	●	●	

Table of Word Study Activities and Lessons (continued)

Page(s)	Activities/Lessons	Blacklines	Balanced Literacy				
			Aloud	Shared	Guided	Independent	Literature Circles
101	**RallyCoach Activity**						
101	Activity 3: Transfer		●	●	●	●	
104	**Lesson 3: *Hamster***						
104	**RallyCoach Activity**						
104	Activity 1: Making Words	• Teacher Transparency Form • Student Form	●	●	●	●	
105	**Find My Rule Activity**						
105	Activity 2: Sorting	• Teacher Transparency Form • Find My Rule Mat	●	●	●	●	
105	**RallyCoach Activity**						
105	Activity 3: Transfer						
111	**Find Someone Who Activities**						
112	Matching Capital and Lower Case Letters, Beginning Word Sounds, Writing Name, Recognizing Bb, Beginning Word Sounds	• Worksheet		●	●		
113	Partner Letters, Adding *a* to Words, /at/ Letter Pattern, Matching Pictures with Words, Recognizing *p* in Words, Recognizing /an/	• Worksheet		●	●		
114	Adding *i* to Words, Matching Capital and Lower Case Letters, Identifying sh Words, Recognizing /an/ in Words	• Worksheet		●	●		
115	Find Someone Who	• Form		●	●		

Table of Word Study Activities and Lessons (continued)

Page(s)	Activities/Lessons	Blacklines	Balanced Literacy				
			Aloud	Shared	Guided	Independent	Literature Circles
116	**Quiz-Quiz-Trade Activities**						
117	Rhyming Words—Yes or No?	• Question/Answer Cards		●	●		
124	Rhyming	• Question/Answer Cards		●	●		
133	Word Parts	• Question/Answer Cards		●	●		
140	Matching Beginning Sounds	• Question/Answer Cards		●	●		
149	Beginning Sounds (Sets #1 and #2)	• Question/Answer Cards		●	●		
163	Ending Sounds	• Question/Answer Cards		●	●		
174	Letter Identification	• Question/Answer Cards		●	●		
181	Capital Letter Identification	• Question/Answer Cards		●	●		
188	Lower Case Letter Identification	• Question/Answer Cards		●	●		
195	Letter Identification—Different Font Styles	• Question/Answer Cards		●	●		
202	**RallyRobin Activities**						
203	Rhyming	• Cards • Alphabet Letter Strips		●	●		
207	**RallyCoach Activities**						
209	Sorting by Syllables	• Cards • Sorting Mat		●	●		
212	Beginning, Middle, End	• Cards		●	●		
216	Phoneme Identification Sort	• Cards • Sorting Mat		●	●		

Table of Word Study Activities and Lessons (continued)

Page(s)	Activities/Lessons	Blacklines	Balanced Literacy				
			Aloud	Shared	Guided	Independent	Literature Circles
207	**RallyCoach Activities** (continued)						
230	Phoneme Blending and Segmenting	• Cards		●	●		
232	Phoneme Segmentation	• Cards • Mat		●	●		
236	Onset and Rime Sorting	• Cards • Mat		●	●		
248	b, p, t, d Spinner	• Spinner • Worksheet		●	●		
250	h, a, r, m, d Spinner	• Spinner • Worksheet		●	●		
252	V, W, Q, Y, J Spinner	• Spinner • Worksheet		●	●		
254	Letter Patterns and Sight Words Game	• Game Board • Word Cards • Blank Cards		●	●		
259	Onset and Rime (f, s, h, d, p, b)	• Cube • Worksheet		●	●		
261	Short Vowel (a, e, i, o, u)	• Cube • Worksheet		●	●		
263	CVC Word Cubes #1, #2, #3	• Cubes • Worksheets		●	●		
267	Onset and Rime #1 and #2	• Spinners • Worksheets		●	●		
273	Word Cards and Vowel Cards	• Word Cards • Letter Cards • Worksheet		●	●		
275	Onset and Rime Cards	• Rime Cards • Letter Cards • Worksheet		●	●		
277	Word Cards and Medial Vowel Cards #1 and #2	• Word Cards • Letter Cards • Worksheet		●	●		
281	Name, Sound, Word	• Student Direction Cards • Letter Cards		●	●		

Table of Word Study Activities and Lessons (continued)

Page(s)	Activities/Lessons	Blacklines	Balanced Literacy				
			Aloud	Shared	Guided	Independent	Literature Circles
287	**Showdown Activities**						
289	Rhyming Strips	• Teacher Transparency Set • Student Cards		●	●		
303	Which One Doesn't Rhyme?	• Teacher Transparency Set • Student Cards		●	●		
308	Word Parts	• Teacher Transparency Cards • Student Cards		●	●		
312	Phoneme Segmentation	• Word List • Mat • Student Cards		●	●		
315	Beginning/Ending Sounds	• Word List • Student Set		●	●		
317	Beginning/Ending Consonant Sounds	• Teacher Transparency Cards • Student Cards		●	●		
321	Phoneme Identification	• Teacher Transparency Strips		●	●		
324	Phoneme Categorization	• Teacher Transparency Strips • Student Cards		●	●		
328	Matching Partner Letters	• Letter Cards		●	●		
330	Beginning Sounds (#1 and #2)	• Teacher Transparency Cards • Student Cards		●	●		
335	Ending Sounds	• Teacher Transparency Cards • Student Cards		●	●		

Balanced Literacy • Kindergarten • Skidmore & Graber
Kagan Publishing • 1 (800) 933-2667 • www.KaganOnline.com

Table of Word Study Activities and Lessons (continued)

Page(s)	Activities/Lessons	Blacklines	Balanced Literacy				
			Aloud	Shared	Guided	Independent	Literature Circles
287	**Showdown Activities** (continued)						
338	Beginning Letter Sound Identification (b, p, t, d)	• Teacher Transparency Cards • Student Cards		●	●		
340	Beginning Letter Sound Identification (v, w, q, y)	• Teacher Transparency Cards • Student Cards		●	●		
342	Beginning Sounds b, p, t, d	• Teacher Word List • Student Cards		●	●		
344	ch, sh, th, wh	• Teacher Transparency Cards • Student Cards		●	●		
347	**Simultaneous RallyTable and CenterPiece Activities**						
348	Letter Identification	• Letter Strips		●	●		
350	Word Pattern Strips	• Word Pattern Strips • Blank Form		●	●		
353	Alphabet Strips	• Letter Strips		●	●		
354	**Numbered Heads Together Activities**						
355	Beginning Word Sounds	• Cards		●	●		
357	Ending Word Sounds	• Cards		●	●		
360	Kindergarten Word Wall Cards	• Word List • Word Wall Cards • Blank Word Wall Cards		●	●		

Word Study
Resources

Phonemic Awareness Resource

Phonemic Awareness is the ability to manipulate the smallest units in spoken words.

"Researchers have found that phonemic awareness and letter knowledge are the two best school-entry predictors of how well children will learn to read during the first two years of instruction." (Share, Jorm, Maclean & Matthews, 1984. Sources of individual differences in reading achievement. *Journal of Education Psychology*, 76, 1309–1324.)

The Word Study Section activities are designed to provide direct instruction and practice as students increase phonemic awareness skills.

Levels of Phonemic Awareness		
Phonemic Awareness Terms	**Definitions**	**Examples**
Rhyming–Awareness and Application	recognition whether or not pairs of words rhyme telling a word that rhymes with a given word	Do *bat* and *cat* rhyme? (yes) What rhymes with *man*?
Syllable Blending/ Segmentation/Deletion	blending word parts into a whole word breaking a word into syllables/beats while tapping each part leaving out a specific part of the word	Say *ta - ble*. (table) Tap the sounds/beats in *robot*. (2) Say *basket*. Take off *ket*. (bas)
Phoneme Isolation	recognition of individual sounds in words (beginning, ending, middle)	Tell me the first sound in *pup*. (/p/) Tell me the sound at the end of *ten*. (/n/) Tell me the sound in the middle of *pet*. (/ĕ/)
Phoneme Identification	recognition of the common sound in different words	Tell me the sound that is the same in *rat*, *rug*, *rice*. (/r/)

—adapted from NICHD, 2000

Phonemic Awareness Resource (continued)

Levels of Phonemic Awareness (continued)

Phonemic Awareness Terms	Definitions	Examples
Phoneme Categorization	recognition of the word with the odd sound in a sequence of three or four words	Which word does not belong? *cat, cake, man* (man, /m/)
Phoneme Blending	ability to listen to a sequence of separately spoken sounds and combine them to form a recognizable word	What word is /t/ /r/ /u/ /k/? *truck*
Phoneme Segmentation	ability to break a word into its sounds by tapping or counting the sounds	How many phonemes in *bake*? (three phonemes: /b/ /ā/ /k/)
Phoneme Deletion/Addition	recognizing what remains when a specified phoneme is removed adding a beginning or ending sound to a word	Say *lake* without the /l/. (/ake/) Add /b/ to the beginning of (/ump/). (bump)
Onset-Rime Manipulation	ability to isolate, identify, segment, blend or delete onsets (The onset is the leading consonant(s) in a syllable; the rime is the vowel(s) and following consonants.)	*b-ump, dr-op, str-ing*

Structures and Phonemic Awareness Activities

Phonemic Awareness Skill	Structures and Terms	Pages
Rhyming–Awareness and Application	**Quiz-Quiz-Trade** • Rhyming Words—Yes or No (Awareness) • Rhyming (Application) **RallyRobin** • Rhyming (Application) **Showdown** • Rhyming Strips (Awareness) • Which One Doesn't Rhyme? (Awareness)	117–123 124–132 203–206 289–302 303–307
Syllable Blending/ Segmentation/Deletion	**Quiz-Quiz-Trade** • Word Parts (Segmentation) **RallyCoach** • Sorting by Syllables (Segmentation) **Showdown** • Word Parts (Segmentation)	133–139 209–211 308–311

Phonemic Awareness Resource (continued)

Word Study Activities and Lessons

Partner Word Study Activities

Match My Word

Structure: Match Mine

Use stand-up folders as buddy barriers. The teacher shows Partner A a slip of paper with a word study word on it. Partner A writes the word on a small dry-erase board, which Partner B cannot see. Partner A tells Partner B how to spell the word on his or her dry-erase board. The directions may include how to form the letters, but the letter names may not be said. Partners switch roles for the next word.

Big Words/Little Words

Structure: RallyCoach

The teacher makes individual letter cards for words. These are packaged in separate bags. Partners take a bag and take turns making as many different words as they can using the letters from the bag. Each word is recorded. A mystery word can be made by using all the letters in the bag.

Computer Typing

Structure: RallyCoach

Partners use a word list to take turns giving each other words to type on a word-processing program on the computer. They change the font style and sizes, so each word looks different. Print out the words to see the finished product.

Foamy Fun

Structure: RallyCoach

Partners sit side by side. The teacher squirts a heap of shaving cream on a protected surface. One at a time, the teacher calls out the word study words. The partners use their fingertips to write the word in the foam. Partners check and praise each other.

Hand Spelling

Structure: RallyCoach

Partner A traces the letters of a word in the palm of Partner B's hand. Partner A says the name of the traced word. Partners take turns tracing the word, praising, coaching, and naming the word. Partners try identifying the word while looking and then with eyes closed.

Illustrating Words

Structure: RallyCoach

Partners take turns giving each other a word from a list. Partner A gives Partner B a word. Partner B writes the word and draws a picture to represent the word. Partner B then explains the picture and spells the word aloud without looking. Partner A praises and coaches. Partner B then gives a word to Partner A. Each word has its own box on the paper.

Partner Word Study Activities

(continued)

Inflatable Ball Spelling

Structure: RallyCoach

Use an inflatable ball with letters printed on it. (You may purchase one with letters already on it or make your own by printing letters with a permanent marker.) Partners take turns tossing the ball back and forth. When the catcher gets the ball, he or she lifts one hand and sees which letter is under it. As quickly as possible, he or she says a word beginning with that letter and spells it. Together partners decide if the word is correctly spelled and record it on paper.

Letter Ladders

Structure: RallyCoach

Partners are given a set of letter cards (one of every consonant and several of every vowel). Partners take turns making new words by changing one letter at a time. The teacher begins by giving the first word (for example, *hat*). Partner A may change the *h* to *c* to make a new word (*cat*) above the first word. Partner B may then change the *t* to *n* to make *can*. Challenge partners to see how tall they can make their ladders.

Memory

Structure: RallyCoach

Partners work together to make two identical word cards for each word on the list. Partners check each other's word cards. The cards are mixed up and placed facedown in rows. Partner A turns over two cards, saying the words. If the cards are a match, he or she removes them, spells the word without looking, and takes another turn. If they are not a match, the cards are turned facedown, and Partner B has a turn. Partners praise and coach each other.

Onsets and Rimes

Structure: RallyCoach

Partners use a container filled with individual onsets. They take turns adding these to rimes provided by the teacher to make new words, which are recorded on paper. Partners check then coach or praise.

On My Back

Structure: RallyCoach

Partner A sits on a chair without a back. Partner B stands in back with a list of words. Partner B "draws" the letters to spell a word on the back of Partner A. Partner A writes the word on paper. Partner B praises and coaches. Partners switch roles.

Partner Word Study Activities

Roll a Word

Structure: RallyCoach

Prepare two large dice by writing onsets on one and rimes on the other. Partners take turns rolling both dice. If a word is rolled, partners praise and both write the word. If the roll does not make a word, the partner rolls the dice again until a word is rolled.

Sit and Spell

Structure: RallyCoach

The teacher writes a word list on the chalkboard. Students sit in two lines facing one another, so that only one line of students can see the word list. Students identify their partners, who are directly across from them. Partners A, who can see the words, are the "callers." Partners B are the "spellers." A caller reads a word aloud and listens carefully as the partner spells the word. If an incorrect spelling is given, the caller repeats the word and the partners spell it together. If a correct spelling is given, the partner praises. Partners switch roles for the next word.

Spelling Takes a Hit

Structure: RallyCoach

Partner A gives Partner B a word to spell by using a flyswatter to "hit" letters printed on a shower curtain hung on a wall. Partner A praises and coaches. Partners take turns giving the word and "hitting" the letters.

Study Buddies

Structure: RallyCoach

Partners take turns giving each other words to spell. A form with three columns is used. Partner A gives a word to Partner B to write in the first column. If the word is spelled correctly the first time, Partner A gives another word, which is written in a new first column. If the word is not spelled correctly, Partner B tries again in the second column. If that word is not correct, Partner A coaches by showing the word. Partner B writes it again in the third column. At any point that the word is correctly spelled, the partner is given a smiley face by the word. Partners switch roles when the words on the list have been spelled correctly or when the teacher indicates it is time to switch roles.

Water Spelling

Structure: RallyCoach

Partner A gives Partner B a word to spell on the sidewalk using a paintbrush and a container of water. Partner A praises and coaches. Partners take turns giving the word and "painting" it. (Note: Water sticks—plastic tubes with sponges on the ends—may also be used to "paint" words on the chalkboard.)

86 Balanced Literacy • Kindergarten • Skidmore & Graber
Kagan Publishing • 1 (800) 933-2667 • www.KaganOnline.com

Partner Word Study Activities
(continued)

Word Search

Structure: RallyCoach

Students use graph paper to create their own word searches, including the words they are focusing on for that week. Students form partners. Using one partner's word search, partners take turns circling one hidden word at a time. Each partner has a different colored pencil. Partners coach and praise. When one word search is completed, the other one is used.

Tic-Tac-Toe—Three Words in a Row

Structure: RallyRobin

Each set of partners is given a set of word cards, a Tic-Tac-Toe worksheet, and two different colors or types of counters. Partner A picks up a card and reads it to Partner B. If Partner B correctly spells the word, he or she places a counter on any open square of the game board. If Partner B gives an incorrect response, Partner A correctly spells the word and coaches Partner B to spell the word correctly. The word card is placed at the bottom of the pile and no counter is placed on the game board. Partner A now has a turn to spell the next word. Partners try to place three counters in a row (horizontally, vertically, or diagonally). Partners celebrate.

Word Family Race

Structure: RallyTable

Partners have a die with rimes (at, an, it, ot, en) and a sheet of paper. Partner A rolls the die and announces the rime it lands on. Partners then take turns writing words in the word family. For example, if the rime was "at," Partner A could write *mat*. Partners then take turns writing words in the word family. For example, Partner A could write *mat*. Partner B could write *flat*. Partners continue to alternate generating written words. When neither partner can think of another word belonging in the word family, the rime die is rolled again and new words are generated.

Spelling Toss

Structure: RallyToss

Partners spell a word while tossing a ball back and forth. Each partner says the next letter of the word until the word is spelled.

Word Toss Game

Structure: RallyToss

Partner A tosses a ball to Partner B at the same time as saying a word. Partner B writes the word on paper and spells it aloud to Partner A. Partner A praises or coaches. Continue by switching roles.

Team Word Study Activities

Spelling Detective

Structure: CenterPiece

Each team needs a page from a newspaper for each teammate and one for the center. Each teammate has a different colored pencil. The teacher calls out a word pattern and students look for a word on their newspaper page, which fits the pattern, and circle it. Students then trade their paper with the one in the center. Students continue circling words which fit the pattern until the teacher calls a new word pattern (examples: beginning /t/, /an/ word pattern, silent *e*, -ing ending, etc.).

Add On Relay

Structure: RoundTable

A team forms a line facing the chalkboard. Teammate #1 gives a word. Teammate #2 goes to the chalkboard and writes the first letter of the word, returning to the line and handing the chalk to Teammate #3, who writes the second letter of the word. Continue in this manner, until the word is spelled. If a student sees that a team member has made a spelling error, he or she may use a turn to correct the error. Teammate #2 gives the second word. (A markerboard could also be used.)

Scrambled Word Problem Solving

Structure: Jigsaw Problem Solving

Each team is given a bag with the individual letters of a word. Teammates each take a letter or letters, until all the letters are taken. Student #1 states his or her letter and where it goes in the sequence. Teammates check, coach, and move letters. Process continues with each teammate until the word is spelled correctly. When the word is spelled correctly, the team receives a new bag with a new word.

Bean Bag Word Family Game

Structure: RoundTable

Each team needs a set of laminated cards with a word family written on the top (for example: ind, ant, ine), a set of word cards, a bean bag, and a different colored transparency pen for each student. Lay out the set of word cards on the floor. Teammate #1 tosses the beanbag at the cards. He or she picks up the card that the bean bag landed on, says the word, and uses a transparency pen to write the word on the correct word family card. The word card goes in a discard pile. The other teammates take turns tossing the beanbag and writing the words on the word family cards.

Word Family Lists

Structure: Jot Thoughts

Teammates cover the table with words, belonging to a word family, written on slips of paper. Each student writes one word per slip of paper and announces the word before placing it in the middle of the table. Each added word needs to be new. (Variation: words that begin or end the same; words that were made plural by adding *es*, words ending with -ing, etc.)

Team Word Study Activities

(continued)

Colorful Team Spelling

Structure: RoundTable

Each team member has a different colored pencil or marker. The teacher gives a word. The team passes a paper around the table. Each student adds one letter to spell the word and passes the paper on to the next student until the word is spelled.

Sentence Writing

Structure: RoundTable

Each student on the team has a different colored pencil. Each person adds a word to a paper, which is passed around the table. The words need to form a complete sentence. When the sentence is completed, the sentence is read to the other teams. Each word study word for the week that is used correctly in the sentence is worth one point for class goal.

Guess the Letters

Structure: Talking Chips

Use a large dry-erase board or chalkboard that all team members can see. Teammate #1 looks at a list of words and chooses one word. He or she makes a line for each letter of the word (_ _ _ _). The other team members take turns putting a talking chip in the middle of the table and guessing a letter or the word. If the word is not guessed and all the talking chips have been used, teammates pick up their talking chips and begin guessing again. When the word has been identified, Teammate #2 chooses a new word. Continue until all teammates have had an opportunity to choose a word.

Do You Know My Word?

Structure: Showdown

One teammate spells aloud a word. Once the word is spelled, teammates pick up a marker and spell the word on individual dry-erase boards. When the Showdown Captain calls, "Showdown," teammates hold up their boards and show their spellings and name the word. They then celebrate or coach.

Find the Errors

Structure: Simultaneous RoundTable

Each team has four teacher-made sentence strips with spelling errors (one for each student). Each student has a different colored pencil. The papers are passed around the table, with each student correcting one error before passing the paper to the next student. Keep passing the sentences around until all the errors have been corrected.

Word Family Web

Structure: RoundTable

Each team works together to create a word family web. A large piece of paper is placed in the center of the team with a word family written in the middle (for example: ick, ate, ip). Each student has a different colored marker. Teammates take turns adding a word to the word family web. The team needs to agree on the spelling of the word before the next person writes.

Team Word Study Activities
(continued)

Body Spelling

Structure: Team Formations

Each team receives a word on a card. Their task is to use their bodies to spell the word. Each person on the team must be part of the spelling. Other teams guess what word was spelled.

Movement Spelling

Structure: Team Formations

The teacher calls out a word. Each team decides on a repetitive movement to use with each letter. For example, one team may decide to hop on one foot for each letter of the word as they spell it. Teams spell the word for the other teams, after practicing their words and movements at least three times. (Variation: Teams may use a different movement for each letter of the word.)

Spelling Cheerleaders

Structure: Team Formations

Students in teams act out the given word with their bodies, showing the tall letters (stretching tall with hands over heads), short letters (putting arms straight out or on hips), and tail letters (squatting or touching toes). For example, "Give me a ____. Give me an ____. Give me a __."

Machine Spelling

Structure: Team Line-Ups

Each student on a team becomes one letter of the word being spelled. They line up in order. The word is spelled orally with each student saying his or her letter while making a body motion. The team becomes a "word machine." Teams demonstrate their machines to the other teams.

Word Line-Ups

Structure: Team Line-Ups

Each team receives a stack of scrambled letters, which spell a word. Each teammate takes one of the letters. (Teammates may need to take more than one letter or share a letter, depending on the length of the word.) Each team tries to be the first to line up holding the letters in the correct order to spell the word. (If a team member has two letters, which are not positioned side by side in the word, the team will need to be creative in solving the problem.) Teams share their words with other teams.

Word Practice

Structure: Team-Pair-Solo

Teams work together to spell a word. Then teams divide into pairs and spell the same word. They compare with the other pair. Finally, individuals spell the word. They come back together as a team and compare. They celebrate or coach and begin the process with a new word.

Team Word Study Activities
(continued)

Spelling Word Collage

Structure: Team Word-Webbing

Roll out a large piece of paper on the floor or tape one to a wall for each team. Each student has a different colored marker. In a set amount of time, each student tries to fit in as many word study words as possible on the paper to create a colorful word collage.

Pick a Letter, Any Letter

Structure: Think-Write-RoundRobin

Each team has a bag of letters. Teammate #1 chooses a letter from the bag without looking and announces the letter to the team, placing it in the middle. Each student thinks about possible words beginning with that letter and then makes a list of words beginning with that letter on individual dry-erase boards. Time is called after a preset time limit. Teammates take turns RoundRobin sharing one of the words on their lists. If a shared word is also on their lists, students may put a mark by it. Words shared aloud must be new words not previously shared. Continue sharing until all new words have been shared. If a teammate does not have a new word on the list to share, he or she may try to come up with another word.

Spelling Walk

Structure: Traveling Heads Together

Teams huddle to make sure all can spell a given word correctly. Use dry-erase boards to practice writing the word. When everyone is confident they can spell the word, the dry-erase boards are cleared and the team sits down. The teacher calls a number and the student with that number travels to a new team with his or her cleared dry-erase board and a marker. At the new team, the student shares the spelling of the word by writing it on the dry-erase board.

Spelling Toss

Structure: Turn Toss

Teammates toss a ball to each other. As each teammate catches the ball, he or she contributes a letter to the spelling of a word called out by the teacher. Teammates continue until the word is spelled. The teacher then gives a new word.

Class Word Study Activities

Add a Word to My Family

Structure: Find Someone Who

Students have bingo sheets. At the top they put a word given by the teacher. They circulate throughout the room looking for someone who can add a word to a square on their paper and sign his or her name below the added word. The word needs to belong to the same family as the given word and needs to be one that is not already on the paper.

Spell My Word

Structure: Inside-Outside Circle

Students form two circles facing each other. Each student has a word list. As either the outside or the inside circle moves one space, students face new partners. Partners take turns having their partner spell a word from the list. Rotate.

What's My Word?

Structure: Who Am I?

Students attempt to determine their secret word (taped on their back) by circulating and asking "yes/ no" questions of classmates. They are allowed three questions per classmate (or unlimited questions until they receive a "no" response). They then find a new classmate to question. When the student guesses his or her word, the student becomes a consultant to give clues to those who have not yet found their identity.

Jumping Words

Structure: Take Off, Touch Down

Give each student a word card. The teacher calls out a vowel sound. If the student's word contains the vowel sound, he or she stands or jumps up. Standing students share their words simultaneously. Teacher and class check for accuracy. The teacher continues to call vowel sounds as students listen for the vowel sound in their words. Variation: The teacher calls out a word and students jump up when they hear a word that rhymes with the word on their word card.

How Many?

Structure: Mix-Freeze-Group

Students make groups with a specific number of students corresponding to answers to questions, asked by the teacher, such as:
- # of total letters in a given word
- # of vowels in a word
- # of a specific letter in a word
- # of syllables in a word

(For example, if the answer to the question is four, when the teacher calls, "Show me," students show the number 4 with their fingers on their chests, quickly form groups of four, and kneel down. Students not finding a group should meet in a predetermined part of the room in "Lost and Found.")

Making Words
Lesson Plans

On the following pages are three lessons designed to help students think about the sounds they hear in words and the letter patterns that make up those sounds. They all involve making words from one longer word. The steps for the three lessons are the same. In each of the three lessons, students proceed through three activities:

- **Activity 1: Making Words** (RallyCoach)
- **Activity 2: Sorting** (Find My Rule)
- **Activity 3: Transfer** (RallyCoach)

Since the steps are the same for all three lesson, we will provide a full description of Lesson 1, then just provide the necessary substitutions for Lessons 2 and 3.

Each lesson has its own set of blacklines, but they all share the Find My Rule Mat on page 108. Also, you will find two forms to plan and create your own Making Words lessons.

- **Making Words Planning Form (p. 109)**
- **Making Words Student Form (p. 110)**

The Magic Word
When done with each lesson, challenge pairs to see if they can discover the "Magic Word." The magic word is the word made from all the letters from each set of student letters.
The magic word from each lesson is:
Lesson 1: plant
Lesson 2: plays
Lesson 3: hamster

Helpful Hints:
- These activities may be done in one day or two days at the beginning of the week. Making Words may be done on day one and the Sorting and Transfer activities on day two.
- Mailing envelopes or plastic sandwich baggies will help students keep their materials organized and accessible.
- These activities are most beneficial when the teacher selects or designs lessons that reinforce letter patterns the students are needing to know or strengthen for their reading and writing.
- All letters on the Making Words form are put in alphabetical order with vowels first, followed by consonants.

Making Words Lessons

Lessons

Making Words
Lesson 1: *Plant*

Activity 1: Making Words

In pairs, students take turns manipulating letter cards to make words.

STRUCTURE
RallyCoach

Activity 1 Steps

1. The teacher makes a transparency of the Making Words (*Plant*) page and cuts out the letters and words.

2. Each pair receives one set of the following letters, *a, l, n, p, t* (the letters from the word *plant*), from the blackline.

3. The teacher asks students to make words as described in the table on page 95, "Words to Make from *Plant*." The teacher reviews the teaching points as indicated on the table.

4. Partner A makes the first word, while Partner B coaches if necessary.

5. The teacher makes the word on the overhead projector.

6. Students write the word in a box on their student form. They will use these words in Activity 2.

7. Partners take turns for each new word and the process is repeated.

Blacklines

Words to Make from *Plant*

Directions	Word	Teaching Point
Make: *ant*	ant	Discuss /an/ letter pattern at the beginning of the word.
Put the *t* at the front of /an/ to make a new word.	tan	Discuss stretching through the word with finger and eyes and saying the word. Discuss the letter pattern at the end of the word.
Change the beginning letter to a *p*.	pan	What word did you make?
Have the beginning letter and ending letter change places.	nap	What word did you make?
Take away the *n*. Put an *l* at the beginning.	lap	Have students stretch through the word to check.
Have the beginning letter and ending letter change places.	pal	What letter pattern do you see now?
Change the ending letter back to an *n*.	pan	
Add a *t* to the end of the word to make a new word.	pant	Locate the /an/ letter pattern in the middle of the word.
Can you use all the letters to make a magic word?	plant	

Activity 2: Sorting

The teacher places words in two different columns on the overhead projector. The challenge is for students to discover the teacher's rules for sorting the words this way. This activity draws the students' attention to visual clues and letter patterns.

Activity 2 Steps

STRUCTURE

Find My Rule

Ideas for Rules

- /ap/ letter pattern
- /ant/ letter pattern
- words beginning with /p/

1. The teacher makes a transparency of the Find My Rule Mat (page 108).

2. The teacher decides on a "rule" to place words in the two different columns of the Mat. For the example below, the rule is **/an/ letter pattern.**

My Rule	Not My Rule
tan	nap
pan	

3. The teacher places one word in each column, and asks, "What is my rule?"

4. Students RallyRobin with their shoulder partners to determine what the rule may be.

5. The teacher adds the next two words, one in each column, and asks again, "What is my rule?"

6. Students RallyRobin again.

7. This continues until students think they know the rule. The teacher calls on students to verbalize the rule. If correct, the teacher congratulates the students, if incorrect the process continues.

8. When done, the activity may be repeated with a new rule. Other rule examples are listed at left.

9. After practice, students can cut apart their word boxes from Activity 1, step 6. They can create their own word sorts and have a partner find the rule.

Blacklines

Activity 3: Transfer

The teacher displays a word card on the overhead projector and discusses the letter pattern. Then the teacher says, "If you can spell this word, you can also spell..." Students work in pairs to spell the new word. This activity helps students "use what they know" from one word and transfer it to a new word that they are trying to read or write.

STRUCTURE
RallyCoach

Activity 3 Steps

1. The teacher places a word card on the overhead projector.
2. The teacher states, "If you can spell this word, you can also spell...." (See the examples below.)
3. Partner A spells the word while Partner B watches, checks, and coaches as needed.
4. The teacher spells the new word for the class, and students praise their partners for correct spelling.
5. Students switch roles of Speller and Coach for each new word.

Using What You Know

If you can spell...	Then you can spell...
tan	man, ran, fan, can, van
lap	cap, map, rap, tap, clap

Making Words (*Plant*)
Teacher Transparency Form

Instructions: Make a transparency of this page. Cut out letters and words to use during Activity 1: Making Words and with Activity 2: Sorting.

	lap	plant				
t	nap	pant				
p	tan	pal				
n						
l						
a	ant	pan				

Making Words (a, l, n, p, t)
Student Form

Instructions: Make one copy per student. Cut apart letters to use during Activity 1: Making Words. Cut apart boxes after words are added to be used during Activity 2: Sorting.

t

p

n

l

a

Lesson 2: Plays
Activity 1: Making Words

The steps for this activity are the same as Lesson 1, Activity 1 but substitute the following words to make from the letters in Plays.

Words to Make from *Plays*

Directions	Word	Teaching Point
Make: *say*	say	Discuss the /ay/ letter pattern.
Take away the *s* and add an *l* to the beginning.	lay	Stretch through the word to check.
Add an *s* to the end of lay to make *lays.* The dog lays on his mat.	lays	Discuss covering up endings to see a familiar letter pattern or word.
Replace the *l* with a *p.* What word did you make?	pays	Have students stretch through the word with their finger and eyes to say the word.
Take away the *s.* Now what word did you make?	pay	
What do you need to add to make the word *play*? Segment the sounds slowly (or) slip the *l* after the *p.*	play	Discuss listening for all sounds. Help student stretch the word orally as they point to the letters.
Use all the letters to spell my magic word.	plays	Cover up the *s* and say the word. Put the *s* back on and say the word.

Activity 2: Sorting

The steps for this activity are the same as Lesson 1, Activity 2. Below is an example for Find My Rule using the Plays words and additional ideas for Find My Rule.

Ideas for Rules

- /ay/ letter pattern
- words beginning with /p/
- words with an *l*

My Rule	Not My Rule
lays	lay
pays	

Example: words ending with /s/

Activity 3: Transfer

The steps for this activity are the same as Lesson 1, Activity 3, except use the following words to spell.

Using What You Know

If you can spell…	Then you can spell…
say	may, bay, hay, way, stay
lays	days, rays, prays

Making Words (*Plays*)
Teacher Transparency Form

Instructions: Make a transparency of this page. Cut out letters and words to use during Activity 1: Making Words.

a	s	pays				
l	y	lays	plays			
p	l	lay	play			
a		say	pay			

Making Words (a, l, p, s, y)
Student Form

Instructions: Make one copy per student. Cut apart letters to use during Activity 1: Making Words.
Cut apart boxes after words are added to be used during Activity 2: Sorting.

y

s

p

l

a

Lesson 3: *Hamster*
Activity 1: Making Words

The steps for this activity are the same as Lesson 1, Activity 1 but substitute the following words to make from the letters in Hamster.

Words to Make from *Hamster*

Directions	Word	Teaching Point
Make: *am*	am	*am* is a word: I am going to the store. It is also a letter pattern that makes a word family: __am
Add an *h* to the beginning to make a new word.	ham	What letter pattern do you see? (am) Cover up from the vowel on and get your mouth ready, say the beginning sound, then uncover and say the rest of the word. What is the word?
Take away the *h* and replace it with the letter *r*.	ram	Cover up the letter pattern, get your mouth ready, say the beginning sound, uncover and say the rest of the word. What word did you make? Who can use the word in a sentence?
Place the *e* and *t* together to make *et*.		We are now going to work on the /et/ letter pattern.
Make: *met* *I met a friend at the movie.*	met	Have the students decode the word and identify the letter pattern as above.
Replace the beginning letter to make the word *set*. *I set the table for dinner.*	set	
Listen closely to the word and change one letter to make the word *sat*. I sat down in my favorite chair.	sat	What letter did you change? (a) What letter pattern do you see? /at/
Replace one letter to make the word *mat*.	mat	Have the students identify the letter pattern by covering the *m* with their fingers.
Now make the word *rat*.	rat	
Make it mean more than one rat.	rats	Discuss adding an *s* to make it mean more than one.
New letter pattern: /ea/ Put the /ea/ letter pattern in front of you.		
Make: *eat*	eat	Have the students slide their finger under the word to stretch through it and say the sounds.

Words to Make from *Hamster* (continued)

Directions	Word	Teaching Point
Add a letter to the beginning to make the word *seat*.	seat	What word/letter pattern do you see? (eat; /ea/)
Replace the *s* and add an *h*.	heat	What word did you make?
Replace the *h* with an *m*.	meat	What word did you make?
Rearrange the beginning and ending letters.	team	What is the new word?
Use all the letters to spell my magic word.	hamster	What letter patterns do you see? Have the students slide their finger under the word and stretch through it to check the word.

Activity 2: Sorting

The steps for this activity are the same as Lesson 1, Activity 2. Below is an example for Find My Rule using the Hamster *words and additional ideas for Find My Rule.*

Ideas for Rules

- /et/ letter pattern
- /am/ letter pattern
- /ea/ letter pattern
- words beginning with /r/ or /s/

My Rule	Not My Rule
sat	eat
rat	

Example: /at/ letter pattern

Activity 3: Transfer

The steps for this activity are the same as Lesson 1, Activity 3, except use the following words to spell.

Using What You Know

If you can spell...	Then you can spell...
ham	jam, yam, Sam
sat	bat, fat, hat, flat, chat
set	jet, pet, vet, let, get, wet

Making Words (*Hamster*)
Teacher Transparency Form

Instructions: Make a transparency of this page. Cut out letters and words to use during Activity 1: Making Words.

t	met	rat	heat		
s r	ram	mat	seat	hamster	
m h	ham	sat	eat	team	
e a	am	set	rats	meat	

Balanced Literacy • Kindergarten • Skidmore & Graber
Kagan Publishing • 1 (800) 933-2667 • www.KaganOnline.com

Making Words (a, e, h, m, r, s, t)
Student Form

Instructions: Make one copy per student. Cut apart letters to use during Activity 1: Making Words. Cut apart boxes after words are added to be used during Activity 2: Sorting.

t

s

r

m

h

e

a

Find My Rule Mat
for Making Words

Instructions: Make a transparency of this mat for Activity 2: Sorting. Make copies for each pair of students for Activity 2: Sorting.

My Rule	Not My Rule

Making Words Planning Form

Letters: _____

Magic Word: _____

Part 1: Making Words (RallyCoach)

Instructions: Use this planning form to create additional Making Words lessons.

Directions	Word	Teaching Point

Part 2: Sorting (Find My Rule)	Sort For:

Part 3: Transfer (RallyCoach)	Using What You Know

Making Words Student Form

Instructions: Use this planning form to create the letters and words for additional Making Words lessons.

Who Knows?

Students mix about the room, finding others who can help them fill out their Find Someone Who word study worksheets.

STRUCTURE

Find Someone Who

Activity Steps

1. Every student receives a Find Someone Who worksheet.

2. Students mix around the room until they find a partner.

3. In pairs, Partner A asks a question from the worksheet; Partner B responds. Partner A records the answer on his or her worksheet.

4. Partner B checks and initials the answer.

5. Partner B asks a question. Partner A responds. Partner B records the answer on his or her worksheet.

6. Partner A checks and initials the answer.

7. Partners shake hands, part, and raise a hand again as they search for a new partner.

8. Students repeat the process until they complete their worksheets.

9. When their worksheets are completed, students sit down; seated students may be approached by others as a resource.

10. In teams, students compare answers; if there is disagreement or uncertainty, they raise four hands to ask a team question.

Blacklines

Matching Capital and Lower Case Letters, Beginning Word Sounds, Writing Name, Recognizing Bb, Beginning Word Sounds

Find Someone Who

Name _____

Instructions: Copy one page per student.

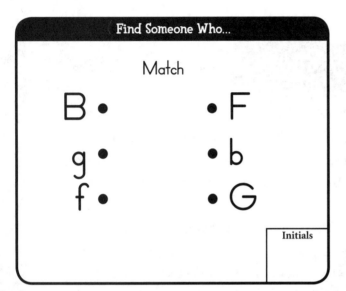

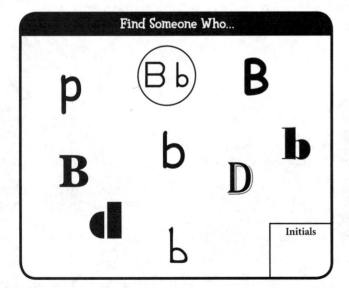

Balanced Literacy • Kindergarten • Skidmore & Graber
Kagan Publishing • 1 (800) 933-2667 • www.KaganOnline.com

Partner Letters, Adding a to Words, /at/ Letter Pattern, Matching Pictures with Words, Recognizing *p* in Words, Recognizing /an/

Find Someone Who

Name _____

Instructions: Copy one page per student.

Find Someone Who...

Partner Letters

D _____

_____t

N _____

Initials

Find Someone Who...

Add *a*

m_p   m_n   m_t

Initials

Find Someone Who...

Add a Letter

_____at

_____at

_____at

Initials

Find Someone Who...

Match

mug

dog

bell

Initials

Find Someone Who...

p

pup

pig

jump

Initials

Find Someone Who...

an   an

and

an   and   an

an

am   at   an   am

Initials

Adding *i* to Words, Matching Capital and Lower Case Letters, Identifying /sh/ Words, Recognizing /an/ in Words

Find Someone Who

Name _____

Instructions: Copy one page per student.

Find Someone Who...

Add *i*

s__t   f__n   l__p

Initials

Find Someone Who...

w   M

N   n

m   W

Initials

Find Someone Who...

sh

Initials

Find Someone Who...

Dan   can

plan   pan   an   hand   fan

van   tan

ant

Initials

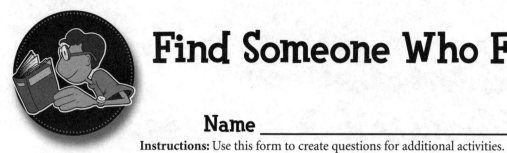

Find Someone Who Form

Name _____

Instructions: Use this form to create questions for additional activities.

Initials

Initials

Initials

Initials

Initials

Initials

Initials

Activity

Phonemic Awareness Letter Identification

To practice phonemic awareness and letter identification skills, students quiz a partner, get quizzed by a partner, and then trade cards to repeat the process with a new partner.

Activity Steps

1. Each student receives a card with a question on the front and answer on the back.

2. All students stand up, put a hand up, and pair up.

3. Partner A quizzes Partner B.

4. Partner B answers.

5. Partner A checks the answer on back and praises or coaches.

6. Partners switch roles and quiz again.

7. After they have quizzed both ways, partners trade cards, and raise their hands to find a new partner. The partner quizzing and trading proceeds for numerous pairings.

STRUCTURE

Quiz-Quiz-Trade

Blacklines

Rhyming Words–Yes or No?
Quiz-Quiz-Trade

Instructions: Copy enough cards so each student has one card. Cut on dotted lines and fold in half.

Rhyming Words–Yes or No? Question: Rhyming Words? 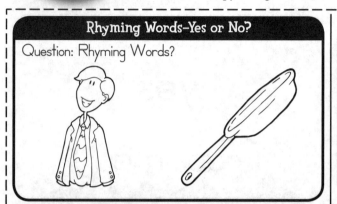	Rhyming Words–Yes or No? Answer: **yes** (man, pan)
Rhyming Words–Yes or No? Question: Rhyming Words? 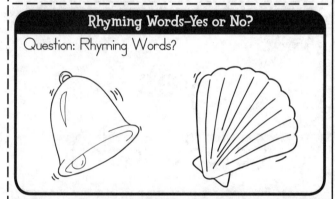	Rhyming Words–Yes or No? Answer: **yes** (bell, shell)
Rhyming Words–Yes or No? Question: Rhyming Words? 	Rhyming Words–Yes or No? Answer: **no** (frog, skunk)
Rhyming Words–Yes or No? Question: Rhyming Words? 	Rhyming Words–Yes or No? Answer: **yes** (box, fox)

Rhyming Words–Yes or No?
Quiz-Quiz-Trade

Instructions: Copy enough cards so each student has one card. Cut on dotted lines and fold in half.

Rhyming Words–Yes or No?	**Rhyming Words–Yes or No?**
Question: Rhyming Words? 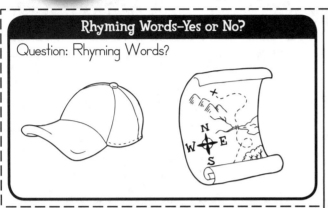	Answer: **yes** (cap, map)
Rhyming Words–Yes or No?	**Rhyming Words–Yes or No?**
Question: Rhyming Words? 	Answer: **yes** (clock, lock)
Rhyming Words–Yes or No?	**Rhyming Words–Yes or No?**
Question: Rhyming Words? 	Answer: **no** (nail, lion)
Rhyming Words–Yes or No?	**Rhyming Words–Yes or No?**
Question: Rhyming Words? 	Answer: **no** (mop, lamp)

Rhyming Words–Yes or No?
Quiz-Quiz-Trade

Instructions: Copy enough cards so each student has one card. Cut on dotted lines and fold in half.

Rhyming Words–Yes or No?
Question: Rhyming Words?

Rhyming Words–Yes or No?
Answer:

no
(fish, fox)

Rhyming Words–Yes or No?
Question: Rhyming Words?

Rhyming Words–Yes or No?
Answer:

yes
(coat, goat)

Rhyming Words–Yes or No?
Question: Rhyming Words?

Rhyming Words–Yes or No?
Answer:

no
(bed, net)

Rhyming Words–Yes or No?
Question: Rhyming Words?

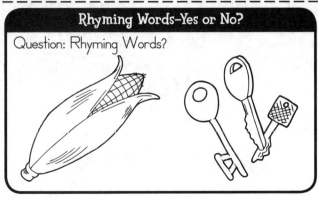

Rhyming Words–Yes or No?
Answer:

no
(corn, keys)

Rhyming Words–Yes or No?
Quiz-Quiz-Trade

Instructions: Copy enough cards so each student has one card. Cut on dotted lines and fold in half.

Rhyming Words–Yes or No?	Rhyming Words–Yes or No?
Question: Rhyming Words? 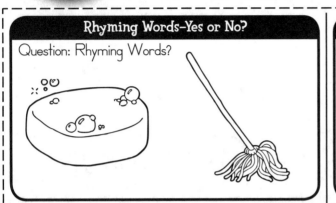	Answer: **no** (soap, mop)
Question: Rhyming Words? 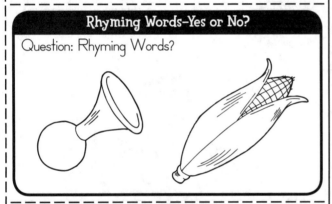	Answer: **yes** (horn, corn)
Question: Rhyming Words? 	Answer: **yes** (cot, pot)
Question: Rhyming Words? 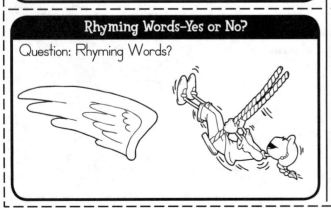	Answer: **yes** (wing, swing)

Balanced Literacy • Kindergarten • Skidmore & Graber
Kagan Publishing • 1 (800) 933-2667 • www.KaganOnline.com

Rhyming Words–Yes or No?
Quiz-Quiz-Trade

Instructions: Copy enough cards so each student has one card. Cut on dotted lines and fold in half.

Rhyming Words–Yes or No?	Rhyming Words–Yes or No?
Question: Rhyming Words? 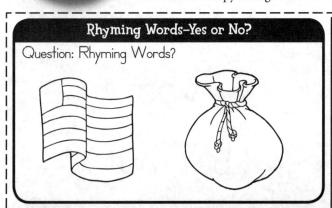	Answer: **yes** (flag, bag)
Question: Rhyming Words? 	Answer: **no** (up, soap)
Question: Rhyming Words? 	Answer: **yes** (chain, train)
Question: Rhyming Words? 	Answer: **yes** (shell, well)

Rhyming Words–Yes or No?
Quiz-Quiz-Trade

Instructions: Copy enough cards so each student has one card. Cut on dotted lines and fold in half.

Rhyming Words–Yes or No?	Rhyming Words–Yes or No?
Question: Rhyming Words? 	Answer: **yes** (bat, hat)
Question: Rhyming Words? 	Answer: **yes** (sock, clock)
Question: Rhyming Words? 	Answer: **yes** (truck, duck)
Question: Rhyming Words? 	Answer: **yes** (bee, tree)

Rhyming Words–Yes or No?
Quiz-Quiz-Trade

Instructions: Copy enough cards so each student has one card. Cut on dotted lines and fold in half.

Rhyming Words–Yes or No?	Rhyming Words–Yes or No?
Question: Rhyming Words? 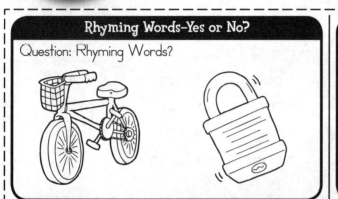	Answer: **no** (bike, lock)
Question: Rhyming Words? 	Answer: **yes** (man, fan)
Question: Rhyming Words? 	Answer: **no** (net, tent)
Question: Rhyming Words? 	Answer: **no** (book, box)

Rhyming
Quiz-Quiz-Trade

Instructions: Copy and cut apart cards so each student has one. Partners give one rhyming word for the answer. Possible options are listed.

Rhyming	Rhyming
Question: What rhymes?  **can**	Answer: • ban • ran • clan • fan • tan • plan • man • van • than • pan • bran
Question: What rhymes? 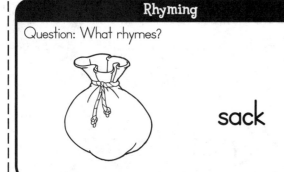 **cake**	Answer: • bake • take • snake • fake • wake • stake • lake • brake • sake • make • flake • rake • shake
Question: What rhymes? 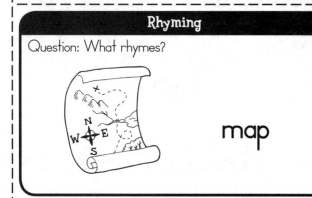 **sack**	Answer: • back • snack • shack • lack • black • stack • pack • clack • track • rack • crack • tack
Question: What rhymes? **map**	Answer: • cap • sap • slap • gap • tap • snap • nap • yap • trap • lap • chap • rap • flap

Rhyming
Quiz-Quiz-Trade

Instructions: Copy and cut apart cards so each student has one. Partners give one rhyming word for the answer. Possible options are listed.

Rhyming	

Question: What rhymes?

cat

Rhyming

Answer:

- bat   • pat   • brat
- fat   • rat   • chat
- hat   • sat   • flat
- mat   • vat   • that

Rhyming	

Question: What rhymes?

tray

Rhyming

Answer:

- bay   • lay   • way
- clay   • may   • stay
- day   • pay   • gray
- hay   • ray   • play
- jay   • say

Rhyming	

Question: What rhymes?

bell

Rhyming

Answer:

- cell   • tell   • spell
- fell   • well   • swell
- jell   • yell
- sell   • smell

Rhyming	

Question: What rhymes?

nest

Rhyming

Answer:

- best   • vest   • chest
- pest   • west   • crest
- rest   • zest
- test

Rhyming
Quiz-Quiz-Trade

Instructions: Copy and cut apart cards so each student has one. Partners give one rhyming word for the answer. Possible options are listed.

Rhyming	Rhyming
Question: What rhymes?  **kick**	Answer: • lick • brick • slick • pick • chick • stick • sick • click • thick • tick • flick • trick • wick
Question: What rhymes?  **hill**	Answer: • bill • sill • frill • fill • till • grill • gill • will • spill • mill • chill • still • pill • drill • thrill
Question: What rhymes? 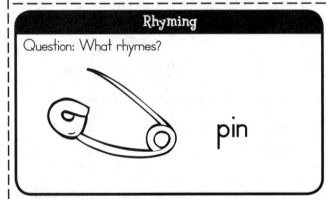 **pin**	Answer: • bin • tin • skin • fin • win • spin • kin • chin • thin • sin • grin • twin
Question: What rhymes?  **sink**	Answer: • link • wink • stink • mink • blink • think • pink • drink • rink • shrink

Balanced Literacy • Kindergarten • Skidmore & Graber
Kagan Publishing • 1 (800) 933-2667 • www.KaganOnline.com

Rhyming
Quiz-Quiz-Trade

Instructions: Copy and cut apart cards so each student has one. Partners give one rhyming word for the answer. Possible options are listed.

Rhyming

Question: What rhymes?

drip

Rhyming

Answer:
- dip
- hip
- lip
- nip
- rip
- sip
- tip
- trip
- zip
- chip
- clip
- flip
- ship

Rhyming

Question: What rhymes?

kit

Rhyming

Answer:
- bit
- fit
- hit
- pit
- lit
- sit
- skit
- slit
- spit
- split

Rhyming

Question: What rhymes?

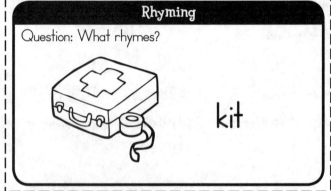

stop

Rhyming

Answer:
- cop
- hop
- mop
- pop
- top
- chop
- crop
- drop
- flop
- plop
- shop
- slop

Rhyming

Question: What rhymes?

hug

Rhyming

Answer:
- bug
- dug
- jug
- mug
- rug
- tug
- chug
- plug
- shrug
- slug
- snug

Rhyming
Quiz-Quiz-Trade

Instructions: Copy and cut apart cards so each student has one. Partners give one rhyming word for the answer. Possible options are listed.

Rhyming
Question: What rhymes?  jump

Rhyming
Answer: • bump • grump • thump   • dump • plump • trump   • lump • slump   • pump • stump

Rhyming
Question: What rhymes? 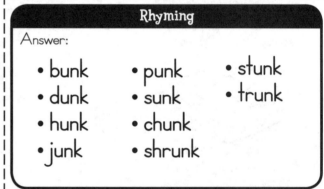 skunk

Rhyming
Answer: • bunk • punk • stunk   • dunk • sunk • trunk   • hunk • chunk   • junk • shrunk

Rhyming
Question: What rhymes?  duck

Rhyming
Answer: • buck • tuck • struck   • luck • cluck • truck   • muck • pluck   • puck • stuck

Rhyming
Question: What rhymes? pail

Rhyming
Answer: • bail • nail • frail   • fail • rail • snail   • hail • sail • trail   • jail • tail   • mail

Rhyming
Quiz-Quiz-Trade

Instructions: Copy and cut apart cards so each student has one. Partners give one rhyming word for the answer. Possible options are listed.

Rhyming

Question: What rhymes?

chain

Rhyming

Answer:

- main
- pain
- rain
- vain
- brain
- drain
- grain
- plain
- stain
- train

Rhyming

Question: What rhymes?

whale

Rhyming

Answer:

- bale
- gale
- male
- pale
- sale
- tale
- scale
- shale
- stale

Rhyming

Question: What rhymes?

flame

Rhyming

Answer:

- came
- fame
- game
- lame
- name
- same
- tame
- blame
- frame
- shame

Rhyming

Question: What rhymes?

tank

Rhyming

Answer:

- bank
- hank
- rank
- sank
- yank
- blank
- crank
- drank
- prank
- shrank
- spank
- thank

Rhyming
Quiz-Quiz-Trade

Instructions: Copy and cut apart cards so each student has one. Partners give one rhyming word for the answer. Possible options are listed.

Rhyming
Question: What rhymes?

trash

Rhyming
Answer:

- bash
- cash
- dash
- gash
- mash
- rash
- clash
- crash
- flash
- smash
- stash

Rhyming
Question: What rhymes?

skate

Rhyming
Answer:

- date
- gate
- hate
- late
- mate
- rate
- crate
- plate
- state

Rhyming
Question: What rhymes?

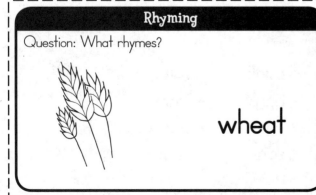

saw

Rhyming
Answer:

- law
- jaw
- paw
- raw
- claw
- draw
- straw

Rhyming
Question: What rhymes?

wheat

Rhyming
Answer:

- beat
- heat
- meat
- neat
- seat
- treat

Rhyming
Quiz-Quiz-Trade

Instructions: Copy and cut apart cards so each student has one. Partners give one rhyming word for the answer. Possible options are listed.

Rhyming	
Question: What rhymes?	

dice

Rhyming
Answer:

- ice
- lice
- mice
- nice
- rice
- price
- slice
- spice
- twice

Rhyming	
Question: What rhymes?	

bride

Rhyming
Answer:

- hide
- ride
- side
- tide
- wide
- glide
- pride
- slide
- stride

Rhyming	
Question: What rhymes?	

light

Rhyming
Answer:

- might
- night
- right
- sight
- tight
- bright
- flight
- fright
- slight

Rhyming	
Question: What rhymes?	

9

nine

Rhyming
Answer:

- dine
- fine
- line
- mine
- pine
- vine
- shine
- spine
- whine

Rhyming
Quiz-Quiz-Trade

Instructions: Copy and cut apart cards so each student has one. Partners give one rhyming word for the answer. Possible options are listed.

Rhyming
Question: What rhymes?

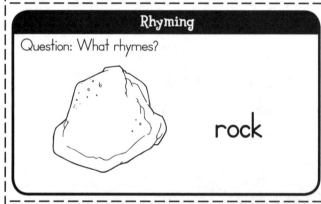

king

Rhyming
Answer:

- ping
- ring
- sing
- wing
- zing
- bring
- cling
- fling
- sling
- spring
- sting
- string
- swing
- thing

Rhyming
Question: What rhymes?

rock

Rhyming
Answer:

- dock
- lock
- sock
- block
- clock
- flock
- shock
- stock

Rhyming
Question: What rhymes?

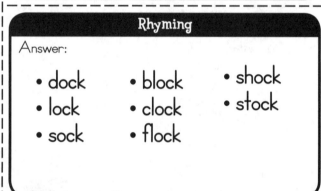

store

Rhyming
Answer:

- core
- more
- sore
- tore
- wore
- chore
- score
- shore
- snore

Rhyming
Question: What rhymes?

log

Rhyming
Answer:

- bog
- dog
- hog
- jog
- blog
- clog
- frog
- smog

Word Parts
Quiz-Quiz-Trade

Instructions: Copy enough cards so each student has one card. Cut on dotted lines and fold in half.

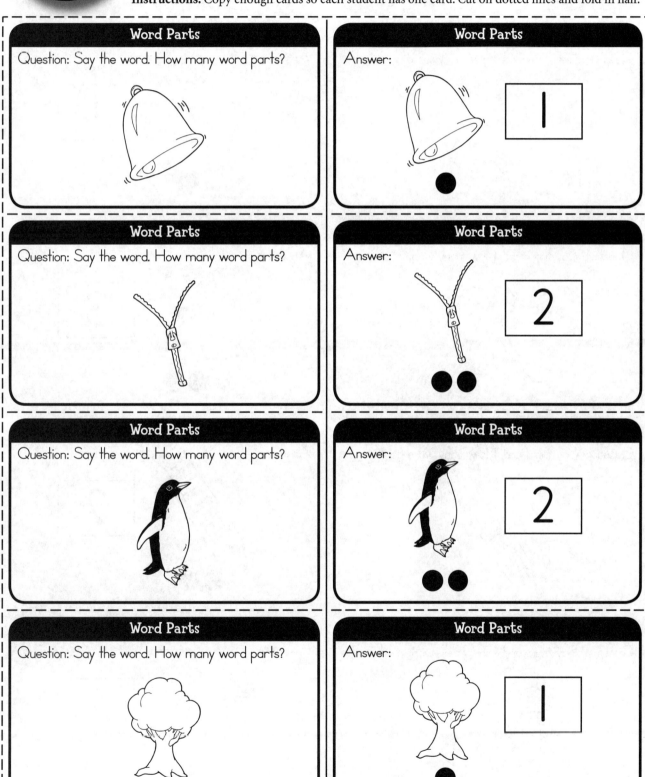

Word Parts	Word Parts
Question: Say the word. How many word parts?	Answer: 1 ●
Question: Say the word. How many word parts?	Answer: 2 ●●
Question: Say the word. How many word parts?	Answer: 2 ●●
Question: Say the word. How many word parts?	Answer: 1 ●

Word Parts
Quiz-Quiz-Trade

Instructions: Copy enough cards so each student has one card. Cut on dotted lines and fold in half.

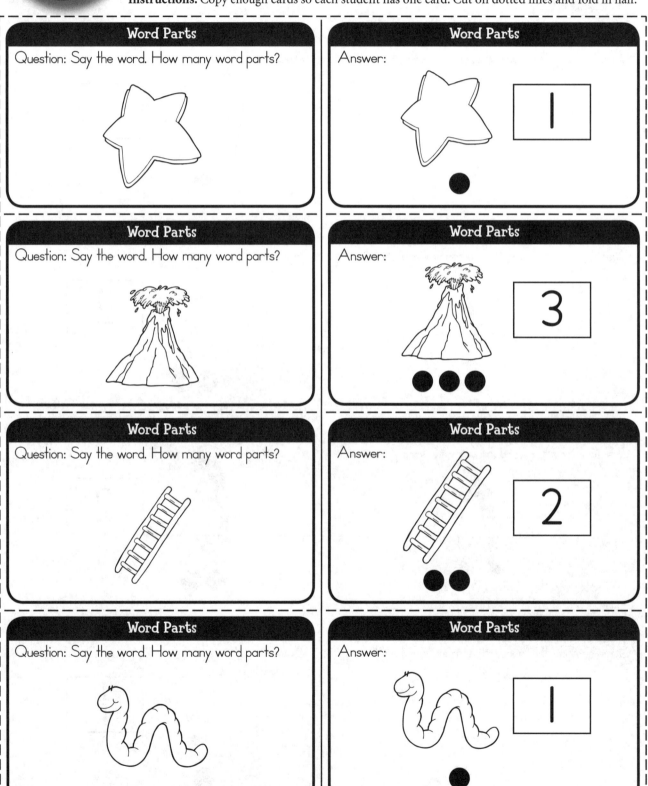

Word Parts	Word Parts
Question: Say the word. How many word parts?	Answer: 1
Word Parts	Word Parts
Question: Say the word. How many word parts?	Answer: 3
Word Parts	Word Parts
Question: Say the word. How many word parts?	Answer: 2
Word Parts	Word Parts
Question: Say the word. How many word parts?	Answer: 1

Word Parts
Quiz-Quiz-Trade

Instructions: Copy enough cards so each student has one card. Cut on dotted lines and fold in half.

Word Parts	Word Parts
Question: Say the word. How many word parts? 	Answer: 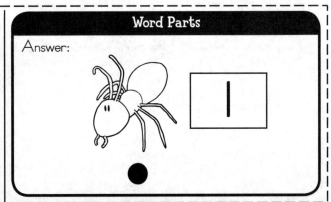
Word Parts	Word Parts
Question: Say the word. How many word parts? 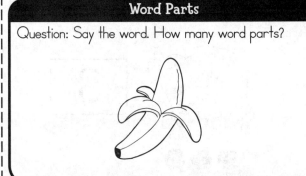	Answer: 
Word Parts	Word Parts
Question: Say the word. How many word parts? 	Answer: 
Word Parts	Word Parts
Question: Say the word. How many word parts? 	Answer: 

Word Parts

Quiz-Quiz-Trade

Instructions: Copy enough cards so each student has one card. Cut on dotted lines and fold in half.

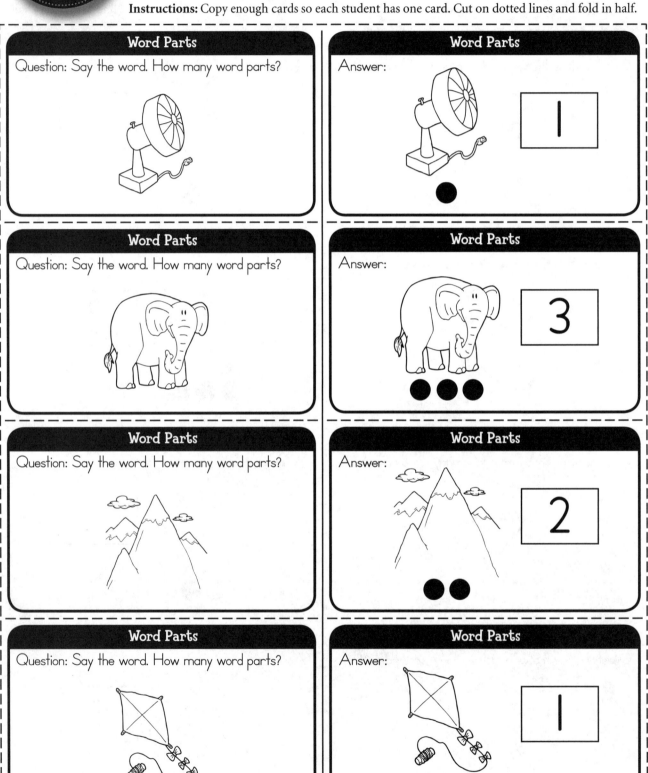

Word Parts	Word Parts
Question: Say the word. How many word parts?	Answer: 1
Question: Say the word. How many word parts?	Answer: 3
Question: Say the word. How many word parts?	Answer: 2
Question: Say the word. How many word parts?	Answer: 1

Word Parts

Quiz-Quiz-Trade

Instructions: Copy enough cards so each student has one card. Cut on dotted lines and fold in half.

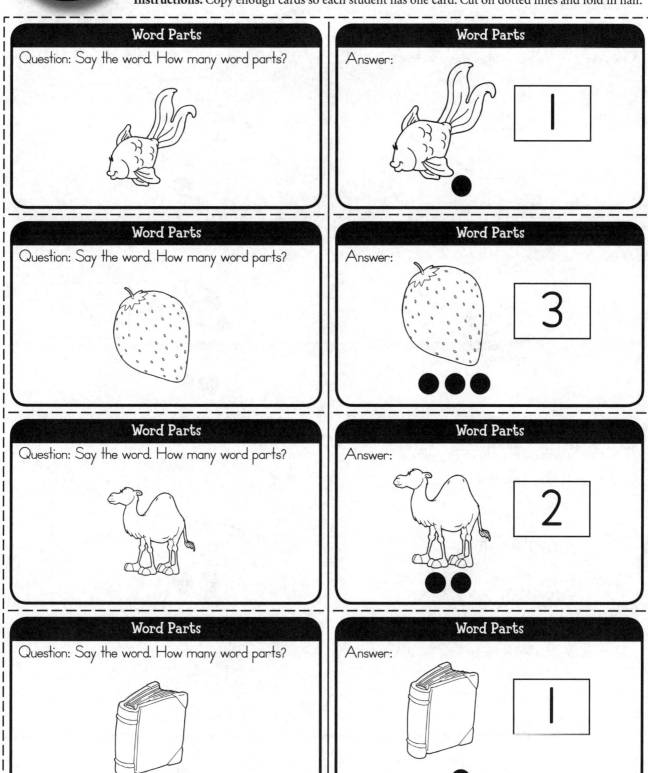

Word Parts
Quiz-Quiz-Trade

Instructions: Copy enough cards so each student has one card. Cut on dotted lines and fold in half.

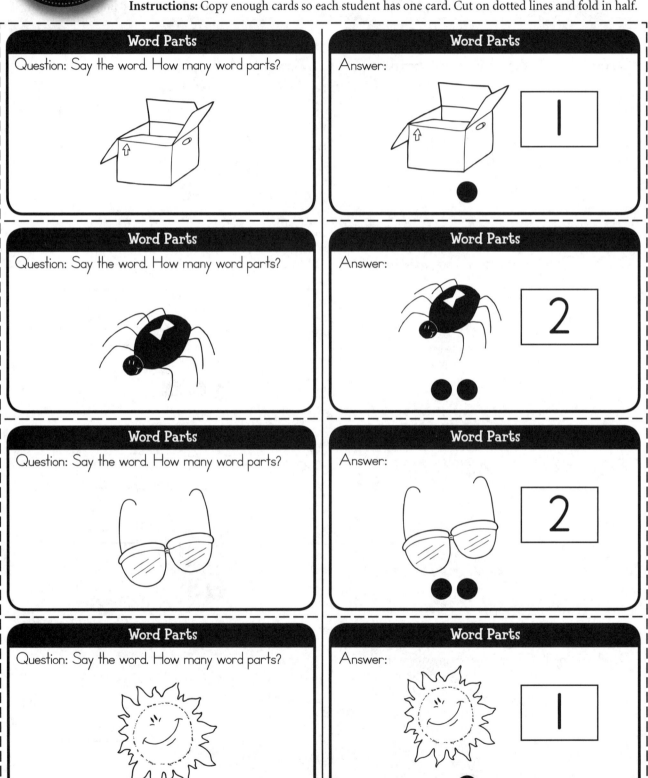

Word Parts
Quiz-Quiz-Trade

Instructions: Copy enough cards so each student has one card. Cut on dotted lines and fold in half.

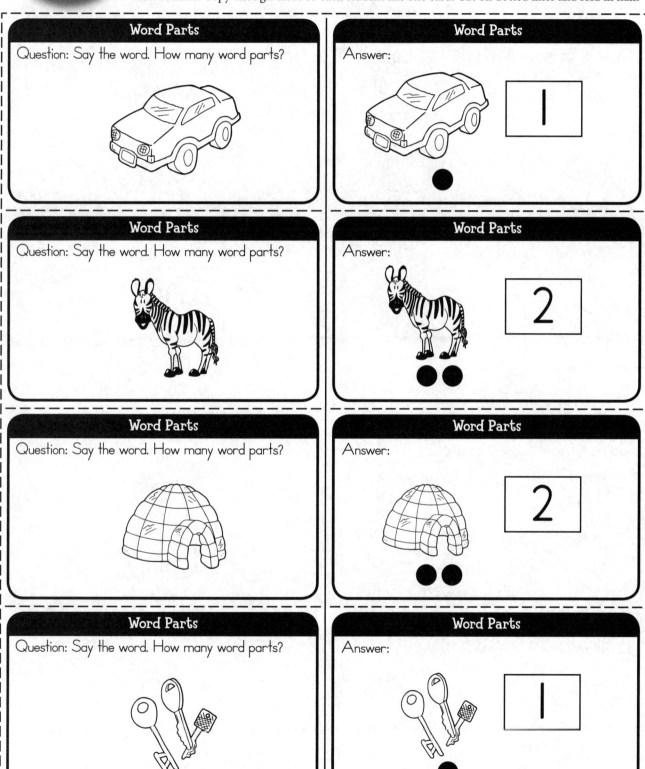

Matching Beginning Sounds
Quiz-Quiz-Trade

Instructions: Copy enough cards so each student has one card. Cut on dotted lines and fold in half.

Matching Beginning Sounds Question: Same beginning sound? 	**Matching Beginning Sounds** Answer: **yes** (b)
Matching Beginning Sounds Question: Same beginning sound? 	**Matching Beginning Sounds** Answer: **no** (b, s)
Matching Beginning Sounds Question: Same beginning sound? 	**Matching Beginning Sounds** Answer: **yes** (sh)
Matching Beginning Sounds Question: Same beginning sound? 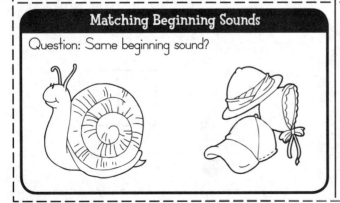	**Matching Beginning Sounds** Answer: **no** (s, h)

Matching Beginning Sounds
Quiz-Quiz-Trade

Instructions: Copy enough cards so each student has one card. Cut on dotted lines and fold in half.

Matching Beginning Sounds	Matching Beginning Sounds
Question: Same beginning sound? 	Answer: **no** **(b, s)**
Matching Beginning Sounds	Matching Beginning Sounds
Question: Same beginning sound? 	Answer: **yes** **(c)**
Matching Beginning Sounds	Matching Beginning Sounds
Question: Same beginning sound? 	Answer: **yes** **(l)**
Matching Beginning Sounds	Matching Beginning Sounds
Question: Same beginning sound? 	Answer: **no** **(g, m)**

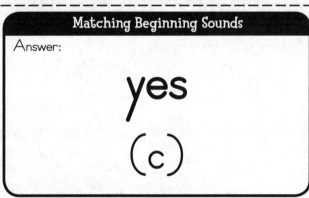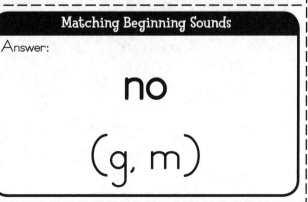

Matching Beginning Sounds
Quiz-Quiz-Trade

Instructions: Copy enough cards so each student has one card. Cut on dotted lines and fold in half.

Matching Beginning Sounds	Matching Beginning Sounds
Question: Same beginning sound? 	Answer: **yes** (h)
Question: Same beginning sound? 	Answer: **yes** (b)
Question: Same beginning sound?	Answer: **no** (p, t)

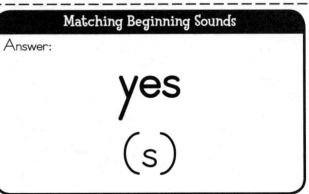

Matching Beginning Sounds
Quiz-Quiz-Trade

Instructions: Copy enough cards so each student has one card. Cut on dotted lines and fold in half.

Matching Beginning Sounds

Question: Same beginning sound?

Matching Beginning Sounds

Answer:

no

(g, f)

Matching Beginning Sounds

Question: Same beginning sound?

Matching Beginning Sounds

Answer:

yes

(w)

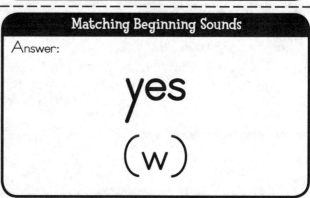

Matching Beginning Sounds

Question: Same beginning sound?

Matching Beginning Sounds

Answer:

yes

(b)

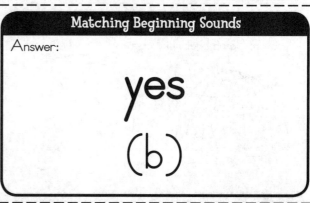

Matching Beginning Sounds

Question: Same beginning sound?

Matching Beginning Sounds

Answer:

no

(p, t)

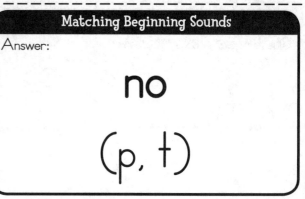

Matching Beginning Sounds
Quiz-Quiz-Trade

Instructions: Copy enough cards so each student has one card. Cut on dotted lines and fold in half.

Matching Beginning Sounds
Question: Same beginning sound?

Matching Beginning Sounds
Answer:

yes
(z)

Matching Beginning Sounds
Question: Same beginning sound?

Matching Beginning Sounds
Answer:

no
(a, o)

Matching Beginning Sounds
Question: Same beginning sound?

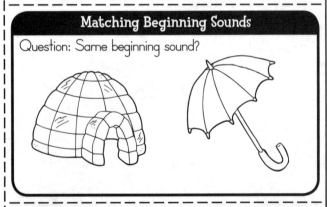

Matching Beginning Sounds
Answer:

no
(i, u)

Matching Beginning Sounds
Question: Same beginning sound?

Matching Beginning Sounds
Answer:

yes
(a)

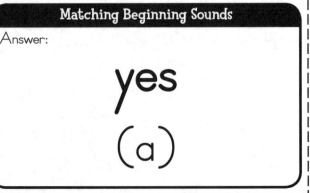

Balanced Literacy • Kindergarten • Skidmore & Graber
Kagan Publishing • 1 (800) 933-2667 • www.KaganOnline.com

Matching Beginning Sounds
Quiz-Quiz-Trade

Instructions: Copy enough cards so each student has one card. Cut on dotted lines and fold in half.

Matching Beginning Sounds Question: Same beginning sound? 	**Matching Beginning Sounds** Answer: **no** **(m, t)**
Matching Beginning Sounds Question: Same beginning sound? 	**Matching Beginning Sounds** Answer: **yes** **(q)**
Matching Beginning Sounds Question: Same beginning sound? 	**Matching Beginning Sounds** Answer: **no** **(p, r)**
Matching Beginning Sounds Question: Same beginning sound? 	**Matching Beginning Sounds** Answer: **no** **(o, e)**

Matching Beginning Sounds
Quiz-Quiz-Trade

Instructions: Copy enough cards so each student has one card. Cut on dotted lines and fold in half.

Matching Beginning Sounds	Matching Beginning Sounds
Question: Same beginning sound? 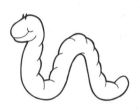 	Answer: **no** (w, x)
Matching Beginning Sounds	Matching Beginning Sounds
Question: Same beginning sound?  	Answer: **yes** (v)
Matching Beginning Sounds	Matching Beginning Sounds
Question: Same beginning sound?  	Answer: **no** (l, h)
Matching Beginning Sounds	Matching Beginning Sounds
Question: Same beginning sound?  	Answer: **yes** (i)

Matching Beginning Sounds
Quiz-Quiz-Trade

Instructions: Copy enough cards so each student has one card. Cut on dotted lines and fold in half.

Matching Beginning Sounds

Question: Same beginning sound?

Matching Beginning Sounds

Answer:

no

(f, v)

Matching Beginning Sounds

Question: Same beginning sound?

Matching Beginning Sounds

Answer:

no

(s, c)

Matching Beginning Sounds

Question: Same beginning sound?

Matching Beginning Sounds

Answer:

yes

(y)

Matching Beginning Sounds

Question: Same beginning sound?

Matching Beginning Sounds

Answer:

no

(r, m)

Matching Beginning Sounds
Quiz-Quiz-Trade

Instructions: Copy enough cards so each student has one card. Cut on dotted lines and fold in half.

Matching Beginning Sounds	Matching Beginning Sounds
Question: Same beginning sound? 	Answer: **no** (k, v) 
Question: Same beginning sound? 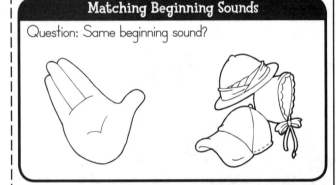	Answer: **yes** (h) 
Question: Same beginning sound? 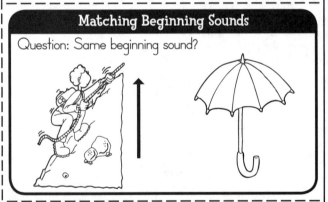	Answer: **yes** (u) 
Question: Same beginning sound? 	Answer: **yes** (e) 

Beginning Sounds #1
Quiz-Quiz-Trade

Instructions: Copy enough cards so each student has one card. Cut on dotted lines and fold in half.

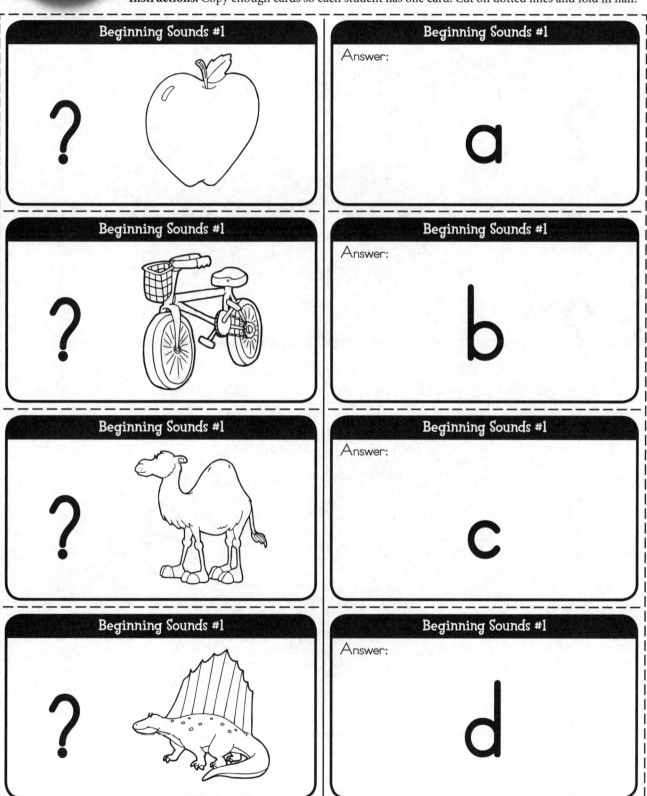

Beginning Sounds #1
Quiz-Quiz-Trade

Instructions: Copy enough cards so each student has one card. Cut on dotted lines and fold in half.

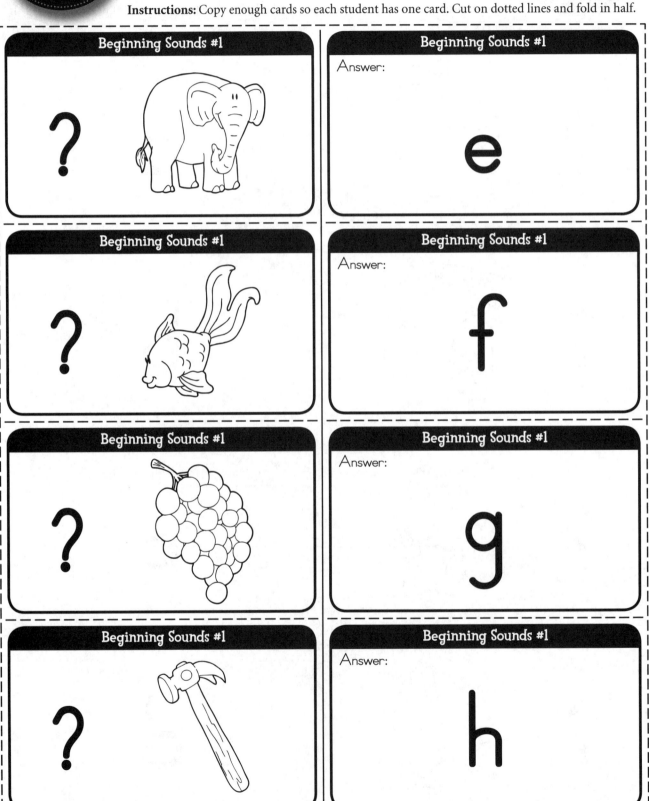

Beginning Sounds #1	Beginning Sounds #1
? (elephant)	Answer: e
Beginning Sounds #1	Beginning Sounds #1
? (fish)	Answer: f
Beginning Sounds #1	Beginning Sounds #1
? (grapes)	Answer: g
Beginning Sounds #1	Beginning Sounds #1
? (hammer)	Answer: h

Balanced Literacy • Kindergarten • Skidmore & Graber
Kagan Publishing • 1 (800) 933-2667 • www.KaganOnline.com

Beginning Sounds #1
Quiz-Quiz-Trade

Instructions: Copy enough cards so each student has one card. Cut on dotted lines and fold in half.

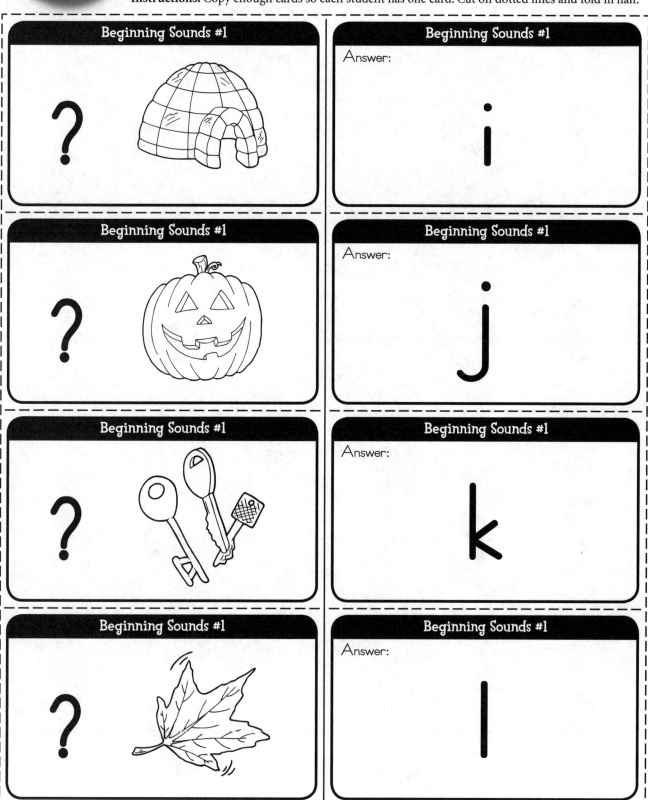

Beginning Sounds #1

?

Beginning Sounds #1

Answer:

i

Beginning Sounds #1

?

Beginning Sounds #1

Answer:

j

Beginning Sounds #1

?

Beginning Sounds #1

Answer:

k

Beginning Sounds #1

?

Beginning Sounds #1

Answer:

l

Beginning Sounds #1
Quiz-Quiz-Trade

Instructions: Copy enough cards so each student has one card. Cut on dotted lines and fold in half.

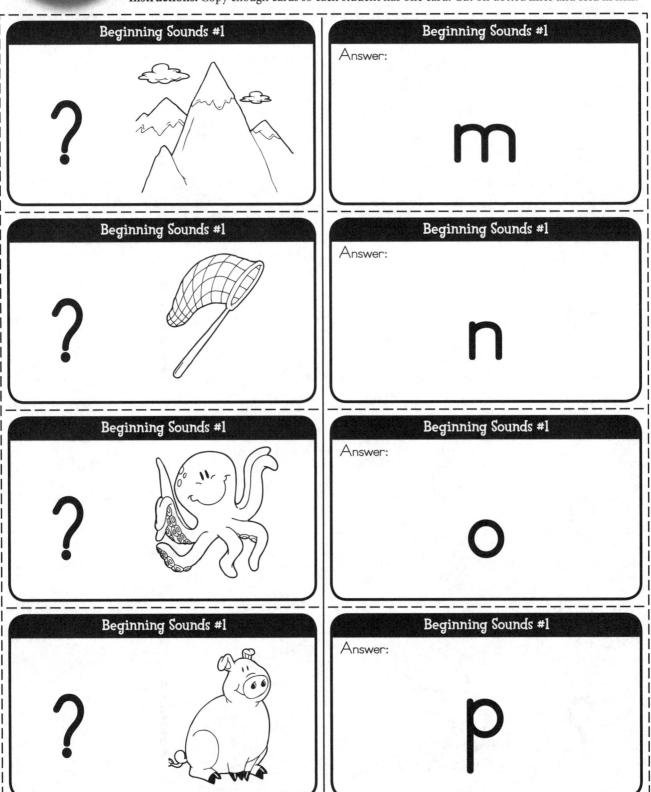

Beginning Sounds #1	Beginning Sounds #1
?	Answer:
	m
Beginning Sounds #1	Beginning Sounds #1
?	Answer:
	n
Beginning Sounds #1	Beginning Sounds #1
?	Answer:
	o
Beginning Sounds #1	Beginning Sounds #1
?	Answer:
	p

Beginning Sounds #1
Quiz-Quiz-Trade

Instructions: Copy enough cards so each student has one card. Cut on dotted lines and fold in half.

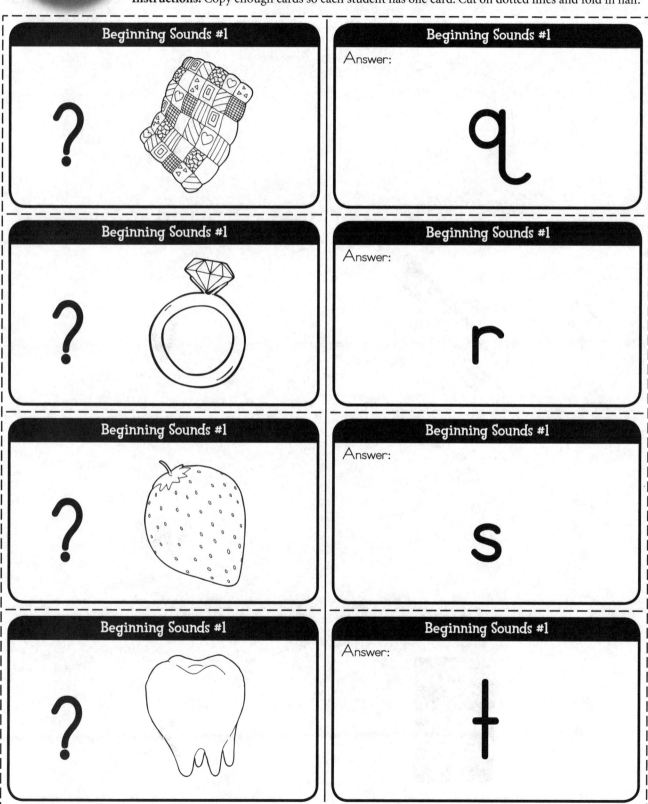

Beginning Sounds #1	Beginning Sounds #1
? (quilt)	Answer: q
? (ring)	Answer: r
? (strawberry)	Answer: s
? (tooth)	Answer: t

Beginning Sounds #1
Quiz-Quiz-Trade

Instructions: Copy enough cards so each student has one card. Cut on dotted lines and fold in half.

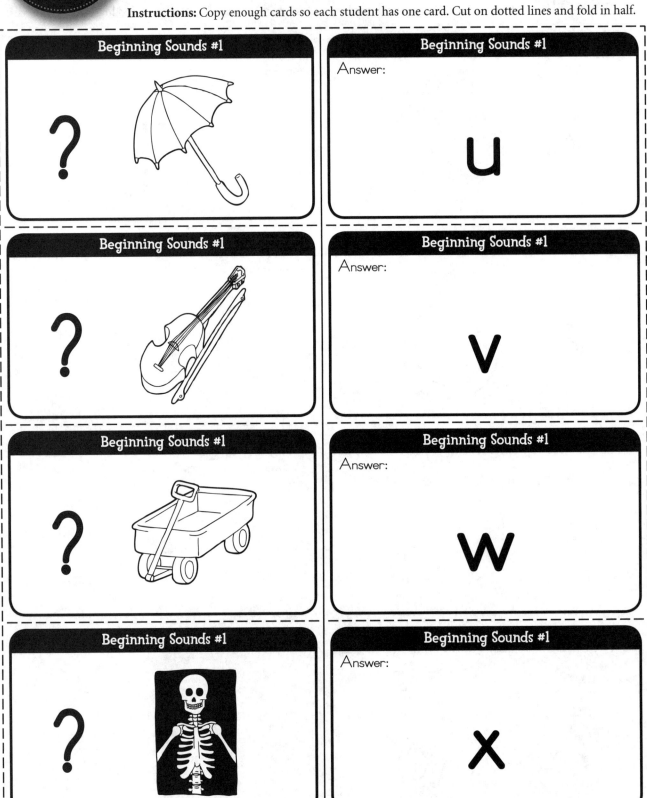

Balanced Literacy • Kindergarten • Skidmore & Graber
Kagan Publishing • 1 (800) 933-2667 • www.KaganOnline.com
154

Beginning Sounds #1
Quiz-Quiz-Trade

Instructions: Copy enough cards so each student has one card. Cut on dotted lines and fold in half.

Beginning Sounds #1	Beginning Sounds #1
?	Answer:
	y
Beginning Sounds #1	Beginning Sounds #1
?	Answer:
	z
Beginning Sounds #1	Beginning Sounds #1
Beginning Sounds #1	Beginning Sounds #1

Beginning Sounds #2
Quiz-Quiz-Trade

Instructions: Copy enough cards so each student has one card. Cut on dotted lines and fold in half.

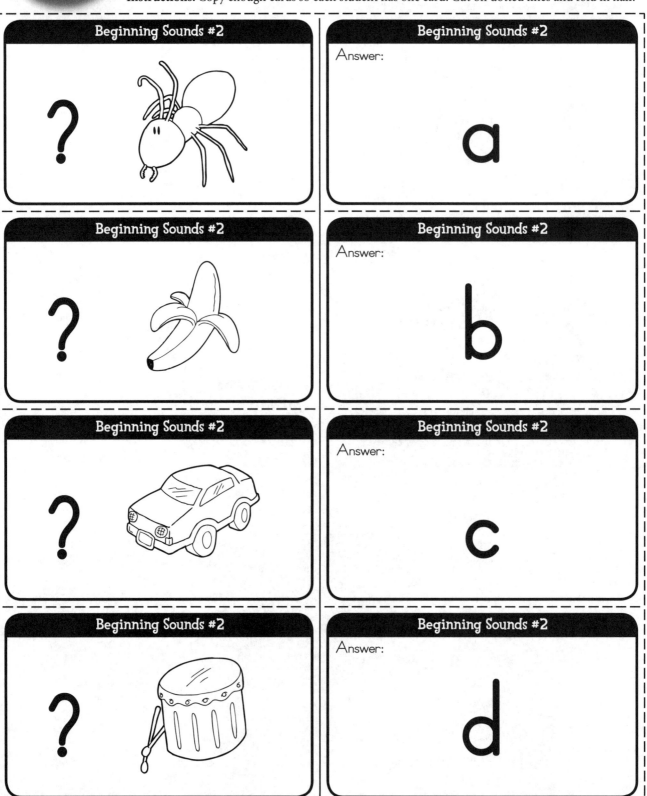

Beginning Sounds #2
Quiz-Quiz-Trade

Instructions: Copy enough cards so each student has one card. Cut on dotted lines and fold in half.

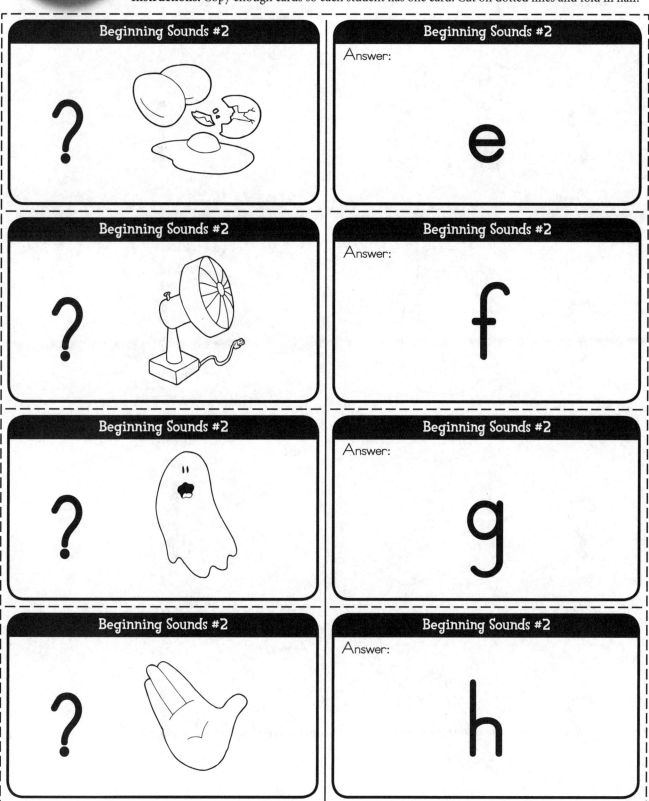

Beginning Sounds #2
Quiz-Quiz-Trade

Instructions: Copy enough cards so each student has one card. Cut on dotted lines and fold in half.

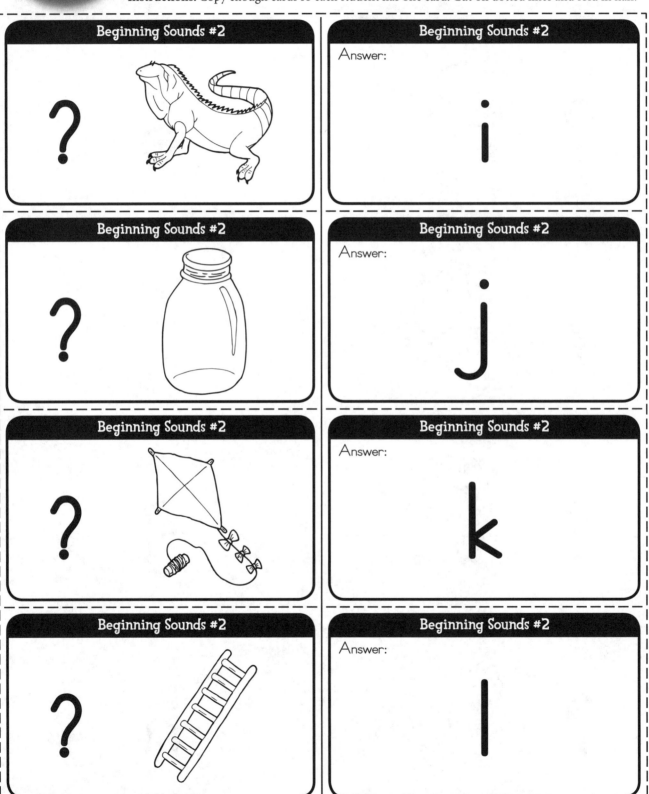

Beginning Sounds #2

? [iguana image]

Beginning Sounds #2

Answer:

i

Beginning Sounds #2

? [jar image]

Beginning Sounds #2

Answer:

j

Beginning Sounds #2

? [kite image]

Beginning Sounds #2

Answer:

k

Beginning Sounds #2

? [ladder image]

Beginning Sounds #2

Answer:

l

Beginning Sounds #2
Quiz-Quiz-Trade

Instructions: Copy enough cards so each student has one card. Cut on dotted lines and fold in half.

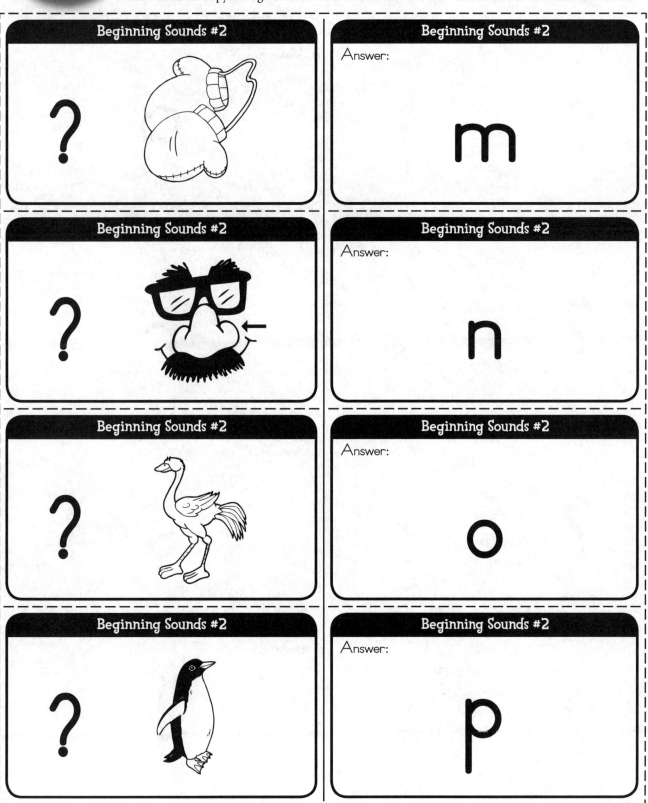

Beginning Sounds #2	Beginning Sounds #2
?	Answer: **m**
Beginning Sounds #2	Beginning Sounds #2
?	Answer: **n**
Beginning Sounds #2	Beginning Sounds #2
?	Answer: **o**
Beginning Sounds #2	Beginning Sounds #2
?	Answer: **p**

Beginning Sounds #2
Quiz-Quiz-Trade

Instructions: Copy enough cards so each student has one card. Cut on dotted lines and fold in half.

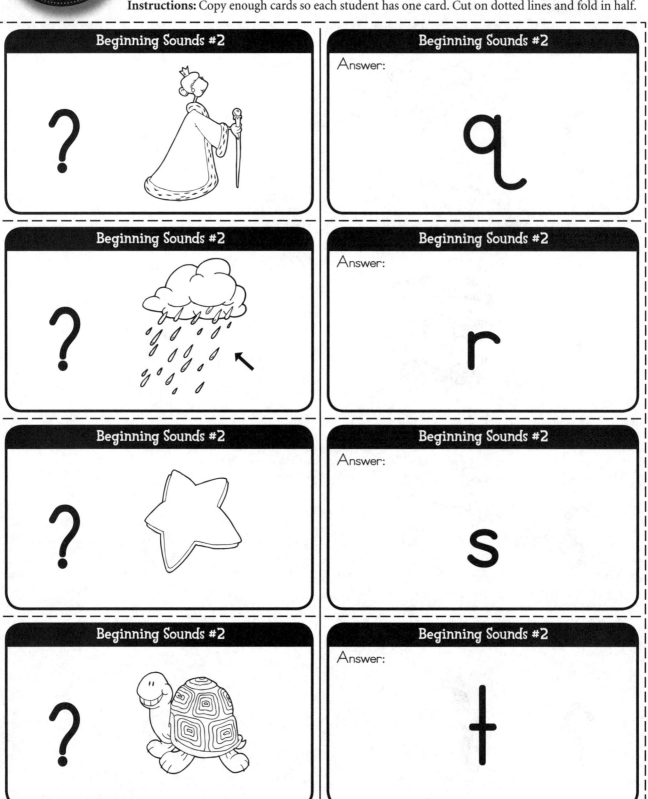

Beginning Sounds #2
Quiz-Quiz-Trade

Instructions: Copy enough cards so each student has one card. Cut on dotted lines and fold in half.

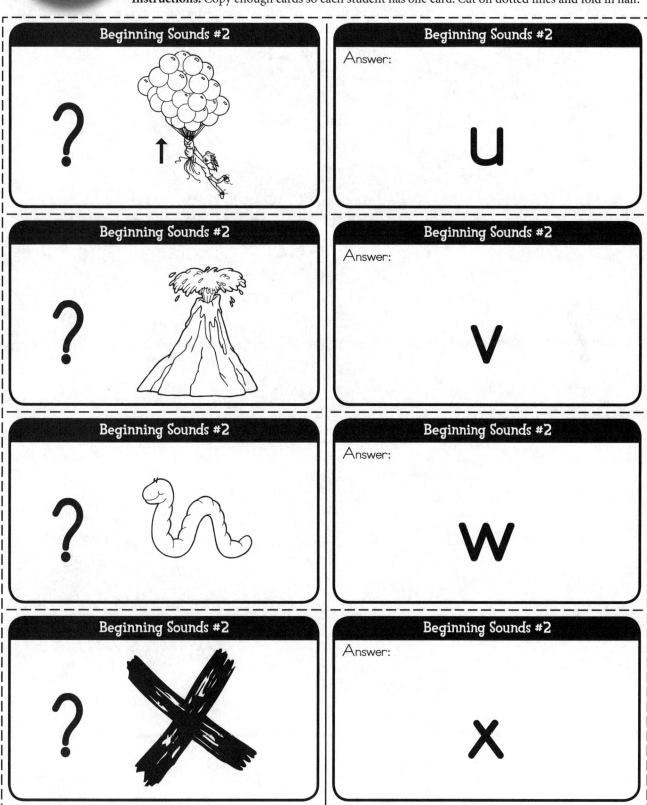

Beginning Sounds #2
Quiz-Quiz-Trade

Instructions: Copy enough cards so each student has one card. Cut on dotted lines and fold in half.

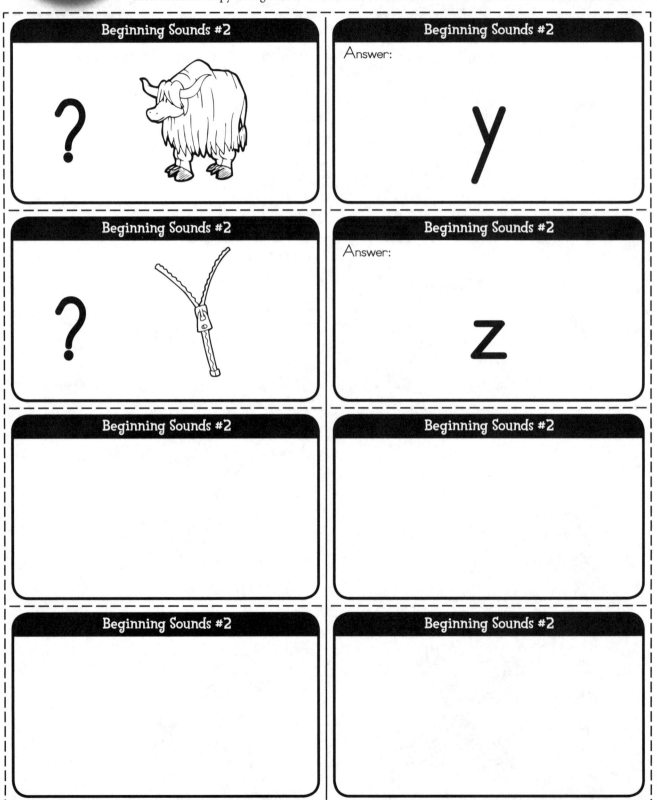

Ending Sounds
Quiz-Quiz-Trade

Instructions: Copy enough cards so each student has one card. Cut on dotted lines and fold in half.

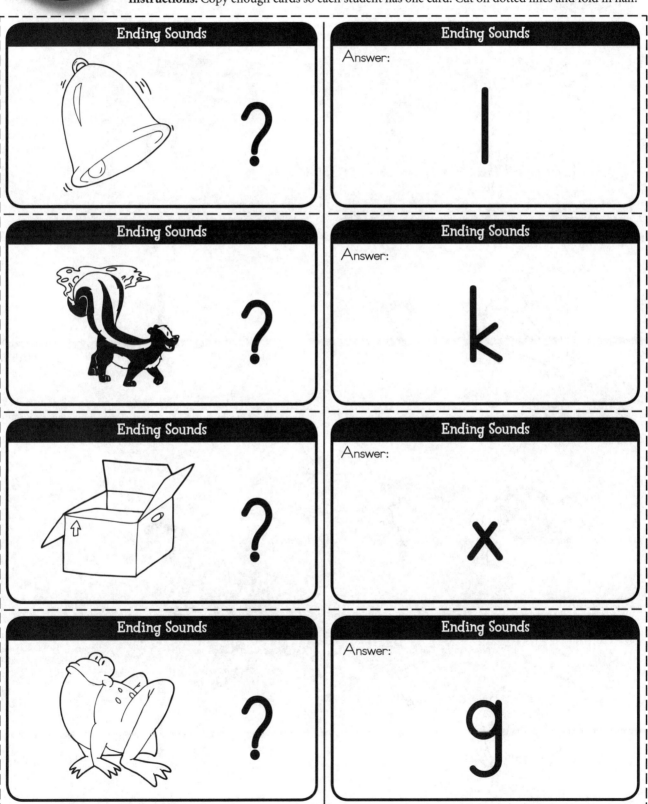

Ending Sounds

?

Ending Sounds

Answer:

l

Ending Sounds

?

Ending Sounds

Answer:

k

Ending Sounds

?

Ending Sounds

Answer:

x

Ending Sounds

?

Ending Sounds

Answer:

g

Ending Sounds
Quiz-Quiz-Trade

Instructions: Copy enough cards so each student has one card. Cut on dotted lines and fold in half.

Ending Sounds	Ending Sounds
?	Answer: n
?	Answer: l
?	Answer: r
?	Answer: l

Ending Sounds
Quiz-Quiz-Trade

Instructions: Copy enough cards so each student has one card. Cut on dotted lines and fold in half.

Ending Sounds	Ending Sounds
?	Answer: **k**
Ending Sounds	Ending Sounds
?	Answer: **t**
Ending Sounds	Ending Sounds
?	Answer: **p**
Ending Sounds	Ending Sounds
?	Answer: **k**

Ending Sounds
Quiz-Quiz-Trade

Instructions: Copy enough cards so each student has one card. Cut on dotted lines and fold in half.

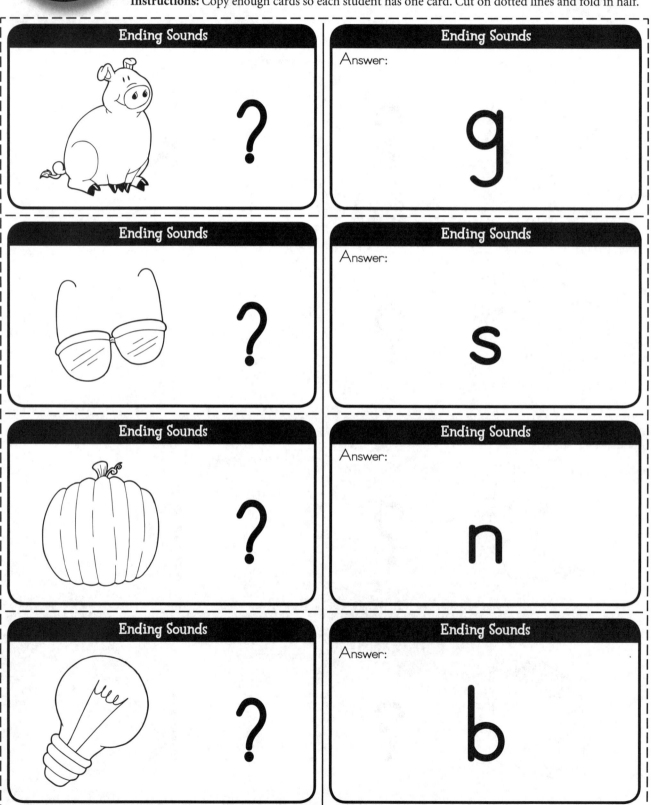

Ending Sounds	Ending Sounds
?	Answer: g
Ending Sounds	Ending Sounds
?	Answer: s
Ending Sounds	Ending Sounds
?	Answer: n
Ending Sounds	Ending Sounds
?	Answer: b

Ending Sounds
Quiz-Quiz-Trade

Instructions: Copy enough cards so each student has one card. Cut on dotted lines and fold in half.

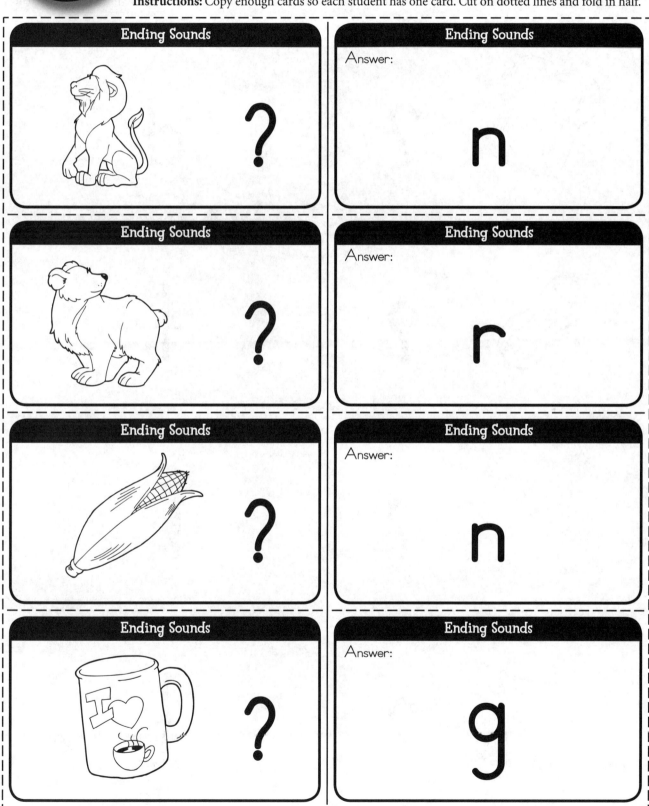

Ending Sounds	Ending Sounds
?	Answer: n
?	Answer: r
?	Answer: n
?	Answer: g

Ending Sounds
Quiz-Quiz-Trade

Instructions: Copy enough cards so each student has one card. Cut on dotted lines and fold in half.

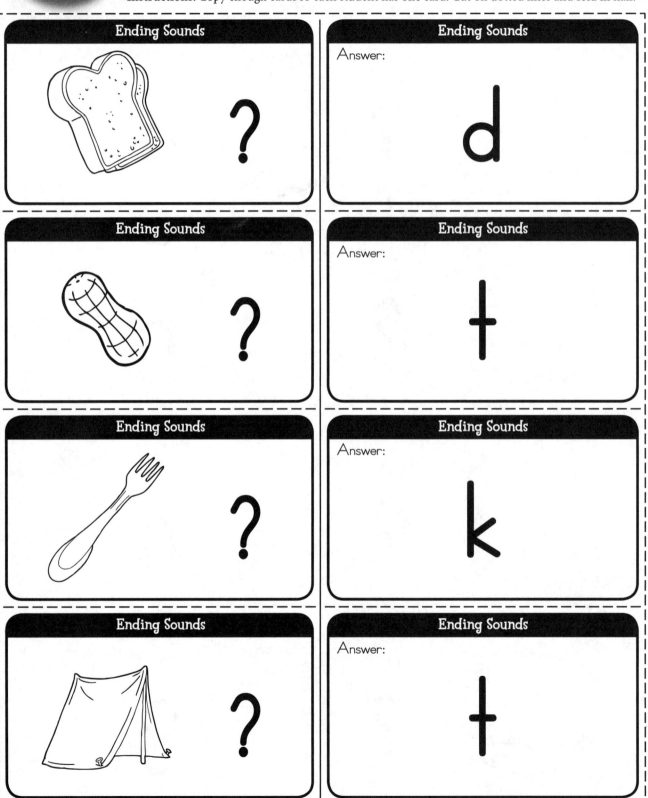

Ending Sounds
Quiz-Quiz-Trade

Instructions: Copy enough cards so each student has one card. Cut on dotted lines and fold in half.

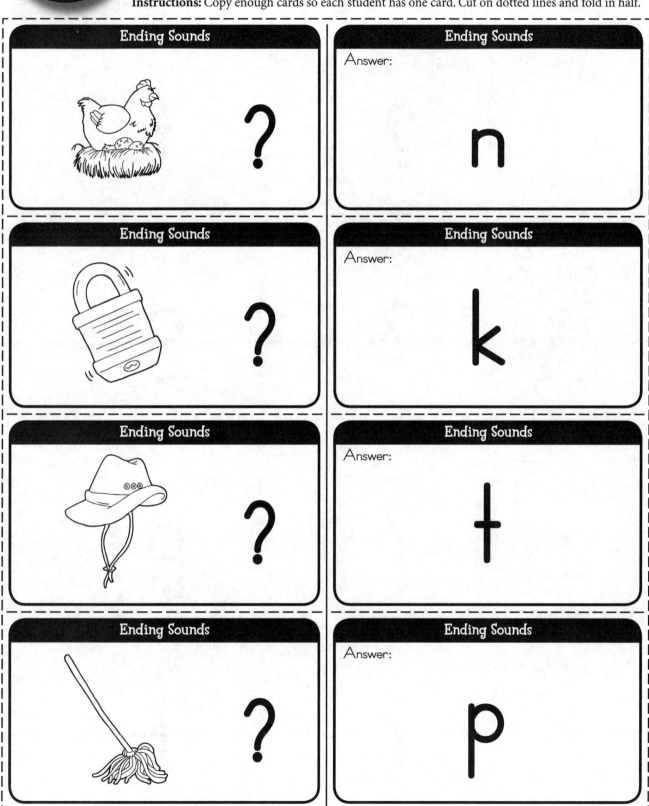

Ending Sounds
Quiz-Quiz-Trade

Instructions: Copy enough cards so each student has one card. Cut on dotted lines and fold in half.

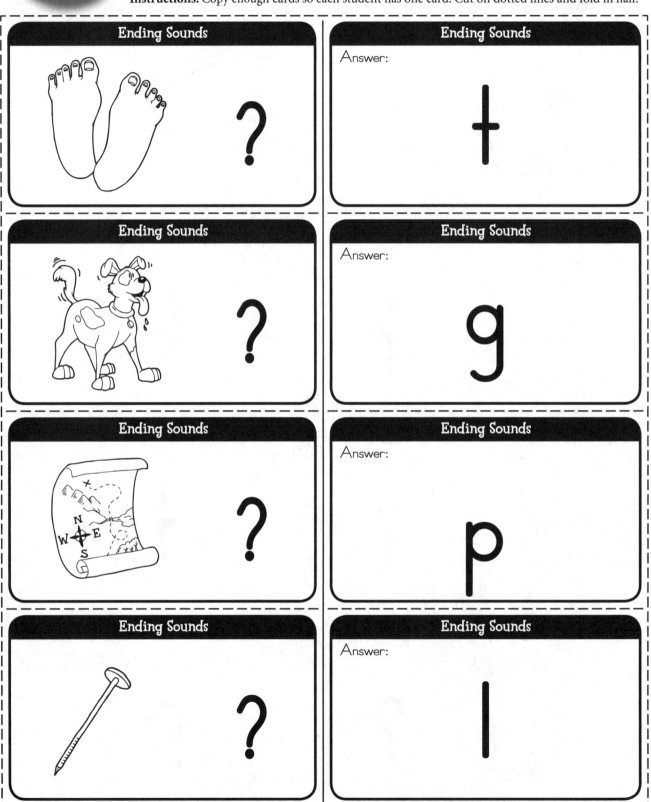

170 Balanced Literacy • Kindergarten • Skidmore & Graber
Kagan Publishing • 1 (800) 933-2667 • www.KaganOnline.com

Ending Sounds
Quiz-Quiz-Trade

Instructions: Copy enough cards so each student has one card. Cut on dotted lines and fold in half.

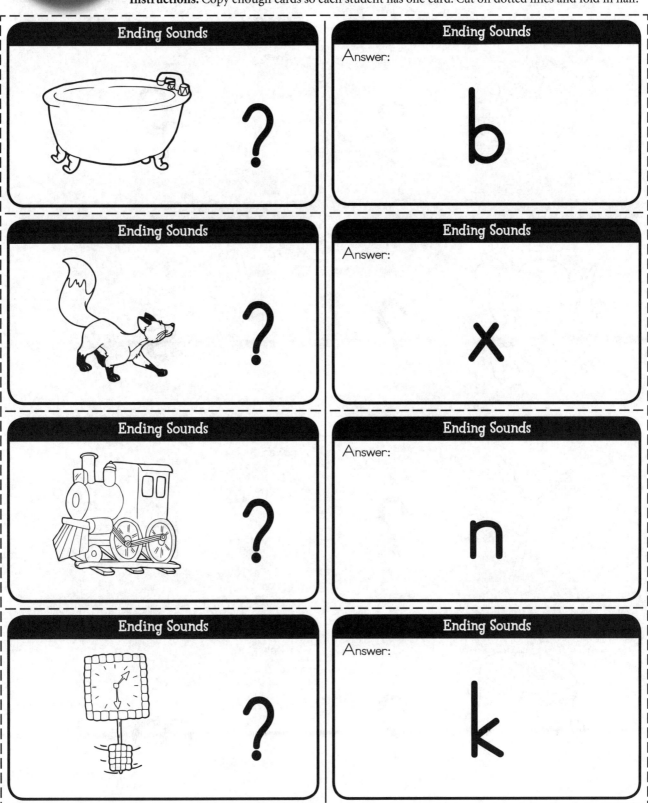

Ending Sounds
Quiz-Quiz-Trade

Instructions: Copy enough cards so each student has one card. Cut on dotted lines and fold in half.

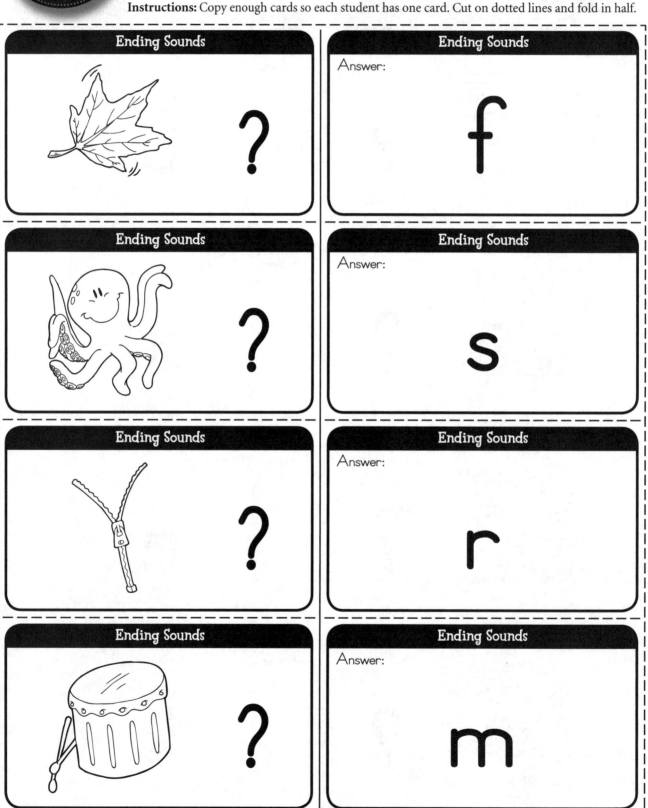

Ending Sounds	Ending Sounds
?	Answer: **f**
?	Answer: **s**
?	Answer: **r**
?	Answer: **m**

Ending Sounds
Quiz-Quiz-Trade

Instructions: Copy enough cards so each student has one card. Cut on dotted lines and fold in half.

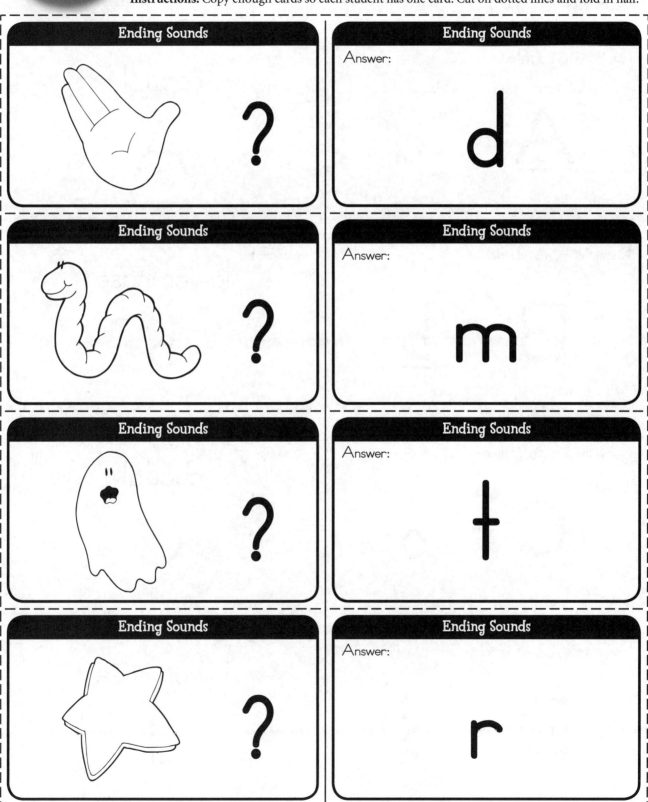

Ending Sounds	Ending Sounds
?	Answer: d
?	Answer: m
?	Answer: t
?	Answer: r

Letter Identification
Quiz-Quiz-Trade

Instructions: Copy enough cards so each student has one card. Cut on dotted lines and fold in half.

Letter Identification	Letter Identification
Name the <u>underlined</u> letter. <u>A</u> a	Answer: capital A
Name the <u>underlined</u> letter. B <u>b</u>	Answer: lower case b
Name the <u>underlined</u> letter. <u>C</u> c	Answer: capital C
Name the <u>underlined</u> letter. D <u>d</u>	Answer: lower case d

Balanced Literacy • Kindergarten • Skidmore & Graber
Kagan Publishing • 1 (800) 933-2667 • www.KaganOnline.com

Letter Identification

Quiz-Quiz-Trade

Instructions: Copy enough cards so each student has one card. Cut on dotted lines and fold in half.

Letter Identification Name the <u>underlined</u> letter. E <u>e</u>	**Letter Identification** Answer: lower case e
Letter Identification Name the <u>underlined</u> letter. F <u>f</u>	**Letter Identification** Answer: lower case f
Letter Identification Name the <u>underlined</u> letter. G <u>g</u>	**Letter Identification** Answer: lower case g
Letter Identification Name the <u>underlined</u> letter. <u>H</u> h	**Letter Identification** Answer: capital H

Letter Identification
Quiz-Quiz-Trade

Instructions: Copy enough cards so each student has one card. Cut on dotted lines and fold in half.

Letter Identification	Letter Identification
Name the <u>underlined</u> letter. I <u>i</u>	Answer: lower case i
Name the <u>underlined</u> letter. <u>J</u> j	Answer: capital J
Name the <u>underlined</u> letter. K <u>k</u>	Answer: lower case k
Name the <u>underlined</u> letter. L <u>l</u>	Answer: lower case l

Balanced Literacy • Kindergarten • Skidmore & Graber
Kagan Publishing • 1 (800) 933-2667 • www.KaganOnline.com

Letter Identification
Quiz-Quiz-Trade

Instructions: Copy enough cards so each student has one card. Cut on dotted lines and fold in half.

Letter Identification	Letter Identification
Name the <u>underlined</u> letter. M <u>m</u>	Answer: lower case m

Letter Identification	Letter Identification
Name the <u>underlined</u> letter. <u>N</u> n	Answer: capital N

Letter Identification	Letter Identification
Name the <u>underlined</u> letter. O <u>o</u>	Answer: lower case o

Letter Identification	Letter Identification
Name the <u>underlined</u> letter. P <u>p</u>	Answer: lower case p

Letter Identification
Quiz-Quiz-Trade

Instructions: Copy enough cards so each student has one card. Cut on dotted lines and fold in half.

Letter Identification	Letter Identification
Name the <u>underlined</u> letter. <u>Q</u> q	Answer: capital Q
Name the <u>underlined</u> letter. R <u>r</u>	Answer: lower case r
Name the <u>underlined</u> letter. S <u>s</u>	Answer: lower case s
Name the <u>underlined</u> letter. T <u>t</u>	Answer: lower case t

Balanced Literacy • Kindergarten • Skidmore & Graber
Kagan Publishing • 1 (800) 933-2667 • www.KaganOnline.com

Letter Identification
Quiz-Quiz-Trade

Instructions: Copy enough cards so each student has one card. Cut on dotted lines and fold in half.

Letter Identification	Letter Identification
Name the <u>underlined</u> letter. <u>U</u> u	Answer: capital U
Name the <u>underlined</u> letter. V <u>v</u>	Answer: lower case v
Name the <u>underlined</u> letter. <u>W</u> w	Answer: capital W
Name the <u>underlined</u> letter. <u>X</u> x	Answer: capital X

Letter Identification
Quiz-Quiz-Trade

Instructions: Copy enough cards so each student has one card. Cut on dotted lines and fold in half.

Letter Identification	Letter Identification
Name the <u>underlined</u> letter. Y y	Answer: capital Y
Name the <u>underlined</u> letter. Z z	Answer: lower case z
Name the <u>underlined</u> letter. B b	Answer: capital B
Name the <u>underlined</u> letter. D d	Answer: capital D

 Balanced Literacy • Kindergarten • Skidmore & Graber
Kagan Publishing • 1 (800) 933-2667 • www.KaganOnline.com

Capital Letter Identification
Quiz-Quiz-Trade

Instructions: Copy enough cards so each student has one card. Cut on dotted lines and fold in half.

Capital Letter Identification	Capital Letter Identification
? A	Answer: capital A
Capital Letter Identification	Capital Letter Identification
? B	Answer: capital B
Capital Letter Identification	Capital Letter Identification
? C	Answer: capital C
Capital Letter Identification	Capital Letter Identification
? D	Answer: capital D

Capital Letter Identification
Quiz-Quiz-Trade

Instructions: Copy enough cards so each student has one card. Cut on dotted lines and fold in half.

Capital Letter Identification	Capital Letter Identification
? E	Answer: capital E
? F	Answer: capital F
? G	Answer: capital G
? H	Answer: capital H

Capital Letter Identification
Quiz-Quiz-Trade

Instructions: Copy enough cards so each student has one card. Cut on dotted lines and fold in half.

Capital Letter Identification	Capital Letter Identification
? I	Answer: capital I
Capital Letter Identification	Capital Letter Identification
? J	Answer: capital J
Capital Letter Identification	Capital Letter Identification
? K	Answer: capital K
Capital Letter Identification	Capital Letter Identification
? L	Answer: capital L

Capital Letter Identification
Quiz-Quiz-Trade

Instructions: Copy enough cards so each student has one card. Cut on dotted lines and fold in half.

Capital Letter Identification	Capital Letter Identification
? M	Answer: capital M
Capital Letter Identification	Capital Letter Identification
? N	Answer: capital N
Capital Letter Identification	Capital Letter Identification
? O	Answer: capital O
Capital Letter Identification	Capital Letter Identification
? P	Answer: capital P

Capital Letter Identification
Quiz-Quiz-Trade

Instructions: Copy enough cards so each student has one card. Cut on dotted lines and fold in half.

Capital Letter Identification	Capital Letter Identification
? Q	Answer: capital **Q**
Capital Letter Identification	Capital Letter Identification
? R	Answer: capital **R**
Capital Letter Identification	Capital Letter Identification
? S	Answer: capital **S**
Capital Letter Identification	Capital Letter Identification
? T	Answer: capital **T**

Capital Letter Identification
Quiz-Quiz-Trade

Instructions: Copy enough cards so each student has one card. Cut on dotted lines and fold in half.

Capital Letter Identification	Capital Letter Identification
? U	Answer: capital U
? V	Answer: capital V
? W	Answer: capital W
? X	Answer: capital X

Capital Letter Identification
Quiz-Quiz-Trade

Instructions: Copy enough cards so each student has one card. Cut on dotted lines and fold in half.

Capital Letter Identification	Capital Letter Identification
? Y	Answer: capital Y
Capital Letter Identification	Capital Letter Identification
? Z	Answer: capital Z
Capital Letter Identification	Capital Letter Identification
Capital Letter Identification	Capital Letter Identification

Lower Case Letter Identification

Quiz-Quiz-Trade

Instructions: Copy enough cards so each student has one card. Cut on dotted lines and fold in half.

Lower Case Letter Identification	Lower Case Letter Identification
? a	Answer: lower case a
Lower Case Letter Identification	Lower Case Letter Identification
? b	Answer: lower case b
Lower Case Letter Identification	Lower Case Letter Identification
? c	Answer: lower case c
Lower Case Letter Identification	Lower Case Letter Identification
? d	Answer: lower case d

Lower Case Letter Identification
Quiz-Quiz-Trade

Instructions: Copy enough cards so each student has one card. Cut on dotted lines and fold in half.

Lower Case Letter Identification	Lower Case Letter Identification
? e	Answer: lower case e
? f	Answer: lower case f
? g	Answer: lower case g
? h	Answer: lower case h

Lower Case Letter Identification

Quiz-Quiz-Trade

Instructions: Copy enough cards so each student has one card. Cut on dotted lines and fold in half.

Lower Case Letter Identification	Lower Case Letter Identification
? i	Answer: lower case i
? j	Answer: lower case j
? k	Answer: lower case k
? l	Answer: lower case l

Lower Case Letter Identification
Quiz-Quiz-Trade
Instructions: Copy enough cards so each student has one card. Cut on dotted lines and fold in half.

Lower Case Letter Identification	Lower Case Letter Identification
? m	Answer: lower case **m**

Lower Case Letter Identification	Lower Case Letter Identification
? n	Answer: lower case **n**

Lower Case Letter Identification	Lower Case Letter Identification
? o	Answer: lower case **o**

Lower Case Letter Identification	Lower Case Letter Identification
? p	Answer: lower case **p**

Lower Case Letter Identification

Quiz-Quiz-Trade

Instructions: Copy enough cards so each student has one card. Cut on dotted lines and fold in half.

Lower Case Letter Identification	Lower Case Letter Identification
? q	Answer: lower case q
Lower Case Letter Identification	Lower Case Letter Identification
? r	Answer: lower case r
Lower Case Letter Identification	Lower Case Letter Identification
? s	Answer: lower case s
Lower Case Letter Identification	Lower Case Letter Identification
? t	Answer: lower case t

Balanced Literacy • Kindergarten • Skidmore & Graber
Kagan Publishing • 1 (800) 933-2667 • www.KaganOnline.com

Lower Case Letter
Identification
Quiz-Quiz-Trade

Instructions: Copy enough cards so each student has one card. Cut on dotted lines and fold in half.

Lower Case Letter Identification	Lower Case Letter Identification
? u	Answer: lower case u
Lower Case Letter Identification	Lower Case Letter Identification
? v	Answer: lower case v
Lower Case Letter Identification	Lower Case Letter Identification
? w	Answer: lower case w
Lower Case Letter Identification	Lower Case Letter Identification
? x	Answer: lower case x

Lower Case Letter Identification
Quiz-Quiz-Trade

Instructions: Copy enough cards so each student has one card. Cut on dotted lines and fold in half.

Lower Case Letter Identification	Lower Case Letter Identification
? y	Answer: lower case y
Lower Case Letter Identification	Lower Case Letter Identification
? z	Answer: lower case z
Lower Case Letter Identification	Lower Case Letter Identification
Lower Case Letter Identification	Lower Case Letter Identification

Letter Identification—
Different Font Styles
Quiz-Quiz-Trade

Instructions: Copy enough cards so each student has one card. Cut on dotted lines and fold in half.

Letter Identification—Different Font Styles	Letter Identification—Different Font Styles
? A A a a	Answer: A a
? B b b B	Answer: B b
? C c C C	Answer: C c
? D d d D	Answer: D d

Letter Identification
Different Font Styles
Quiz-Quiz-Trade

Instructions: Copy enough cards so each student has one card. Cut on dotted lines and fold in half.

Letter Identification—Different Font Styles

? **E** e **e** **E**

Letter Identification—Different Font Styles

Answer:

E e

Letter Identification—Different Font Styles

? f **F** **f** f

Letter Identification—Different Font Styles

Answer:

F f

Letter Identification—Different Font Styles

? **G** g G **g**

Letter Identification—Different Font Styles

Answer:

G g

Letter Identification—Different Font Styles

? **H** h h H

Letter Identification—Different Font Styles

Answer:

H h

Letter Identification
Different Font Styles
Quiz-Quiz-Trade

Instructions: Copy enough cards so each student has one card. Cut on dotted lines and fold in half.

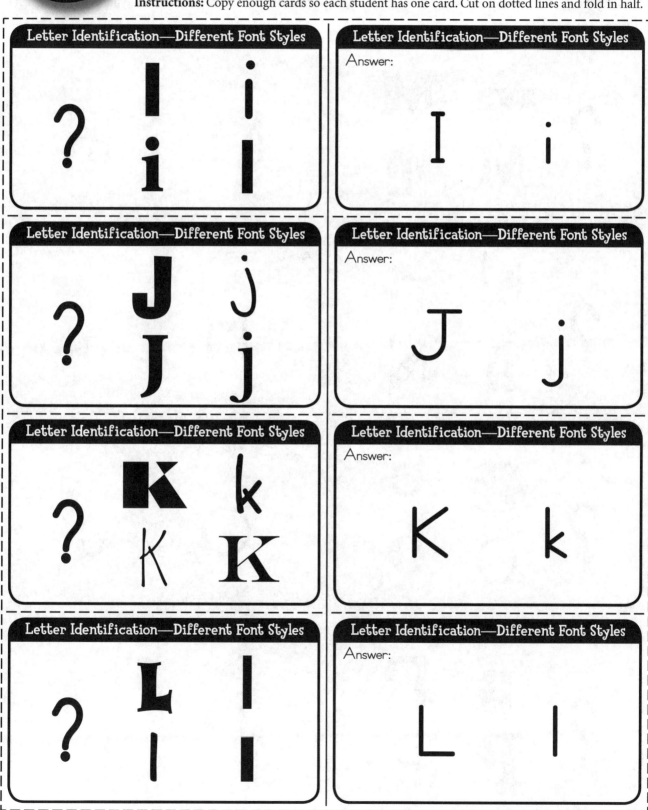

Letter Identification
Different Font Styles
Quiz-Quiz-Trade

Instructions: Copy enough cards so each student has one card. Cut on dotted lines and fold in half.

Letter Identification—Different Font Styles	Letter Identification—Different Font Styles
? **m** **M** **M** **m**	Answer: M m
Letter Identification—Different Font Styles	Letter Identification—Different Font Styles
? N n n N	Answer: N n
Letter Identification—Different Font Styles	Letter Identification—Different Font Styles
? ● o O **o**	Answer: O o
Letter Identification—Different Font Styles	Letter Identification—Different Font Styles
? **p** P P p	Answer: P p

Letter Identification
Different Font Styles
Quiz-Quiz-Trade
Instructions: Copy enough cards so each student has one card. Cut on dotted lines and fold in half.

Letter Identification—Different Font Styles

? q Q
Q q

Letter Identification—Different Font Styles

Answer:

Q q

Letter Identification—Different Font Styles

? R r
r R

Letter Identification—Different Font Styles

Answer:

R r

Letter Identification—Different Font Styles

? S s
S S

Letter Identification—Different Font Styles

Answer:

S s

Letter Identification—Different Font Styles

? T t
t T

Letter Identification—Different Font Styles

Answer:

T t

Letter Identification
Different Font Styles
Quiz-Quiz-Trade

Instructions: Copy enough cards so each student has one card. Cut on dotted lines and fold in half.

Letter Identification—Different Font Styles	Letter Identification—Different Font Styles
? **u U** **U U**	Answer: U u
? V V V V	Answer: V v
? **w W** **W W**	Answer: W w
? **x x** **X X**	Answer: X x

Letter Identification
Different Font Styles
Quiz-Quiz-Trade

Instructions: Copy enough cards so each student has one card. Cut on dotted lines and fold in half.

Letter Identification—Different Font Styles	Letter Identification—Different Font Styles
? y Y Y y Y	Answer: Y y
Letter Identification—Different Font Styles	Letter Identification—Different Font Styles
? Z z z Z z Z	Answer: Z z
Letter Identification—Different Font Styles	Letter Identification—Different Font Styles
Letter Identification—Different Font Styles	Letter Identification—Different Font Styles

Activity

Pictures and Words

In pairs, students alternate generating oral responses.

Activity Steps

1. Partner A chooses a picture card and identifies it.

2. Partner B gives a word that rhymes.

3. Partner A gives a different word that rhymes.

4. In pairs, students take turns naming different rhyming words.

5. When students have listed as many rhyming words as they can, repeat from Step 1 with Partner B choosing a picture card.

STRUCTURE
RallyRobin

Note:
Students may use the alphabet letter strips as a reference for possible beginning letter sounds for rhyming words.

Blacklines

Rhyming Picture Cards
RallyRobin

Instructions: Copy and cut out a set of picture cards for each pair of students. A picture card is turned over and identified. Partners take turns orally giving words that rhyme.

Rhyming Picture Cards — **fan**

Rhyming Picture Cards — **man**

Rhyming Picture Cards — **cap**

Rhyming Picture Cards — **hat**

Rhyming Picture Cards — **chin**

Rhyming Picture Cards — **ship**

Rhyming Picture Cards — **pit**

Rhyming Picture Cards — **mop**

Rhyming Picture Cards — **dot**

Rhyming Picture Cards — **jug**

Rhyming Picture Cards — **crash**

Rhyming Picture Cards — **sack**

Rhyming Picture Cards
RallyRobin

Instructions: Copy and cut out a set of picture cards for each pair of students. A picture card is turned over and identified. Partners take turns orally giving words that rhyme.

Rhyming Picture Cards	Rhyming Picture Cards	Rhyming Picture Cards
ring	wink	sock
shell	vest	truck
chick	pump	skunk
drill	pay	vine

Rhyming Picture Cards
RallyRobin

Instructions: Copy and cut out a set of picture cards for each pair of students. A picture card is turned over and identified. Partners take turns orally giving words that rhyme.

Rhyming Picture Cards	Rhyming Picture Cards	Rhyming Picture Cards
snail	rain	snake
whale	game	smoke
gate	saw	meat
ice	slide	night

Alphabet Strips
RallyRobin

Instructions: Copy and cut out one alphabet strip for each pair of students.
Note: This page includes alphabet strips for four pairs of students.

z	z	z	z
y	y	y	y
x	x	x	x
w	w	w	w
v	v	v	v
u	u	u	u
t	t	t	t
s	s	s	s
r	r	r	r
q	q	q	q
p	p	p	p
o	o	o	o
n	n	n	n
m	m	m	m
l	l	l	l
k	k	k	k
j	j	j	j
i	i	i	i
h	h	h	h
g	g	g	g
f	f	f	f
e	e	e	e
d	d	d	d
c	c	c	c
b	b	b	b
a	a	a	a

Activity

Coach Me

A variety of word study RallyCoach activities are provided for phonemic awareness and for phonics. Using the materials provided, one partner completes the task while the other is the coach. They switch roles for each new problem.

STRUCTURE
RallyCoach

Activity Steps

1. Each pair receives the materials associated with the activity (see blacklines below and on the following page).

2. First, Partner A completes the task.
   • Sorting Mat: Partner sorts an item on the mat.
   • Fill in the Blanks: Partner fills in missing letters.
   • Gameboards: Partner performs task and moves gamepiece.
   • Cube: Partner rolls cube and uses result to fill in worksheet.
   • Spinner: Partner spins spinner and uses result to fill in worksheet.

3. Partner B watches and listens, checks, and praises.

4. Then Partner B completes the next task.

5. Partner A watches and listens, checks, and praises.

6. The process continues until they complete their worksheet or sort all word/letter cards.

Blacklines

Coach Me (continued)

A variety of word study RallyCoach activities are provided for phonemic awareness and for phonics. Using the materials provided, one partner completes the task while the other is the coach. They switch roles for each new problem.

Blacklines (continued)

Sorting by Syllables
RallyCoach

Instructions: Copy and cut apart one set of syllable sorting picture cards for each pair of students. Partners take turns sorting pictures under heading on syllable sorting mat by number of syllables heard when word represented on picture cards is clapped or tapped.

Sorting by Syllables
RallyCoach

Instructions: Copy and cut apart one set of syllable sorting picture cards for each pair of students. Partners take turns sorting pictures under heading on syllable sorting mat by number of syllables heard when word represented on picture cards is clapped or tapped.

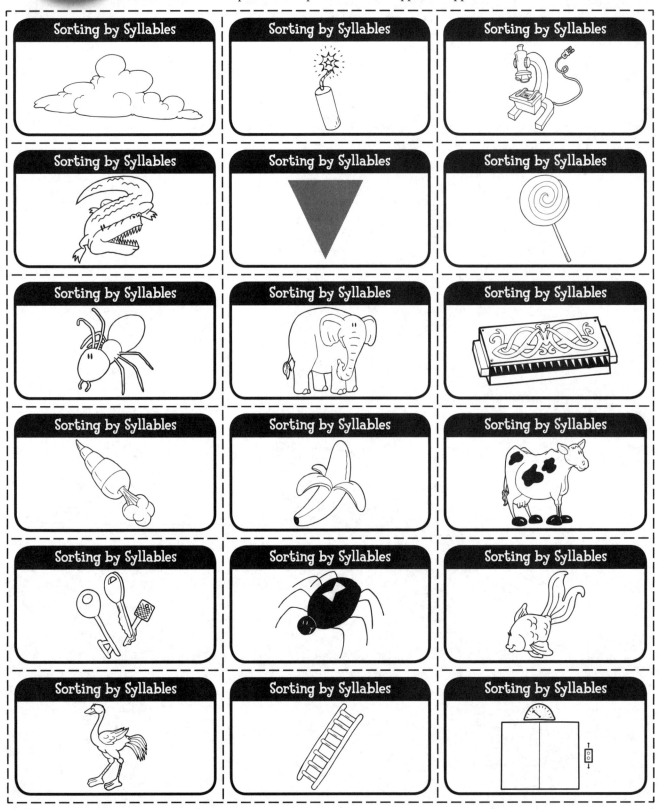

Sorting by Syllables
Sorting Mat
RallyCoach

Instructions: Copy one Syllable Sorting Mat for each pair of students.

4	
3	
2	
1	

Beginning, Middle, End
RallyCoach

Instructions: Copy, laminate, and cut apart one set of cards for each pair of students or slip the entire sheet into a page protector. Partners take turns segmenting the three sounds in each word as it is said and writing the letters of the sounds on the lines under the pictures with a dry-erase marker.

Beginning, Middle, End

Beginning, Middle, End

Beginning, Middle, End

Beginning, Middle, End

Beginning, Middle, End

Beginning, Middle, End

Beginning, Middle, End

Beginning, Middle, End

Beginning, Middle, End

Beginning, Middle, End
RallyCoach

Instructions: Copy, laminate, and cut apart one set of cards for each pair of students or slip the entire sheet into a page protector. Partners take turns segmenting the three sounds in each word as it is said and writing the letters of the sounds on the lines under the pictures with a dry-erase marker.

Beginning, Middle, End

Beginning, Middle, End

Beginning, Middle, End

Beginning, Middle, End

Beginning, Middle, End

Beginning, Middle, End

Beginning, Middle, End

Beginning, Middle, End

Beginning, Middle, End

Beginning, Middle, End
RallyCoach

Instructions: Copy, laminate, and cut apart one set of cards for each pair of students or slip the entire sheet into a page protector. Partners take turns segmenting the three sounds in each word as it is said and writing the letters of the sounds on the lines under the pictures with a dry-erase marker.

Beginning, Middle, End
RallyCoach

Instructions: Copy, laminate, and cut apart one set of cards for each pair of students or slip the entire sheet into a page protector. Partners take turns segmenting the three sounds in each word as it is said and writing the letters of the sounds on the lines under the pictures with a dry-erase marker.

Phoneme Identification
RallyCoach

Instructions: Copy and cut apart one set of cards for each pair of students. **Note:** Copy only the letter and following picture cards for the sorts you want students to participate in.

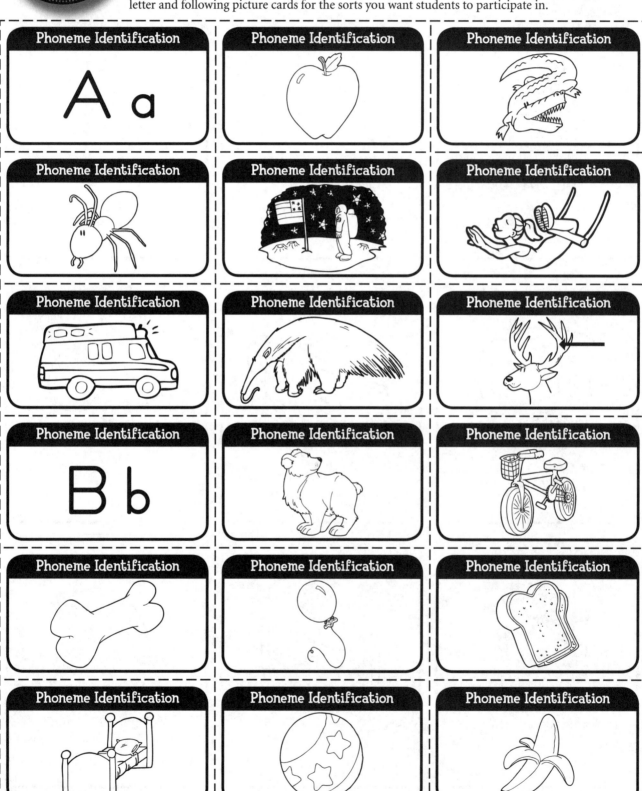

Phoneme Identification
RallyCoach

Instructions: Copy and cut apart one set of cards for each pair of students. **Note:** Copy only the letter and following picture cards for the sorts you want students to participate in.

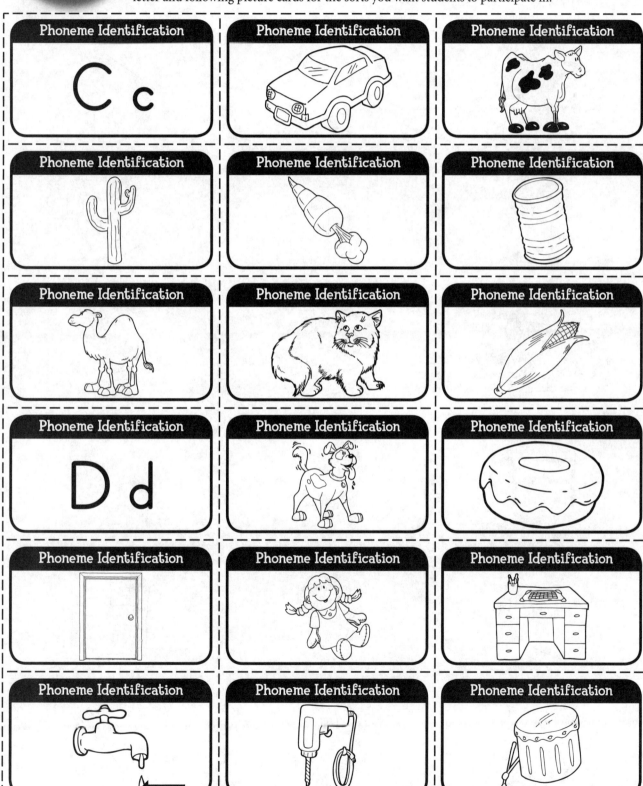

Phoneme Identification	Phoneme Identification	Phoneme Identification
C c		
Phoneme Identification	Phoneme Identification	Phoneme Identification
Phoneme Identification	Phoneme Identification	Phoneme Identification
Phoneme Identification	Phoneme Identification	Phoneme Identification
D d		
Phoneme Identification	Phoneme Identification	Phoneme Identification
Phoneme Identification	Phoneme Identification	Phoneme Identification

Phoneme Identification
RallyCoach

Instructions: Copy and cut apart one set of cards for each pair of students. **Note:** Copy only the letter and following picture cards for the sorts you want students to participate in.

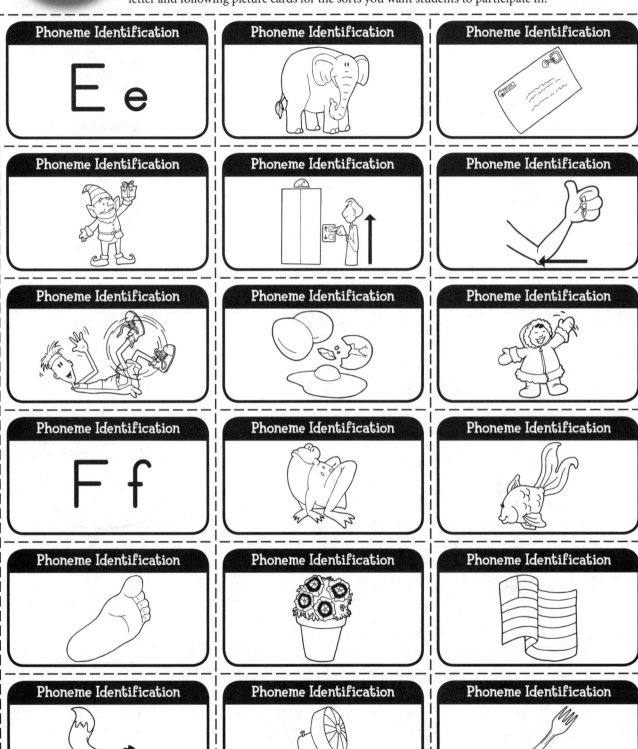

Phoneme Identification
RallyCoach

Instructions: Copy and cut apart one set of cards for each pair of students. **Note:** Copy only the letter and following picture cards for the sorts you want students to participate in.

Phoneme Identification
RallyCoach

Instructions: Copy and cut apart one set of cards for each pair of students. **Note:** Copy only the letter and following picture cards for the sorts you want students to participate in.

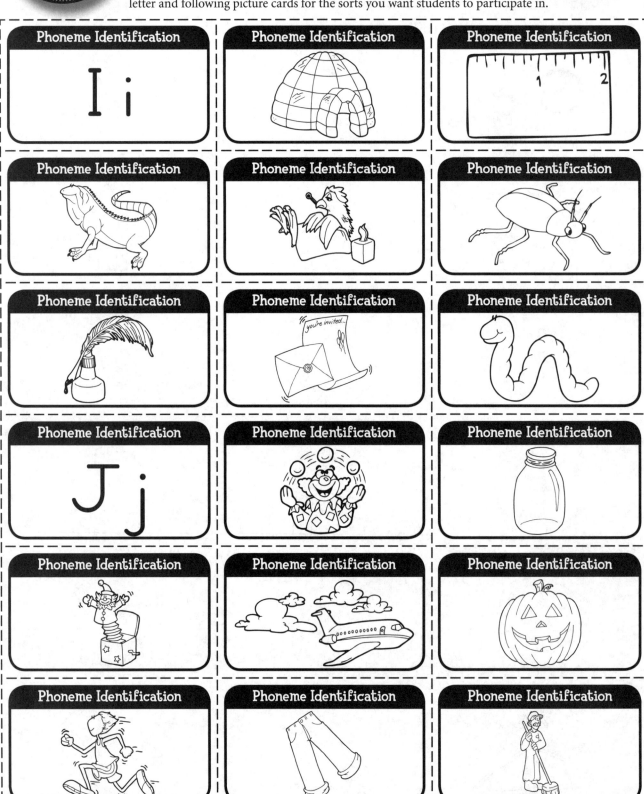

Balanced Literacy • Kindergarten • Skidmore & Graber
Kagan Publishing • 1 (800) 933-2667 • www.KaganOnline.com

Phoneme Identification
RallyCoach

Instructions: Copy and cut apart one set of cards for each pair of students. **Note:** Copy only the letter and following picture cards for the sorts you want students to participate in.

Phoneme Identification — **K k**

Phoneme Identification

Phoneme Identification

Phoneme Identification

Phoneme Identification

Phoneme Identification

Phoneme Identification

Phoneme Identification

Phoneme Identification

Phoneme Identification — **L l**

Phoneme Identification

Phoneme Identification

Phoneme Identification

Phoneme Identification

Phoneme Identification

Phoneme Identification

Phoneme Identification

Phoneme Identification

Phoneme Identification
RallyCoach

Instructions: Copy and cut apart one set of cards for each pair of students. **Note:** Copy only the letter and following picture cards for the sorts you want students to participate in.

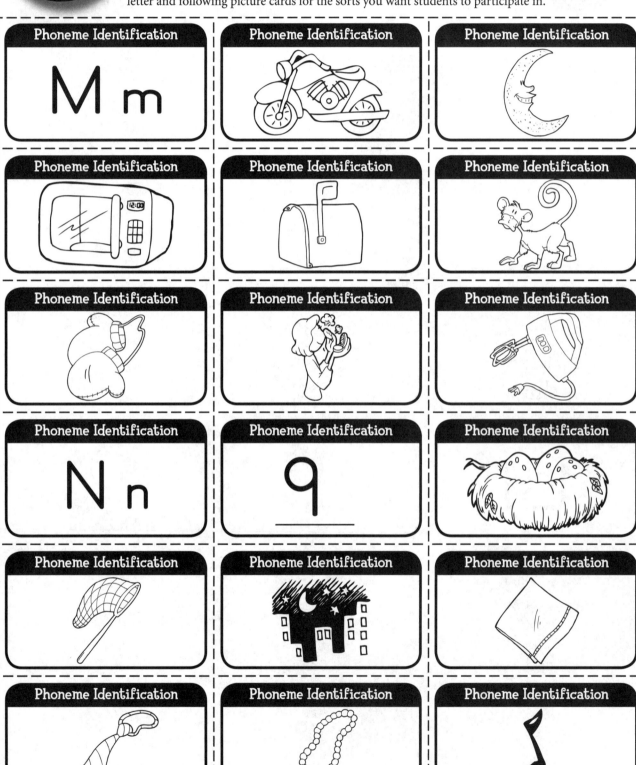

Phoneme Identification	Phoneme Identification	Phoneme Identification
M m		
Phoneme Identification	Phoneme Identification	Phoneme Identification
Phoneme Identification	Phoneme Identification	Phoneme Identification
Phoneme Identification	Phoneme Identification	Phoneme Identification
N n	9	
Phoneme Identification	Phoneme Identification	Phoneme Identification
Phoneme Identification	Phoneme Identification	Phoneme Identification

Balanced Literacy • Kindergarten • Skidmore & Graber
Kagan Publishing • 1 (800) 933-2667 • www.KaganOnline.com

Phoneme Identification
RallyCoach

Instructions: Copy and cut apart one set of cards for each pair of students. **Note:** Copy only the letter and following picture cards for the sorts you want students to participate in.

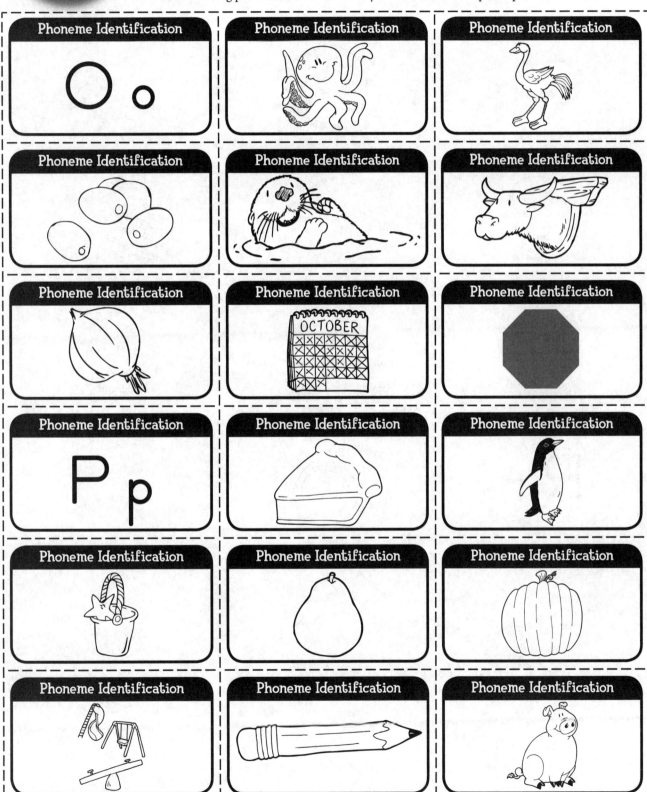

Phoneme Identification	Phoneme Identification	Phoneme Identification
O o		
Phoneme Identification	Phoneme Identification	Phoneme Identification
Phoneme Identification	Phoneme Identification	Phoneme Identification
Phoneme Identification	Phoneme Identification	Phoneme Identification
P p		
Phoneme Identification	Phoneme Identification	Phoneme Identification
Phoneme Identification	Phoneme Identification	Phoneme Identification

Phoneme Identification
RallyCoach

Instructions: Copy and cut apart one set of cards for each pair of students. **Note:** Copy only the letter and following picture cards for the sorts you want students to participate in.

Phoneme Identification
RallyCoach

Instructions: Copy and cut apart one set of cards for each pair of students. **Note:** Copy only the letter and following picture cards for the sorts you want students to participate in.

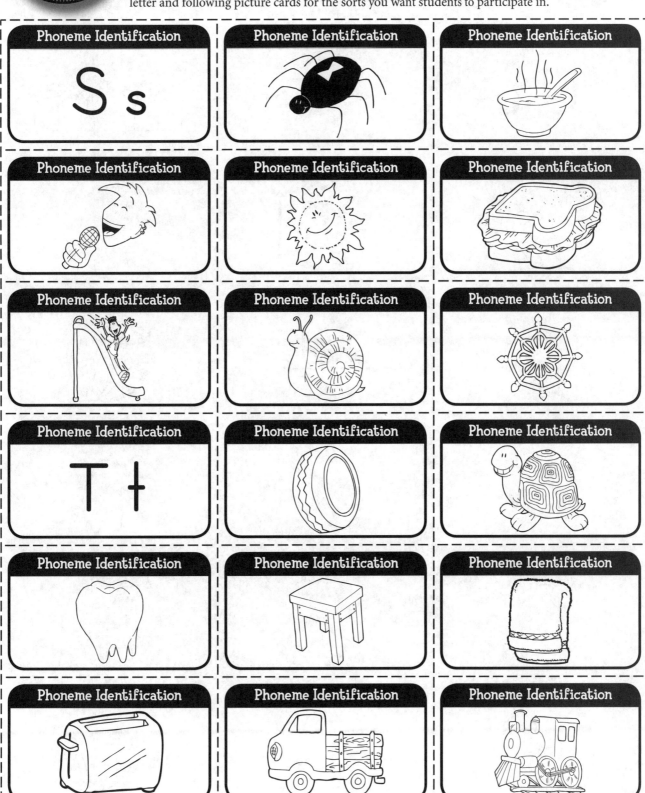

Phoneme Identification
RallyCoach

Instructions: Copy and cut apart one set of cards for each pair of students. **Note:** Copy only the letter and following picture cards for the sorts you want students to participate in.

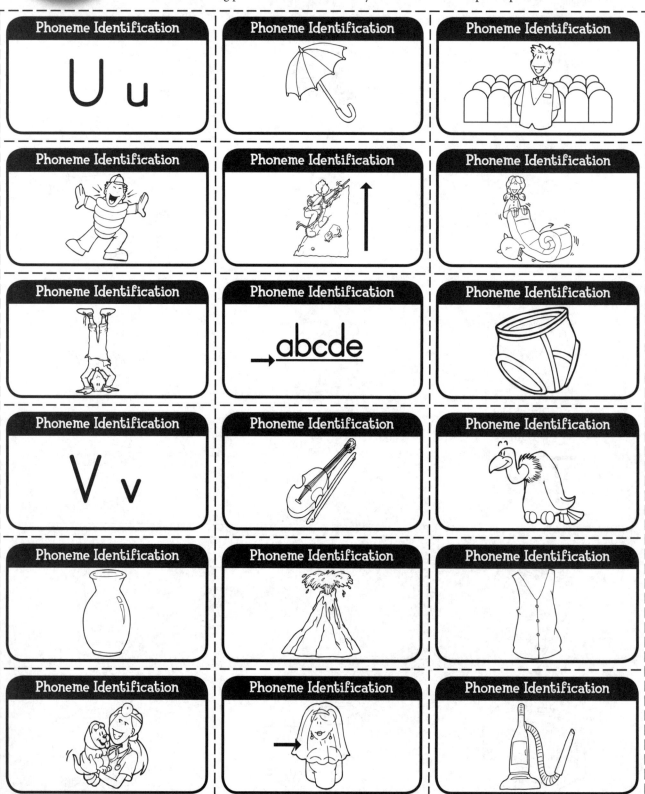

Phoneme Identification	Phoneme Identification	Phoneme Identification
U u		
Phoneme Identification	Phoneme Identification	Phoneme Identification
Phoneme Identification	Phoneme Identification	Phoneme Identification
	abcde	
Phoneme Identification	Phoneme Identification	Phoneme Identification
V v		
Phoneme Identification	Phoneme Identification	Phoneme Identification
Phoneme Identification	Phoneme Identification	Phoneme Identification

Phoneme Identification
RallyCoach

Instructions: Copy and cut apart one set of cards for each pair of students. **Note:** Copy only the letter and following picture cards for the sorts you want students to participate in.

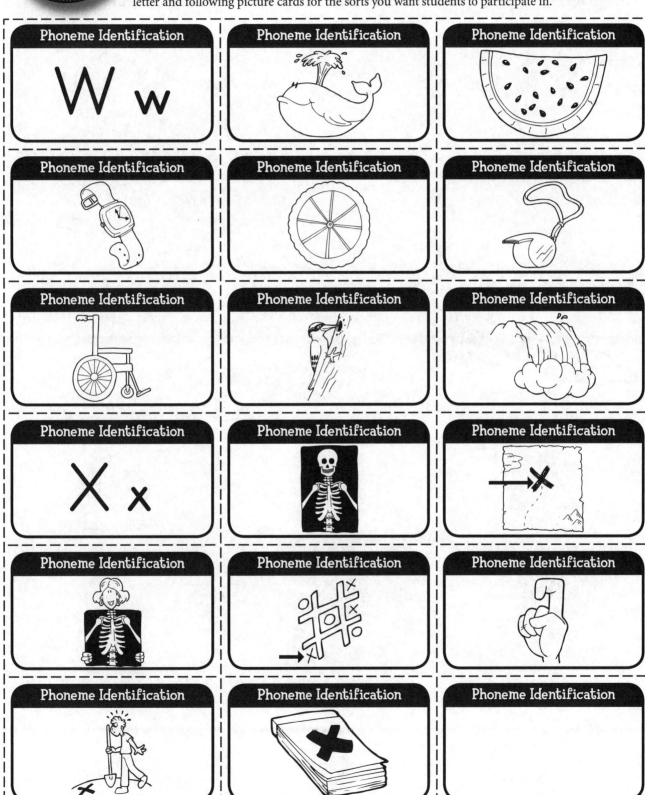

Phoneme Identification
RallyCoach

Instructions: Copy and cut apart one set of cards for each pair of students. **Note:** Copy only the letter and following picture cards for the sorts you want students to participate in.

Phoneme Identification — Y y

Phoneme Identification

Phoneme Identification

Phoneme Identification

Phoneme Identification

Phoneme Identification

Phoneme Identification — yellow

Phoneme Identification

Phoneme Identification

Phoneme Identification — Z z

Phoneme Identification

Phoneme Identification

Phoneme Identification

Phoneme Identification

Phoneme Identification

Phoneme Identification

Phoneme Identification — 0

Phoneme Identification

Phoneme Identification Sorting Mat

RallyCoach

Instructions: Copy one mat per pair of students. Attach beginning letter card or picture card to the top of each column. Partners take turns taking a picture card, saying its name, and placing it on the sorting mat under the correct column matching the beginning letter sound.

Phoneme Blending and Segmenting
RallyCoach

Instructions: Copy and cut apart a set of cards for each pair of students. Partner A picks up picture card from a stack of cards placed facedown. Without letting Partner B see the card, Partner A slowly says the word represented by the picture, breaking the word apart by phonemes. (For example, d-o-g.) Partner B blends the sounds together and says, *dog*. Continue with Partner B choosing the next card.

Phoneme Blending and Segmenting

RallyCoach

Instructions: Copy and cut apart a set of cards for each pair of students. Partner A picks up picture card from a stack of cards placed facedown. Without letting Partner B see the card, Partner A slowly says the word represented by the picture, breaking the word apart by phonemes. (For example, d-o-g.) Partner B blends the sounds together and says, *dog*. Continue with Partner B choosing the next card.

Phoneme Segmentation Cards
RallyCoach

Instructions: Copy and cut apart a set of cards for each pair of students. Partners take turns choosing a picture card, saying the word represented, and using the Phoneme Segmentation Mat to push up a chip for each sound heard in the word.

Phoneme Segmentation Cards
RallyCoach

Instructions: Copy and cut apart a set of cards for each pair of students. Partners take turns choosing a picture card, saying the word represented, and using the Phoneme Segmentation Mat to push up a chip for each sound heard in the word.

Phoneme Segmentation Cards
RallyCoach

Instructions: Copy and cut apart a set of cards for each pair of students. Partners take turns choosing a picture card, saying the word represented, and using the Phoneme Segmentation Mat to push up a chip for each sound heard in the word.

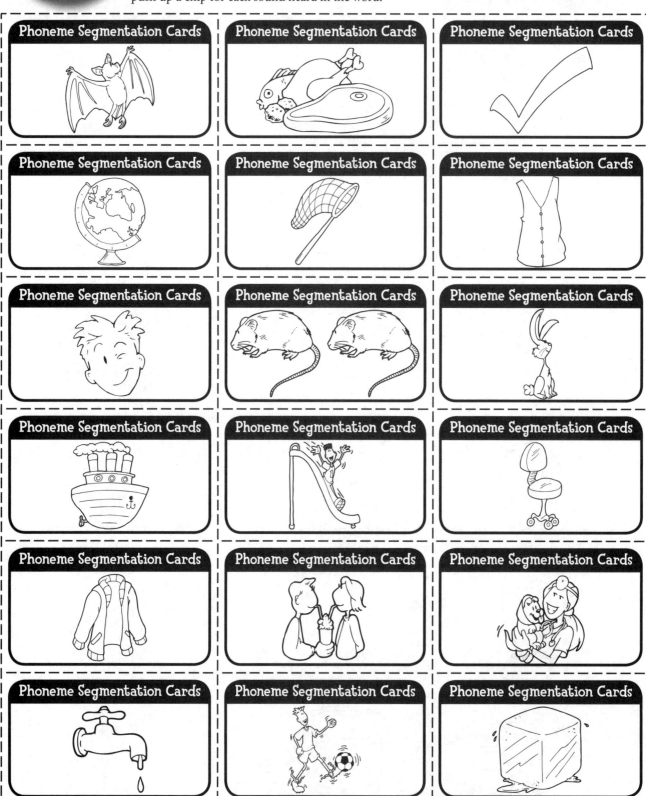

Phoneme Segmentation Mat
RallyCoach

Instructions: Copy one mat per pair of students. Place chips on circles. Partners take turns choosing a picture card, saying the word represented, and pushing one chip up into a top box for each phoneme heard in the word. **Note:** This page contains mats for three pairs.

Onset and Rime Sorting
RallyCoach

Instructions: Copy and cut apart one set of cards for each pair of students.

Note: Teacher may want to copy only the rimes and picture cards for the sorts being assigned.

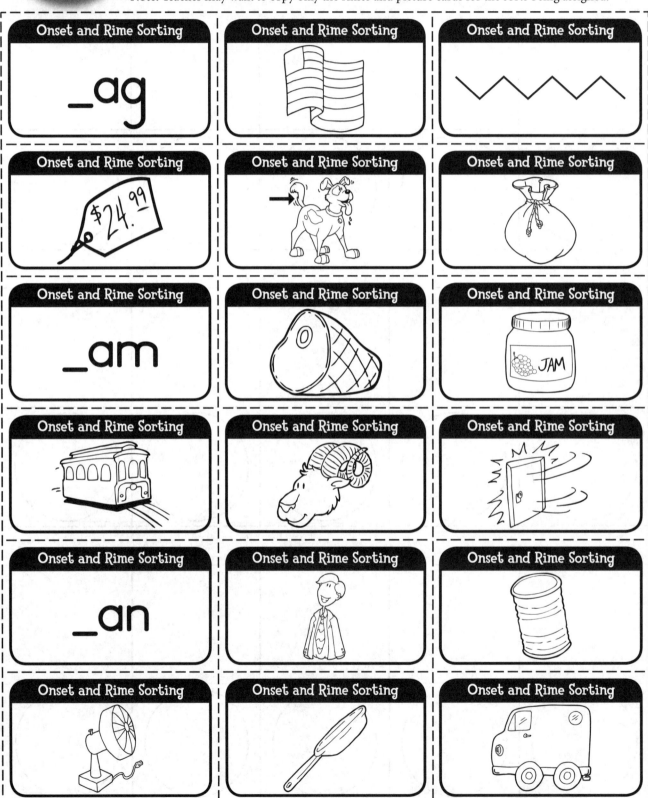

Onset and Rime Sorting	Onset and Rime Sorting	Onset and Rime Sorting
_ag		
Onset and Rime Sorting	Onset and Rime Sorting	Onset and Rime Sorting
$24.99		
Onset and Rime Sorting	Onset and Rime Sorting	Onset and Rime Sorting
_am		JAM
Onset and Rime Sorting	Onset and Rime Sorting	Onset and Rime Sorting
Onset and Rime Sorting	Onset and Rime Sorting	Onset and Rime Sorting
_an		
Onset and Rime Sorting	Onset and Rime Sorting	Onset and Rime Sorting

Onset and Rime Sorting
RallyCoach

Instructions: Copy and cut apart one set of cards for each pair of students.
Note: Teacher may want to copy only the rimes and picture cards for the sorts being assigned.

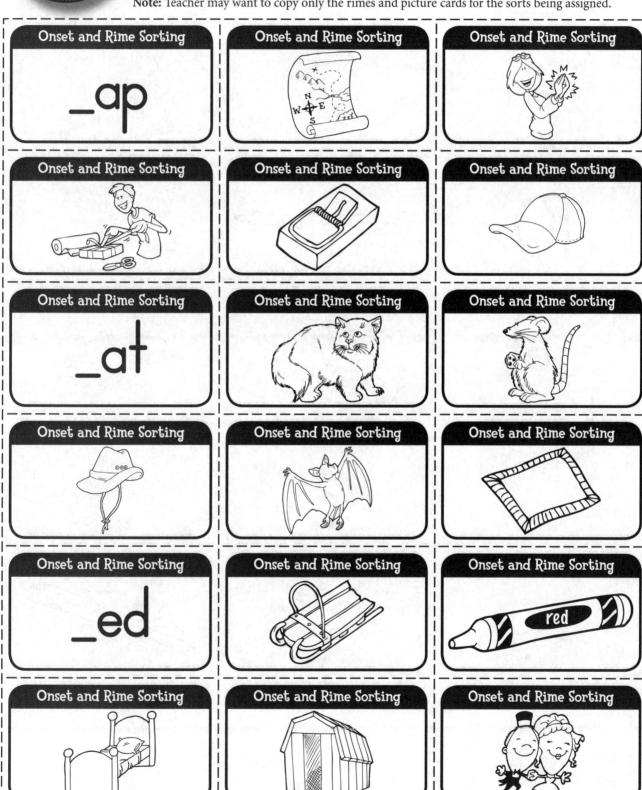

Onset and Rime Sorting

RallyCoach

Instructions: Copy and cut apart one set of cards for each pair of students.

Note: Teacher may want to copy only the rimes and picture cards for the sorts being assigned.

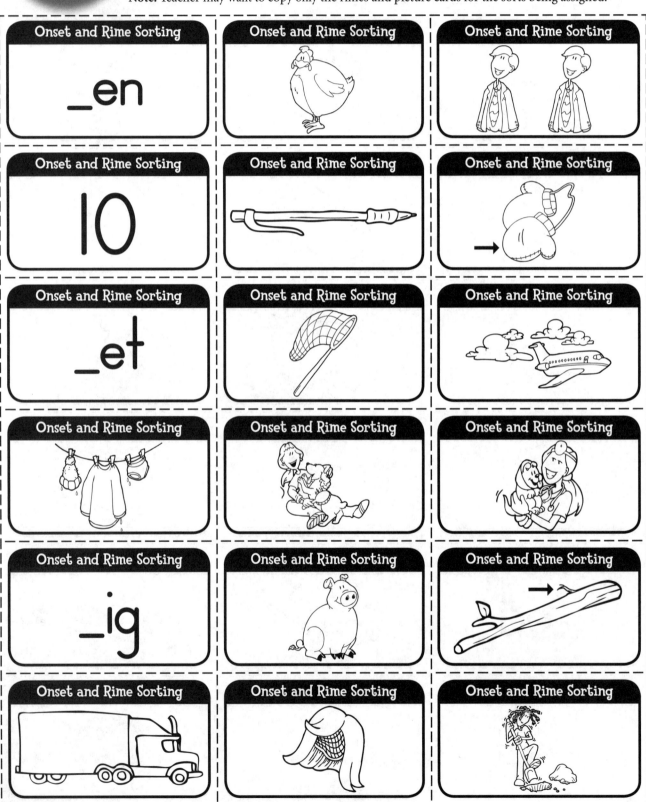

Onset and Rime Sorting	Onset and Rime Sorting	Onset and Rime Sorting
_en		
10		
_et		
_ig		

Onset and Rime Sorting
RallyCoach

Instructions: Copy and cut apart one set of cards for each pair of students.
Note: Teacher may want to copy only the rimes and picture cards for the sorts being assigned.

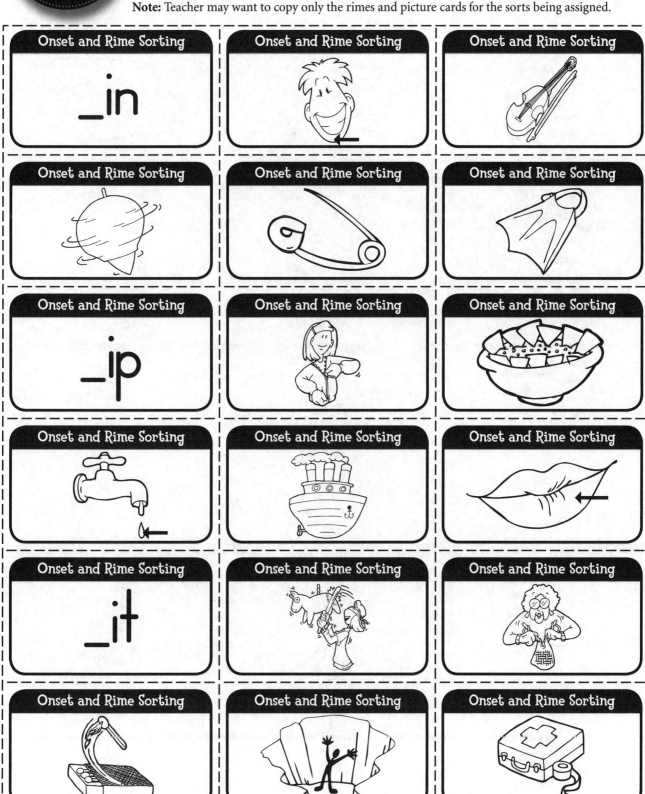

Onset and Rime Sorting	Onset and Rime Sorting	Onset and Rime Sorting
_in		
Onset and Rime Sorting	Onset and Rime Sorting	Onset and Rime Sorting
Onset and Rime Sorting	Onset and Rime Sorting	Onset and Rime Sorting
_ip		
Onset and Rime Sorting	Onset and Rime Sorting	Onset and Rime Sorting
Onset and Rime Sorting	Onset and Rime Sorting	Onset and Rime Sorting
_it		
Onset and Rime Sorting	Onset and Rime Sorting	Onset and Rime Sorting

Onset and Rime Sorting
RallyCoach

Instructions: Copy and cut apart one set of cards for each pair of students.
Note: Teacher may want to copy only the rimes and picture cards for the sorts being assigned.

Onset and Rime Sorting
RallyCoach

Instructions: Copy and cut apart one set of cards for each pair of students.
Note: Teacher may want to copy only the rimes and picture cards for the sorts being assigned.

Onset and Rime Sorting
RallyCoach

Instructions: Copy and cut apart one set of cards for each pair of students. **Note:** Teacher may want to copy only the rimes and picture cards for the sorts being assigned.

Balanced Literacy • Kindergarten • Skidmore & Graber
Kagan Publishing • 1 (800) 933-2667 • www.KaganOnline.com

Onset and Rime Sorting
RallyCoach

Instructions: Copy and cut apart one set of cards for each pair of students.
Note: Teacher may want to copy only the rimes and picture cards for the sorts being assigned.

Onset and Rime Sorting	Onset and Rime Sorting	Onset and Rime Sorting
_eck		
Onset and Rime Sorting	Onset and Rime Sorting	Onset and Rime Sorting
Onset and Rime Sorting	Onset and Rime Sorting	Onset and Rime Sorting
_est		
Onset and Rime Sorting	Onset and Rime Sorting	Onset and Rime Sorting
Onset and Rime Sorting	Onset and Rime Sorting	Onset and Rime Sorting
_ick		
Onset and Rime Sorting	Onset and Rime Sorting	Onset and Rime Sorting

Onset and Rime Sorting
RallyCoach

Instructions: Copy and cut apart one set of cards for each pair of students.

Note: Teacher may want to copy only the rimes and picture cards for the sorts being assigned.

Onset and Rime Sorting
RallyCoach

Instructions: Copy and cut apart one set of cards for each pair of students.
Note: Teacher may want to copy only the rimes and picture cards for the sorts being assigned.

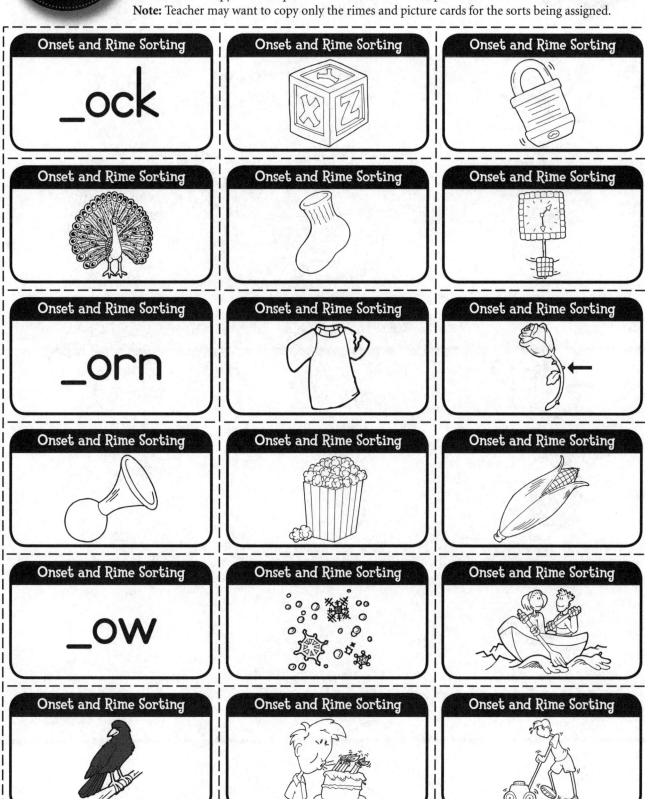

Onset and Rime Sorting
RallyCoach

Instructions: Copy and cut apart one set of cards for each pair of students.
Note: Teacher may want to copy only the rimes and picture cards for the sorts being assigned.

Onset and Rime Sorting	Onset and Rime Sorting	Onset and Rime Sorting
_uck		
Onset and Rime Sorting	Onset and Rime Sorting	Onset and Rime Sorting
		GOOD LUCK
Onset and Rime Sorting	Onset and Rime Sorting	Onset and Rime Sorting
_eep		
Onset and Rime Sorting	Onset and Rime Sorting	Onset and Rime Sorting
Onset and Rime Sorting	Onset and Rime Sorting	Onset and Rime Sorting
_ice		
Onset and Rime Sorting	Onset and Rime Sorting	Onset and Rime Sorting

Onset and Rime Sorting Mat
RallyCoach

Instructions: Copy one mat per pair of students. Attach rime card or picture card to the top of each column. Partners take turns taking a picture card, saying its name, and placing it on the sorting mat under the correct column matching the rime.

b, p, t, d Spinner
RallyCoach

Instructions: Copy the spinner on cardstock. Add a plastic/metal spinner in the middle or use a spinner made from a paper clip and a pencil. Partners take turns spinning the spinner and choosing a matching capital letter card or picture card beginning with the letter on the spinner. **Note:** To make a paper clip spinner: Place a paper clip over the center of the spinner. Place the pencil point on the center point of the spinner, through the paper clip. Using the other hand, spin the paper clip around the pencil point.

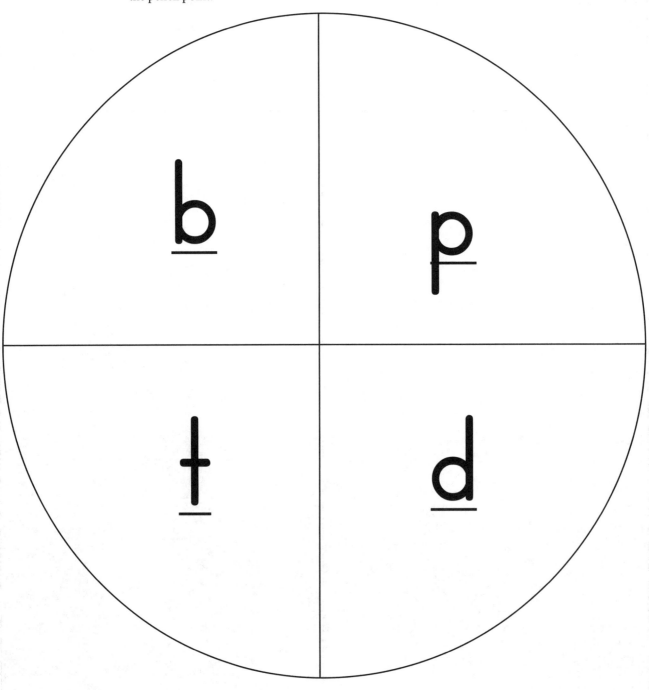

Capital Letter and Picture Cards (for b, p, t, d Spinner)

RallyCoach

Instructions: Cut apart letter and picture cards. Partners take turns matching card to letter on spinner.

Capital Letter and Picture Cards	Capital Letter and Picture Cards	Capital Letter and Picture Cards
B	P	T
Capital Letter and Picture Cards	Capital Letter and Picture Cards	Capital Letter and Picture Cards
D		
Capital Letter and Picture Cards	Capital Letter and Picture Cards	Capital Letter and Picture Cards
Capital Letter and Picture Cards	Capital Letter and Picture Cards	Capital Letter and Picture Cards
Capital Letter and Picture Cards	Capital Letter and Picture Cards	Capital Letter and Picture Cards
Capital Letter and Picture Cards	Capital Letter and Picture Cards	Capital Letter and Picture Cards

h, a, r, m, d Spinner
RallyCoach

Instructions: Copy the spinner on cardstock. Add a plastic/metal spinner in the middle or use a spinner made from a paper clip and a pencil. Partners take turns spinning the spinner and choosing a matching capital letter card or picture card beginning with the letter on the spinner. **Note:** To make a paper clip spinner: Place a paper clip over the center of the spinner. Place the pencil point on the center point of the spinner, through the paper clip. Using the other hand, spin the paper clip around the pencil point.

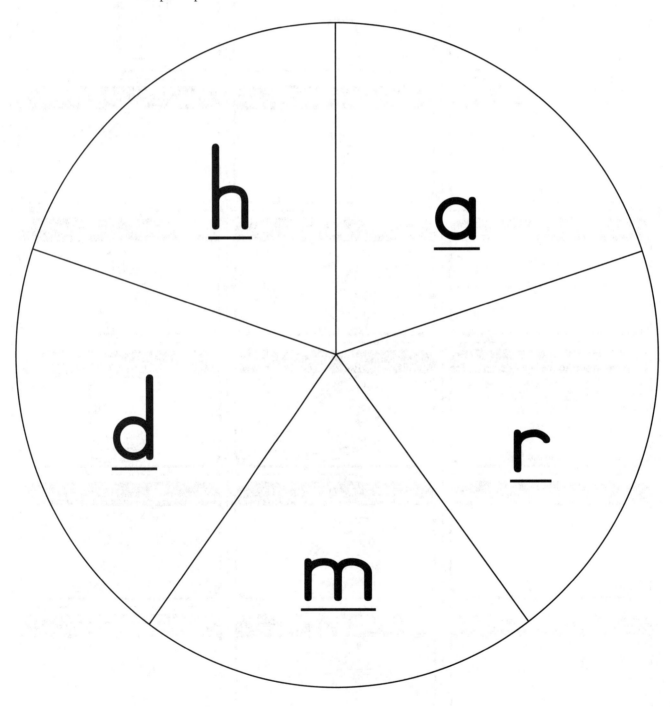

Capital Letter and Picture Cards (for h, a, r, m, d Spinner)
RallyCoach

Instructions: Cut apart letter and picture cards. Partners take turns matching card to letter on spinner.

Capital Letter and Picture Cards	Capital Letter and Picture Cards	Capital Letter and Picture Cards
H	A	R
M	D	(hamburger)
(horse)	(helicopter)	(apple)
(ant)	(alligator)	(ring)
(robot)	(rainbow)	(monkey)
(mailbox)	(doll)	(drum)

V, W, Q, Y, J Spinner
RallyCoach

Instructions: Copy the spinner on cardstock. Add a plastic/metal spinner in the middle or use a spinner made from a paper clip and a pencil. Partners take turns spinning the spinner and choosing a matching capital letter card or picture card beginning with the letter on the spinner. **Note:** To make a paper clip spinner: Place a paper clip over the center of the spinner. Place the pencil point on the center point of the spinner, through the paper clip. Using the other hand, spin the paper clip around the pencil point.

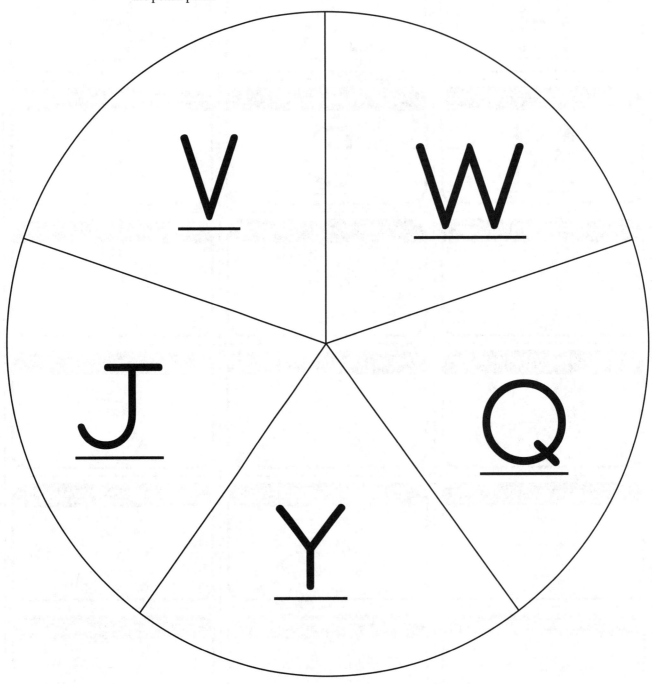

Capital Letter and Picture Cards (for V, W, Q, Y, J Spinner)

RallyCoach

Instructions: Cut apart letter and picture cards. Partners take turns matching card to letter on spinner.

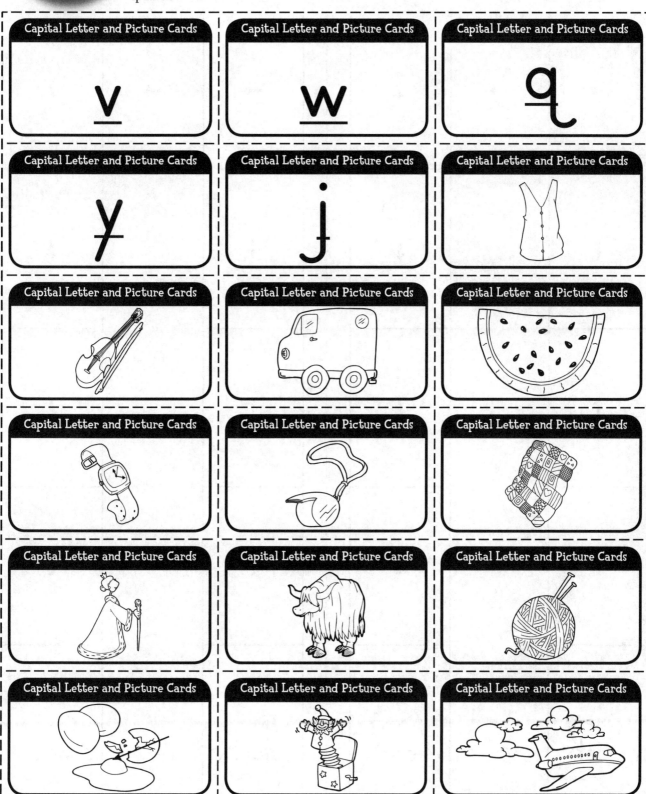

Letter Patterns and
Sight Word Cards Game Board
RallyCoach

Instructions: Copy a game board for each pair of students. Partners take turns reading the word cards and moving a gamepiece or token spaces on the game board. **Note:** This page contains two game boards.

→	→	↓		→	→	↓
↑		↓		↑		↓
↑		↓		↑		↓
↑		↓		↑		↓
start		end		start		end

Letter Pattern Word Cards for Game Board

RallyCoach

Instructions: Cut out set of cards for each pair of students. Partners take turns reading the words and moving spaces on the game board.

Letter Pattern Word Card	Letter Pattern Word Card	Letter Pattern Word Card
fan	tan	jet
ten	ham	rat
let	red	tap
men	sap	jam
pat	pan	bed
man	net	can
zap	fed	den

Sight Word Cards
for Game Board

RallyCoach

Instructions: Cut out set of cards for each pair of students. Partners take turns reading the words and moving spaces on the game board.

Sight Word Cards	Sight Word Cards	Sight Word Cards
a	am	an
and	at	can
come	do	go
he	I	in
is	it	like
me	my	no
said	see	she

Balanced Literacy • Kindergarten • Skidmore & Graber
Kagan Publishing • 1 (800) 933-2667 • www.KaganOnline.com

Sight Word Cards for Game Board

RallyCoach

Instructions: Cut out set of cards for each pair of students. Partners take turns reading the words and moving spaces on the game board.

Sight Word Cards	Sight Word Cards	Sight Word Cards
so	the	to
Sight Word Cards	Sight Word Cards	Sight Word Cards
up	we	you
Sight Word Cards	Sight Word Cards	Sight Word Cards
look	not	us
Sight Word Cards	Sight Word Cards	Sight Word Cards
yes	they	them
Sight Word Cards	Sight Word Cards	Sight Word Cards
their	our	your
Sight Word Cards	Sight Word Cards	Sight Word Cards
are	be	have
Sight Word Cards	Sight Word Cards	Sight Word Cards
what	who	on

Blank Word Cards
for Game Board
RallyCoach

Instructions: Add words in the blank words cards. Copy. Cut out set of cards for each pair of students. Partners take turns reading the words and moving spaces on the game board.

Blank Word Cards	Blank Word Cards	Blank Word Cards
Blank Word Cards	Blank Word Cards	Blank Word Cards
Blank Word Cards	Blank Word Cards	Blank Word Cards
Blank Word Cards	Blank Word Cards	Blank Word Cards
Blank Word Cards	Blank Word Cards	Blank Word Cards
Blank Word Cards	Blank Word Cards	Blank Word Cards
Blank Word Cards	Blank Word Cards	Blank Word Cards

 Balanced Literacy • Kindergarten • Skidmore & Graber
Kagan Publishing • 1 (800) 933-2667 • www.KaganOnline.com

Onset Cube (f, s, h, d, p, b)
RallyCoach

Instructions: Copy the cube pattern onto cardstock for each pair. Cut out, fold, and tape together to form a cube. Partners take turns rolling the cube. The student rolling the cube chooses one incomplete word on the worksheet to make a word.

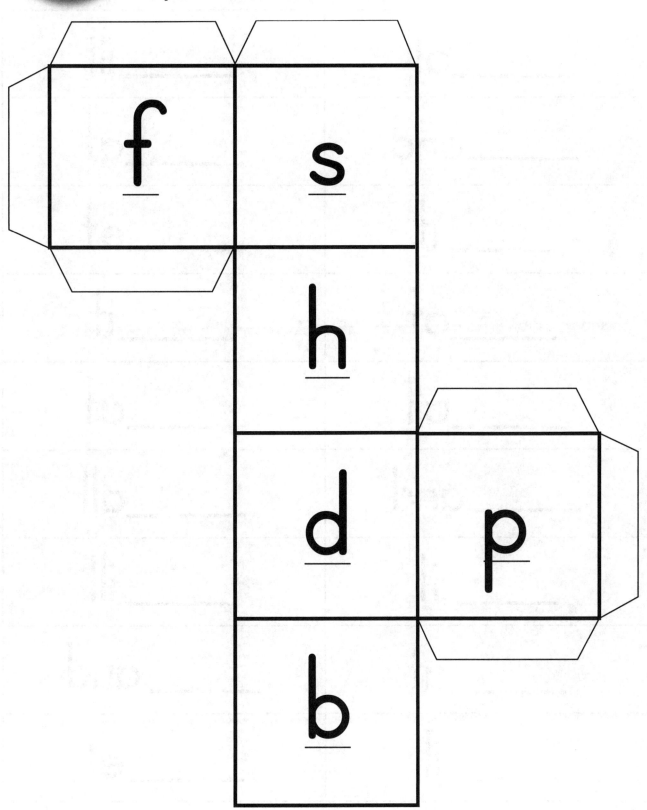

Onset Cube (f, s, h, d, p, b) Worksheet

RallyCoach

Instructions: Partners use worksheet with prefix cube.

_____all	_____ill
_____and	_____at
_____it	_____et
_____at	_____it
_____all	_____at
_____and	_____all
_____it	_____ill
_____at	_____and
_____ill	_____et

Short Vowel Cube (a, e, i, o, u)
RallyCoach

Instructions: Copy the cube pattern onto cardstock for each pair. Cut out, fold, and tape together to form a cube. Partners take turns rolling the cube. The student rolling the cube chooses one incomplete word on the worksheet to make a word.

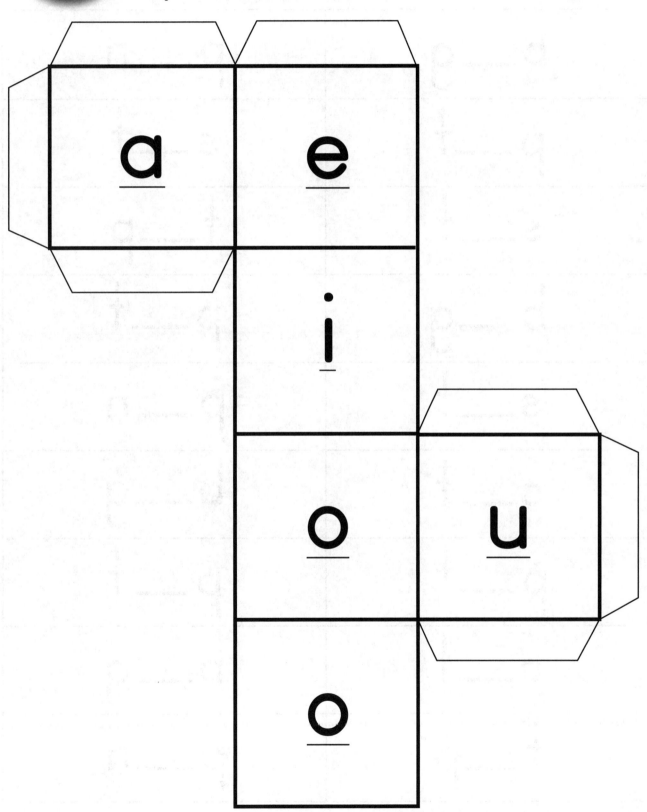

Short Vowel
(a, e, i, o, u) Worksheet

RallyCoach

Instructions: Partners use worksheet with short vowel cube.

b __ g	p __ n
p __ t	s __ t
s __ t	t __ p
b __ g	p __ t
s __ t	p __ n
c __ t	b __ g
p __ t	p __ t
c __ t	b __ g
t __ p	p __ n

Balanced Literacy • Kindergarten • Skidmore & Graber
Kagan Publishing • 1 (800) 933-2667 • www.KaganOnline.com

CVC Word Cube #1
RallyCoach

Instructions: Copy the cube patterns 1, 2, 3 onto cardstock for each pair. Cut out, fold, and tape to form a cube. Partners take turns rolling all the cubes. The student rolling the cubes puts the letters in order according to the numbers on the cubes (1, 2, 3). If a word is formed, both students write it on his or her worksheet.

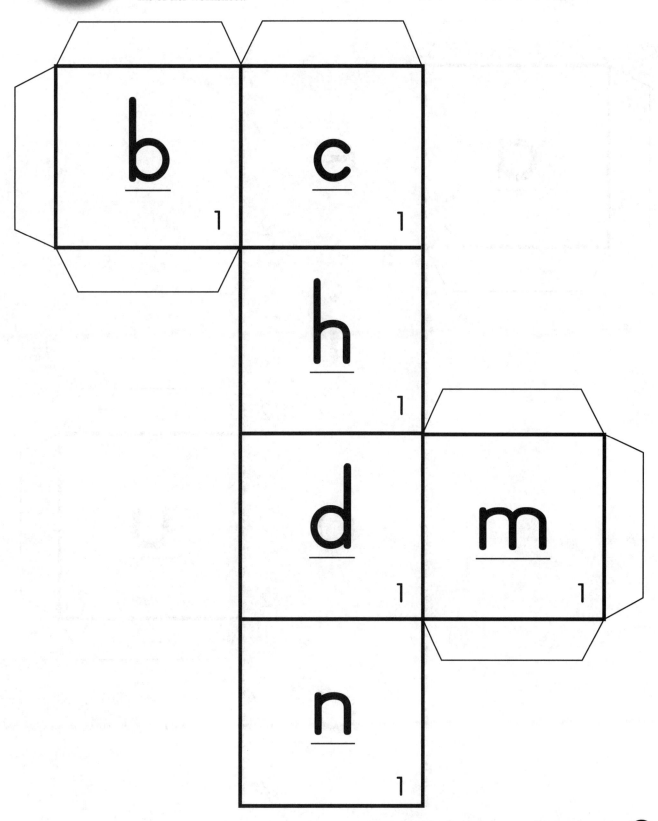

CVC Word Cube #2

RallyCoach

Instructions: Copy the cube patterns 1, 2, 3 onto cardstock for each pair. Cut out, fold, and tape to form a cube. Partners take turns rolling all the cubes. The student rolling the cubes puts the letters in order according to the numbers on the cubes (1, 2, 3). If a word is formed, both students write it on his or her worksheet.

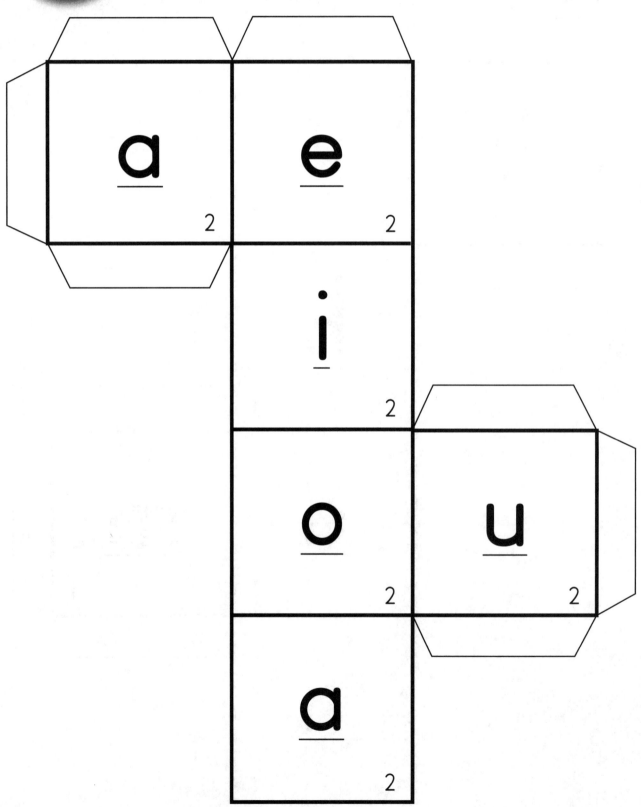

Balanced Literacy • Kindergarten • Skidmore & Graber
Kagan Publishing • 1 (800) 933-2667 • www.KaganOnline.com

CVC Word Cube #3
RallyCoach

Instructions: Copy the cube patterns 1, 2, 3 onto cardstock for each pair. Cut out, fold, and tape to form a cube. Partners take turns rolling all the cubes. The student rolling the cubes puts the letters in order according to the numbers on the cubes (1, 2, 3). If a word is formed, both students write it on his or her worksheet.

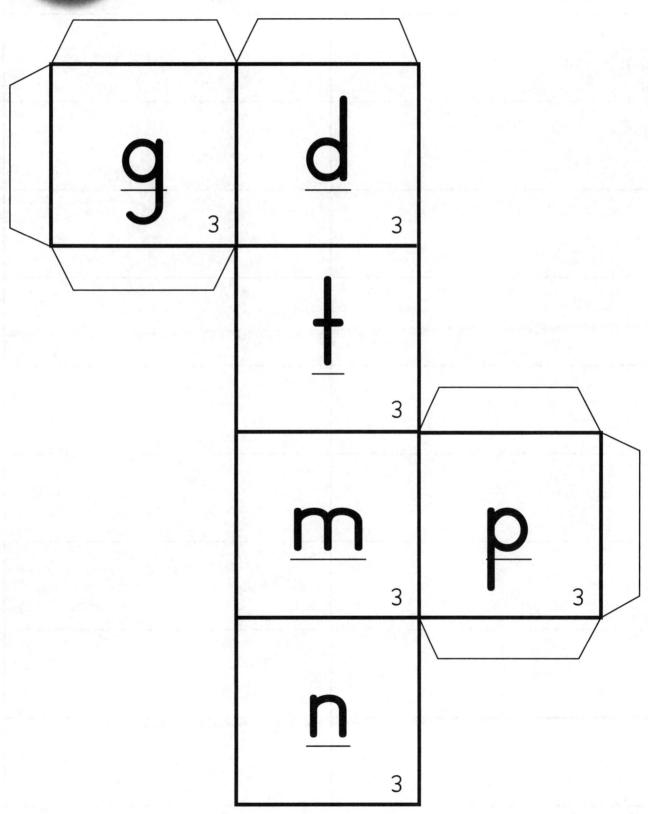

CVC Word Cubes Worksheet

RallyCoach

Instructions: Make one copy for each student.

Balanced Literacy • Kindergarten • Skidmore & Graber
Kagan Publishing • 1 (800) 933-2667 • www.KaganOnline.com

Onset Spinner #1
RallyCoach

Instructions: Copy the spinner patterns onto cardstock for each pair. Add a plastic/metal spinner in the middle or use a spinner made from a paper clip and a pencil. (To make a paper clip spinner: Place a paper clip over the center of the spinner. Place the pencil point on the center point of the spinner, through the paper clip. Using the other hand, spin the paper clip around the pencil point.) Partners take turns spinning the spinners and saying the word made. Both partners write the word on their worksheet.

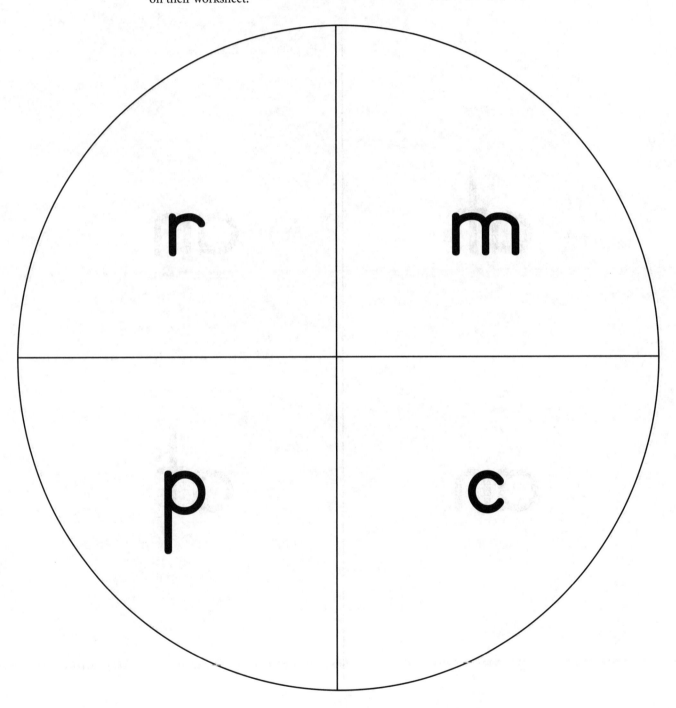

Rime Spinner #1
RallyCoach

Instructions: Copy the spinner patterns onto cardstock for each pair. Add a plastic/metal spinner in the middle or use a spinner made from a paper clip and a pencil. (To make a paper clip spinner: Place a paper clip over the center of the spinner. Place the pencil point on the center point of the spinner, through the paper clip. Using the other hand, spin the paper clip around the pencil point.) Partners take turns spinning the spinners and saying the word made. Both partners write the word on their worksheet.

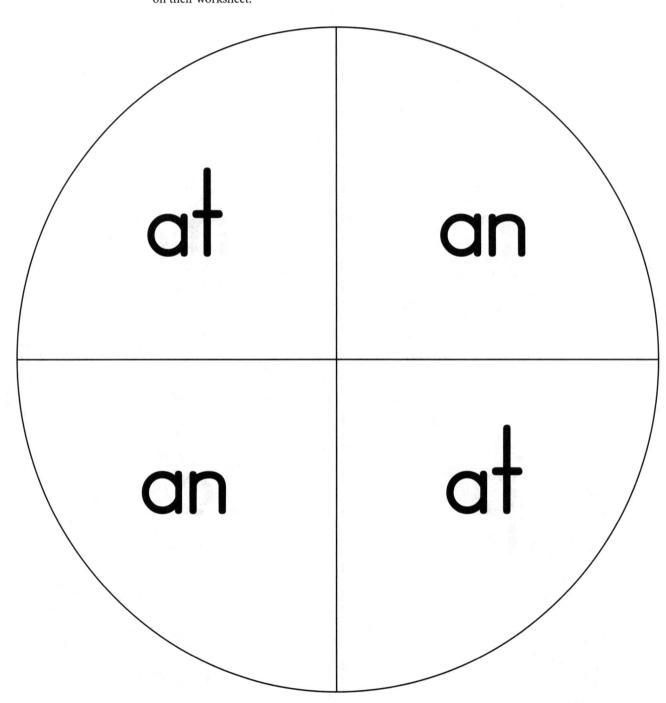

Onset and Rime Worksheet

RallyCoach

Instructions: Make a copy for student.

Onset Spinner #2
RallyCoach

Instructions: Copy the spinner patterns onto cardstock for each pair. Add a plastic/metal spinner in the middle or use a spinner made from a paper clip and a pencil. (To make a paper clip spinner: Place a paper clip over the center of the spinner. Place the pencil point on the center point of the spinner, through the paper clip. Using the other hand, spin the paper clip around the pencil point.) Partners take turns spinning the spinners and saying the word made. Both partners write the word on their worksheet.

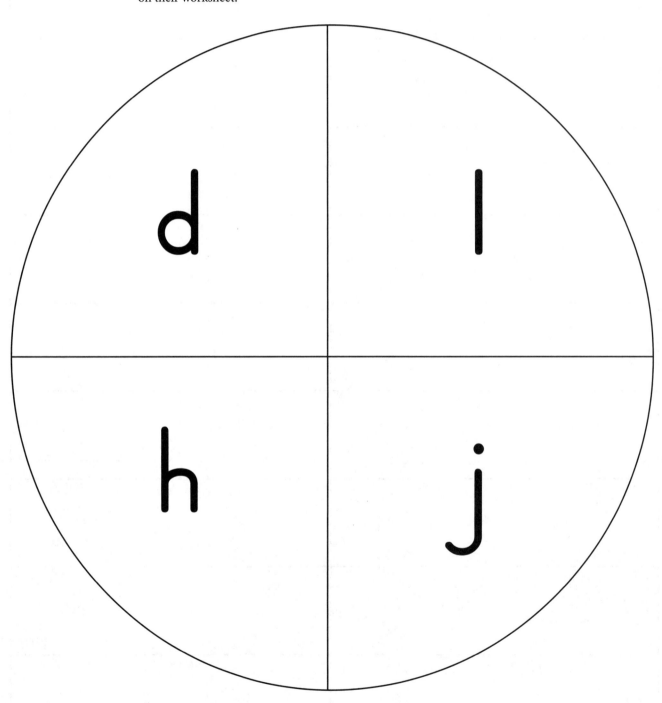

Rime Spinner #2
RallyCoach

Instructions: Copy the spinner patterns onto cardstock for each pair. Add a plastic/metal spinner in the middle or use a spinner made from a paper clip and a pencil. (To make a paper clip spinner: Place a paper clip over the center of the spinner. Place the pencil point on the center point of the spinner, through the paper clip. Using the other hand, spin the paper clip around the pencil point.) Partners take turns spinning the spinners and saying the word made. Both partners write the word on their worksheet.

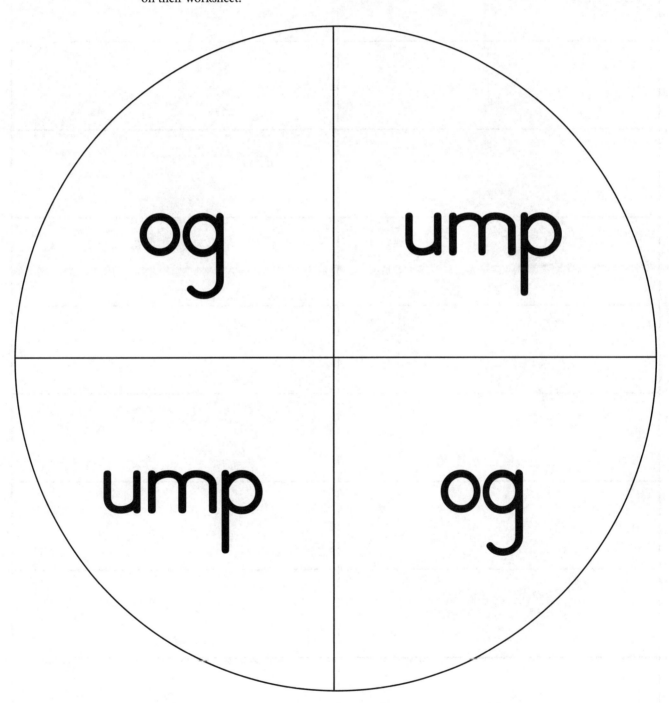

Balanced Literacy • Kindergarten • Skidmore & Graber
Kagan Publishing • 1 (800) 933-2667 • www.KaganOnline.com 271

Onset and Rime Worksheet
RallyCoach

Instructions: Make a copy for student.

Balanced Literacy • Kindergarten • Skidmore & Graber
Kagan Publishing • 1 (800) 933-2667 • www.KaganOnline.com

Word Cards and Vowel Cards
(Adding Medial Vowels)
RallyCoach

Instructions: Partners take turns placing letter cards in the blanks to make words. The words are written on the worksheet.

c___t

p___t

a e i o u

Worksheet for Word Cards
and Vowel Cards
RallyCoach

Instructions: Use the spaces below to write the words made with the vowel cards and word cards.

Onset and Rime Cards
RallyCoach

Instructions: Partners take turns placing letter cards in the blanks to make words. The words are written on the worksheet.

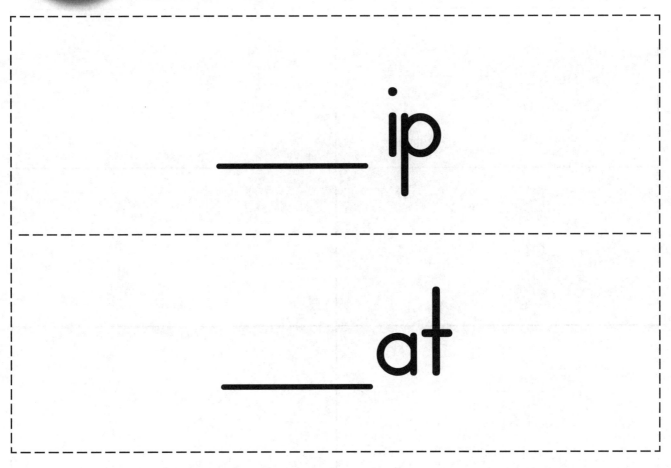

___ip

___at

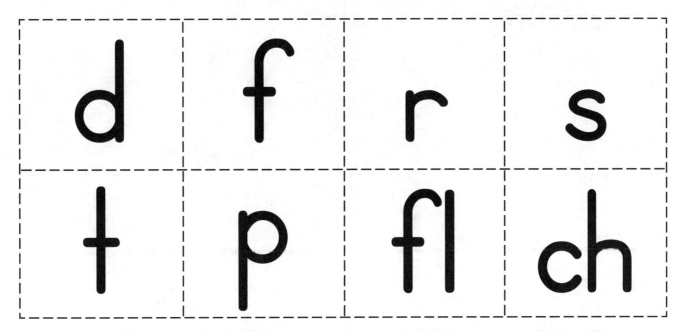

d	f	r	s
t	p	fl	ch

Worksheet for Onset and Rime Cards

RallyCoach

Instructions: Use the spaces below to write the words made with the vowel cards and word cards.

Word Cards and Medial Vowel Cards #1

RallyCoach

Instructions: Partners take turns placing letter cards in the blanks to make words. The words are written on the worksheet.

b___g	h___t
f___x	t___p
s___t	w___g

a e i o u

Word Cards and Medial Vowel Cards #2

RallyCoach

Instructions: Partners take turns placing letter cards in the blanks to make words. The words are written on the worksheet.

f __ n	p __ __ n
n __ __ t	r __ __ p
p __ __ t	r __ __ g

a e i o u

Worksheet for Word Cards
and Medial Vowel Cards
RallyCoach

Instructions: Use the spaces below to write the words made with the vowel cards and word cards.

RALLYCOACH

Activity

Name, Sound, Word

Partners take turns, one solving a problem while the other checks, coaches, and praises.

Activity Steps

1. Partner A chooses a letter card. Partner A says the name of the letter, gives its sound, and gives a word beginning with the sound. (*Partners may refer to the Student Direction Card.*)

2. Partner B watches and listens, checks, and praises.

3. Partner B chooses a letter card. Partner B says the name of the letter, gives its sound, and gives a word beginning with the sound.

4. Partner A watches and listens, checks, and praises.

5. Repeat starting at Step 1.

STRUCTURE
RallyCoach

Variation

Pairs may respond to only one or two of the three directions on the Student Direction Card, depending on teacher directions.

Blacklines

Student Direction Cards

RallyCoach

Instructions: Copy one card per pair. Page contains four cards.

- name  **C c**

- sound

- word  →cat

- name **C c**

- sound

- word  →cat

- name  **C c**

- sound

- word  →cat

- name  **C c**

- sound

- word  →cat

Letter Cards
(Letter Names, Sounds, and Words)
RallyCoach

Instructions: Copy one set of cards for each pair. Cut apart.

Letter Cards	Letter Cards	Letter Cards
a	b	c

Letter Cards	Letter Cards	Letter Cards
d	e	f

Letter Cards	Letter Cards	Letter Cards
g	h	i

Letter Cards	Letter Cards	Letter Cards
j	k	l

Letter Cards
(Letter Names, Sounds, and Words)
RallyCoach

Instructions: Copy one set of cards for each pair. Cut apart.

Letter Cards	Letter Cards	Letter Cards
m	n	o
Letter Cards	**Letter Cards**	**Letter Cards**
p	q	r
Letter Cards	**Letter Cards**	**Letter Cards**
s	t	u
Letter Cards	**Letter Cards**	**Letter Cards**
v	w	x

Letter Cards
(Letter Names, Sounds, and Words)
RallyCoach

Instructions: Copy one set of cards for each pair. Cut apart.

Letter Cards	Letter Cards	Letter Cards
y	z	A
B	C	D
E	F	G
H	I	J

Letter Cards
(Letter Names, Sounds, and Words)
RallyCoach

Instructions: Copy one set of cards for each pair. Cut apart.

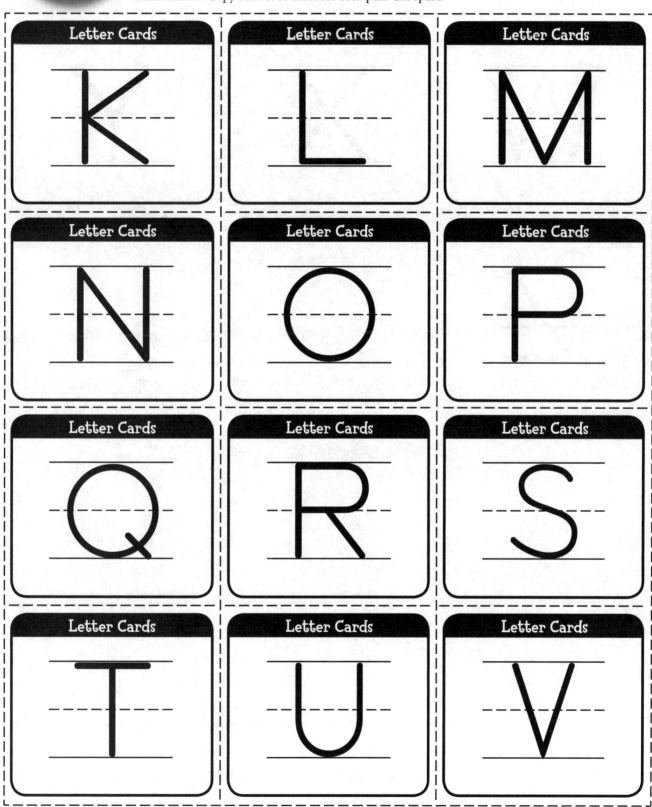

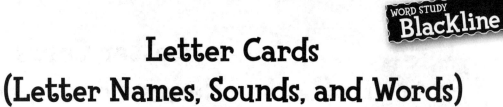

Letter Cards
(Letter Names, Sounds, and Words)
RallyCoach

Instructions: Copy one set of cards for each pair. Cut apart.

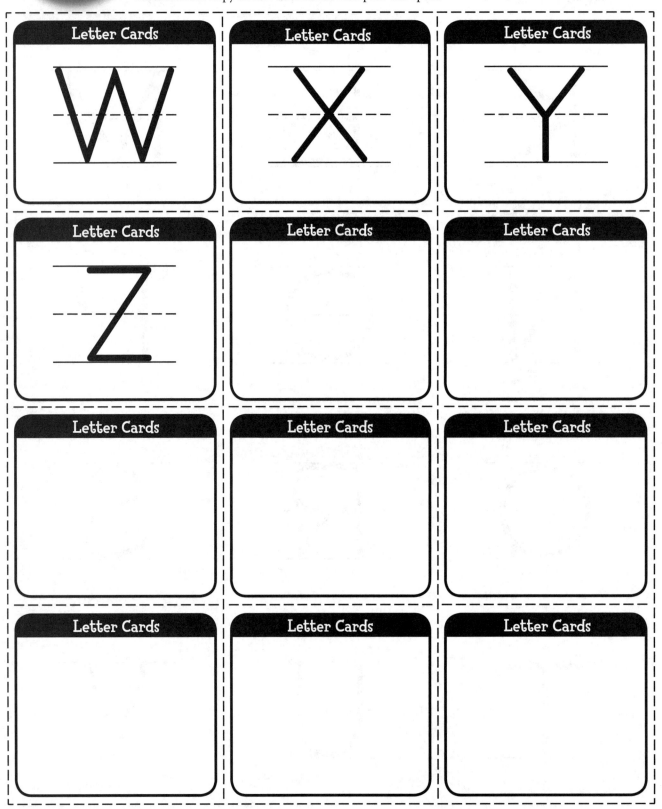

Letter Cards	Letter Cards	Letter Cards
W	X	Y

Letter Cards	Letter Cards	Letter Cards
Z		

Letter Cards	Letter Cards	Letter Cards

Letter Cards	Letter Cards	Letter Cards

Word Study Showdown

Teammates each write or choose an answer. Then there is a "showdown" as they show their answers to each other. Teammates verify answers.

Activity Steps

STRUCTURE

Showdown

Note:
The teacher is the Showdown Captain, rather than rotating the responsibility among the team.

1. Teacher Cards are made into transparencies for teacher use on the overhead projector or the teacher has a list of words to orally read.

2. Each student holds Student Card Set in his or her hand.

3. Teacher is the Showdown Captain.

4. Showdown Captain (teacher) shows the first card on the overhead or reads a word orally.

5. Working alone, students individually identify an answer from Student Cards.

6. When finished, teammates signal they are ready.

7. Showdown Captain (teacher) calls, "Showdown!"

8. Teammates show their answers at the same time.

9. Showdown Captain (teacher) leads checking.

10. If correct, the team celebrates. If not, the teammates coach, then celebrate.

11. The teacher is the Showdown Captain for the remaining rounds.

Blacklines

Word Study Showdown (continued)

Teammates each write or choose an answer. Then there is a "showdown" as they show their answers to each other. Teammates verify answers.

Blacklines (continued)

Rhyming Strips
Showdown (Teacher Set)

Instructions: Make into a transparency and cut apart. Students indicate "Yes" if word pictures rhyme and "No" if they do not rhyme.

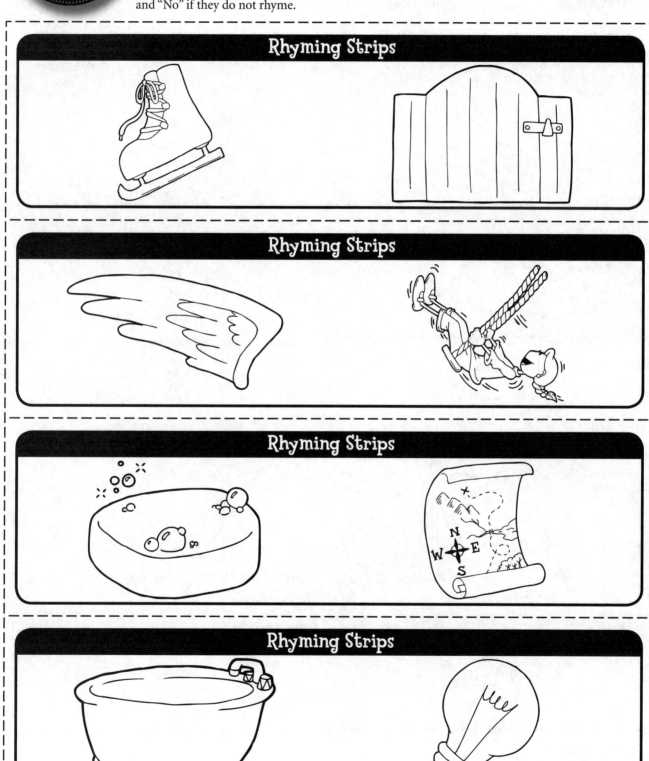

Rhyming Strips

Rhyming Strips

Rhyming Strips

Rhyming Strips

Rhyming Strips
Showdown (Teacher Set)

Instructions: Make into a transparency and cut apart. Students indicate "Yes" if word pictures rhyme and "No" if they do not rhyme.

Rhyming Strips

Rhyming Strips

Rhyming Strips

Rhyming Strips

Rhyming Strips
Showdown (Teacher Set)

Instructions: Make into a transparency and cut apart. Students indicate "Yes" if word pictures rhyme and "No" if they do not rhyme.

Rhyming Strips

Rhyming Strips

Rhyming Strips

Rhyming Strips

Rhyming Strips
Showdown (Teacher Set)

Instructions: Make into a transparency and cut apart. Students indicate "Yes" if word pictures rhyme and "No" if they do not rhyme.

Rhyming Strips

Rhyming Strips

Rhyming Strips

Rhyming Strips

Rhyming Strips
Showdown (Teacher Set)

Instructions: Make into a transparency and cut apart. Students indicate "Yes" if word pictures rhyme and "No" if they do not rhyme.

Rhyming Strips

Showdown (Teacher Set)

Instructions: Make into a transparency and cut apart. Students indicate "Yes" if word pictures rhyme and "No" if they do not rhyme.

Rhyming Strips

Rhyming Strips

Rhyming Strips

Rhyming Strips

Rhyming Strips
Showdown (Teacher Set)

Instructions: Make into a transparency and cut apart. Students indicate "Yes" if word pictures rhyme and "No" if they do not rhyme.

Rhyming Strips
Showdown (Teacher Set)

Instructions: Make into a transparency and cut apart. Students indicate "Yes" if word pictures rhyme and "No" if they do not rhyme.

Rhyming Strips

Rhyming Strips

Rhyming Strips

Rhyming Strips

Balanced Literacy • Kindergarten • Skidmore & Graber
Kagan Publishing • 1 (800) 933-2667 • www.KaganOnline.com

Rhyming Strips
Showdown (Teacher Set)

Instructions: Make into a transparency and cut apart. Students indicate "Yes" if word pictures rhyme and "No" if they do not rhyme.

Rhyming Strips
Showdown (Teacher Set)

Instructions: Make into a transparency and cut apart. Students indicate "Yes" if word pictures rhyme and "No" if they do not rhyme.

Rhyming Strips

Rhyming Strips

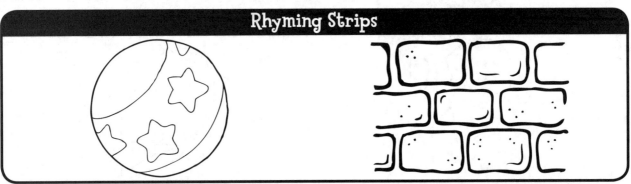

Rhyming Strips

Rhyming Strips

Rhyming Strips
Showdown (Teacher Set)

Instructions: Make into a transparency and cut apart. Students indicate "Yes" if word pictures rhyme and "No" if they do not rhyme.

Rhyming Strips
Showdown (Teacher Set)

Instructions: Make into a transparency and cut apart. Students indicate "Yes" if word pictures rhyme and "No" if they do not rhyme.

Rhyming Strips

Rhyming Strips

Rhyming Strips

Rhyming Strips

Rhyming Strips
Showdown (Teacher Set)

Instructions: Make into a transparency and cut apart. Students indicate "Yes" if word pictures rhyme and "No" if they do not rhyme.

Rhyming Strips
Showdown (Student Set)

Instructions: Copy and cut apart a Yes and No card for each student. This page has cards for four students.

Rhyming Strips
Student Set

yes

Rhyming Strips
Student Set

no

Rhyming Strips
Student Set

yes

Rhyming Strips
Student Set

no

Rhyming Strips
Student Set

yes

Rhyming Strips
Student Set

no

Rhyming Strips
Student Set

yes

Rhyming Strips
Student Set

no

Which One Doesn't Rhyme?
Showdown (Teacher Set)

Instructions: Make a transparency for the teacher, who is the Showdown Captain. Students indicate the picture that does not rhyme with a "1," "2," or "3" student card.

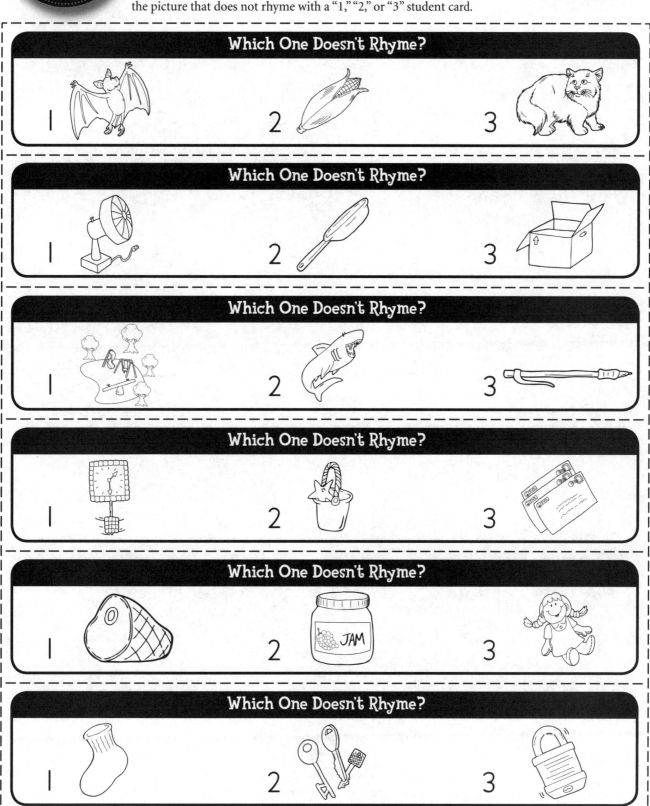

Which One Doesn't Rhyme?

Showdown (Teacher Set)

Instructions: Make a transparency for the teacher, who is the Showdown Captain. Students indicate the picture that does not rhyme with a "1," "2," or "3" student card.

 Balanced Literacy • Kindergarten • Skidmore & Graber
Kagan Publishing • 1 (800) 933-2667 • www.KaganOnline.com

Which One Doesn't Rhyme?
Showdown (Teacher Set)

Instructions: Make a transparency for the teacher, who is the Showdown Captain. Students indicate the picture that does not rhyme with a "1," "2," or "3" student card.

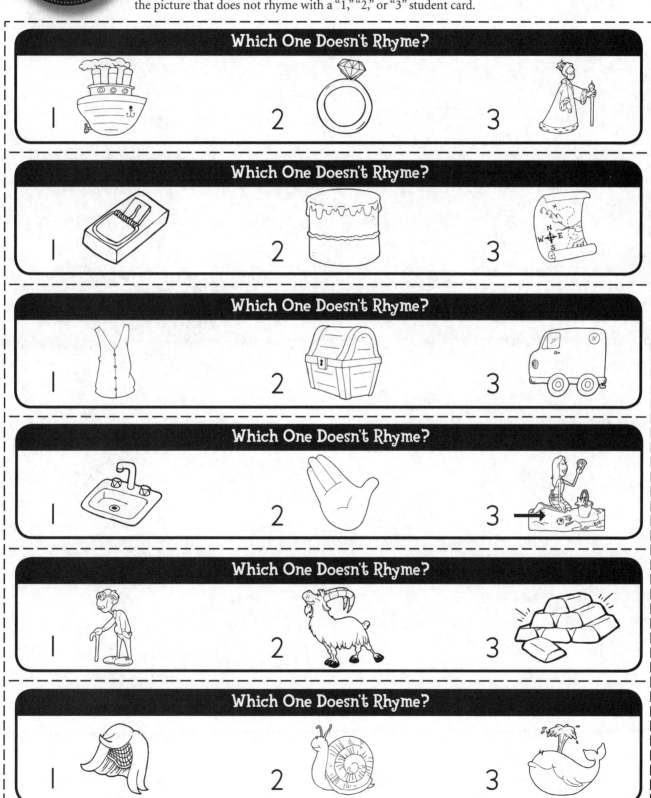

Which One Doesn't Rhyme?

Showdown (Teacher Set)

Instructions: Make a transparency for the teacher, who is the Showdown Captain. Students indicate the picture that does not rhyme with a "1," "2," or "3" student card.

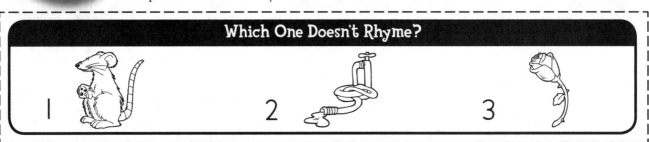

Which One Doesn't Rhyme?
Showdown (Student Set)

Instructions: Copy a set of cards 1–3 for each student. This page has cards for two students. The teacher is the Showdown Captain and shows three numbered pictures. Students use the numbered cards to indicate the picture that does not rhyme with the others.

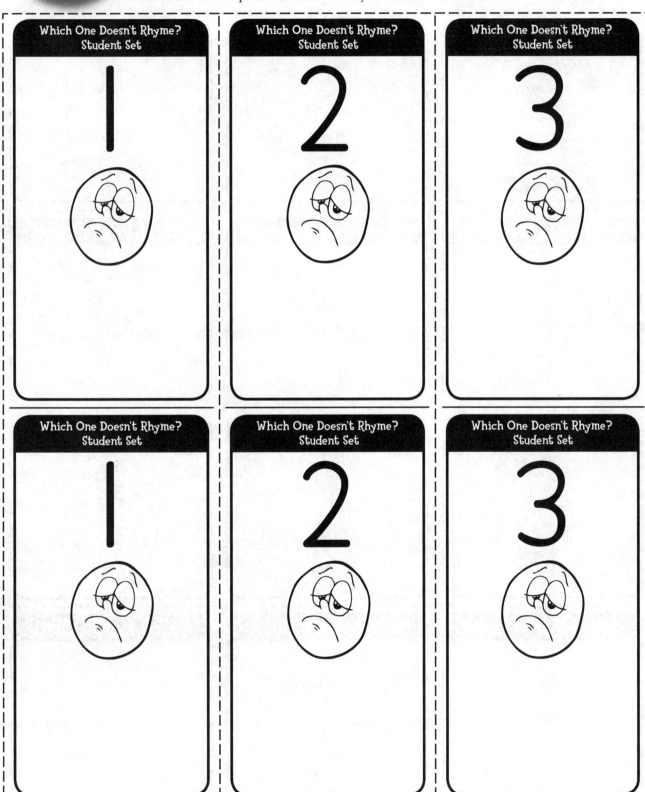

Word Parts

Showdown (Teacher Set)

Instructions: Make into a transparency and cut apart. The teacher shows a picture card and students use the numbered cards to indicate the number of the word parts (syllables) in the word after saying the word and clapping or tapping the parts.

Word Parts Card	Word Parts Card	Word Parts Card
Word Parts Card	Word Parts Card	Word Parts Card
Word Parts Card	Word Parts Card	Word Parts Card
Word Parts Card	Word Parts Card	Word Parts Card

Word Parts
Showdown (Teacher Set)

Instructions: Make into a transparency and cut apart. The teacher shows a picture card and students use the numbered cards to indicate the number of the word parts (syllables) in the word after saying the word and clapping or tapping the parts.

Word Parts Card	Word Parts Card	Word Parts Card
Word Parts Card	Word Parts Card	Word Parts Card
Word Parts Card	Word Parts Card	Word Parts Card
Word Parts Card	Word Parts Card	Word Parts Card

Word Parts

Showdown (Teacher Set)

Instructions: Make into a transparency and cut apart. The teacher shows a picture card and students use the numbered cards to indicate the number of the word parts (syllables) in the word after saying the word and clapping or tapping the parts.

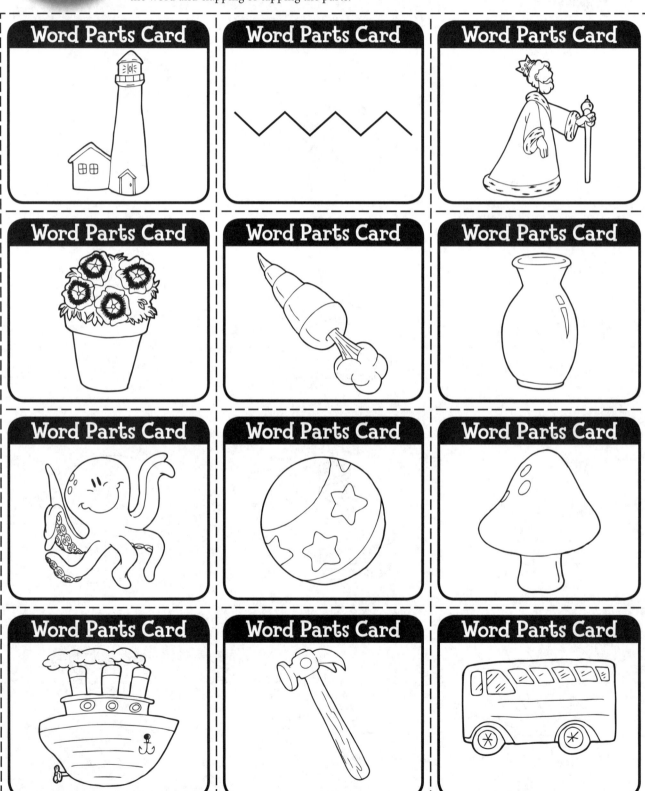

Word Parts Card	Word Parts Card	Word Parts Card
Word Parts Card	Word Parts Card	Word Parts Card
Word Parts Card	Word Parts Card	Word Parts Card
Word Parts Card	Word Parts Card	Word Parts Card

Balanced Literacy • Kindergarten • Skidmore & Graber
Kagan Publishing • 1 (800) 933-2667 • www.KaganOnline.com

Word Parts
Showdown (Student Set)

Instructions: Copy and cut apart a set of cards 1–3 for each student. This page has cards for two students. The teacher is the Showdown Captain and shows a picture card. Students use the numbered cards to indicate the number of word parts (syllables) in the word after saying the word and clapping or tapping the parts.

Word Parts Student Set	Word Parts Student Set	Word Parts Student Set
1	2	3

Word Parts Student Set	Word Parts Student Set	Word Parts Student Set
1	2	3

Words for Phoneme Segmentation
Showdown

Instructions: The Showdown Captain (teacher) says a word from the list. Students individually repeat the word. On the Phoneme Segmentation Mat, students push one chip up into a top box for each phoneme heard in the word. They individually count the number of chips pushed up (number of phonemes) and choose a corresponding Showdown card with a 1, 2, 3, or 4 indicating their answer. Students hold up the chosen number card when the Showdown Captain calls for the answer.

log	(3)		dish	(3)
mom	(3)		wet	(3)
funny	(4)		rats	(4)
say	(2)		space	(4)
wheel	(3)		jump	(4)
toss	(3)		bean	(3)
shed	(3)		lake	(3)
help	(4)		house	(3)
den	(3)		hot	(3)
clock	(4)		play	(3)
food	(3)		box	(3)
chin	(3)		me	(2)
name	(3)		flash	(4)
paw	(2)		snake	(4)
tea	(2)		pail	(3)
bump	(4)		not	(3)
truck	(4)		rug	(3)
see	(2)		smash	(4)
pop	(3)		knee	(2)
yank	(4)		mail	(3)
to	(2)		plan	(4)
sheet	(3)		do	(2)
spill	(4)		thin	(3)
quit	(3)		drip	(4)
zoo	(2)		run	(3)
west	(4)		shop	(3)

 Balanced Literacy • Kindergarten • Skidmore & Graber
Kagan Publishing • 1 (800) 933-2667 • www.KaganOnline.com

Phoneme Segmentation Mat

Showdown

Instructions: Copy one mat for each student. Place chips on circles. Students listen to Showdown Captain (teacher) say a word. Then they individually repeat the word and push one chip up into a top box for each phoneme heard in the word. They individually count the number of chips pushed up (number of phonemes) and choose a Showdown Card with a 1, 2, 3, or 4 indicating their answer to show when the Showdown Captain calls for the answer. **Note:** This page contains mats for three students.

Phoneme Segmentation
Showdown

Instructions: Copy a set of cards 1–4 for each student. The teacher is the Showdown Captain and orally says a word. Students use the numbered cards to indicate the number of phonemes they heard in each word after manipulating chips on the Phoneme Segmentation Mat.
Note: This page has cards for two students.

Phoneme Segmentation	Phoneme Segmentation	Phoneme Segmentation	Phoneme Segmentation
1	2	3	4

Phoneme Segmentation	Phoneme Segmentation	Phoneme Segmentation	Phoneme Segmentation
1	2	3	4

Beginning/Ending Sounds
Showdown (Teacher List)

Instructions: The teacher reads these words orally, one at a time, as individual students in teams slide a pointer finger along the arrow on the student cards as he or she repeats the word. If the identified sound is heard at the beginning of the word, a clothespin is clipped to the green circle. If the identified sound is heard at the end of the word, the clothespin is clipped to the red triangle at the end of the arrow. Students hold up their arrows when the teacher calls, "Showdown."

1. /m/ **m**op	14. /l/ **l**id	27. /c/ **c**at
2. /l/ dol**l**	15. /k/ tac**k**	28. /k/ des**k**
3. /k/ **k**ite	16. /t/ car**t**	29. /d/ ki**d**
4. /j/ ca**g**e	17. /s/ bu**s**	30. /f/ wi**f**e
5. /h/ **h**am	18. /w/ **w**et	31. /f/ **f**an
6. /g/ **g**um	19. /b/ **b**at	32. /t/ foo**t**
7. /t/ ma**t**	20. /b/ ca**b**	33. /g/ **g**ap
8. /p/ **p**ig	21. /d/ be**d**	34. /h/ **h**en
9. /s/ rug**s**	22. /b/ we**b**	35. /j/ **g**em
10. /f/ **f**ox	23. /s/ **s**ub	36. /m/ **m**oon
11. /r/ **r**oof	24. /n/ ca**n**	37. /l/ tel**l**
12. /d/ **d**uck	25. /k/ **c**art	38. /n/ pe**n**
13. /g/ do**g**	26. /p/ ca**p**	39. /b/ **b**ook

Beginning/Ending Sounds
Showdown (Student Set)

Instructions: Copy and cut out an arrow for each student. On the arrow, color the circle green and the triangle red. Each student will slide a pointer finger along the arrow as he or she repeats the word said by the teacher. If the indicated sound is located at the beginning of the word, a clothespin is clipped to the green circle. If the indicated sound is located at the end of the word, a clothespin is clipped to the red triangle part of the arrow. Students hold up their arrows when the teacher calls, "Showdown." **Note:** This page has arrows for four students.

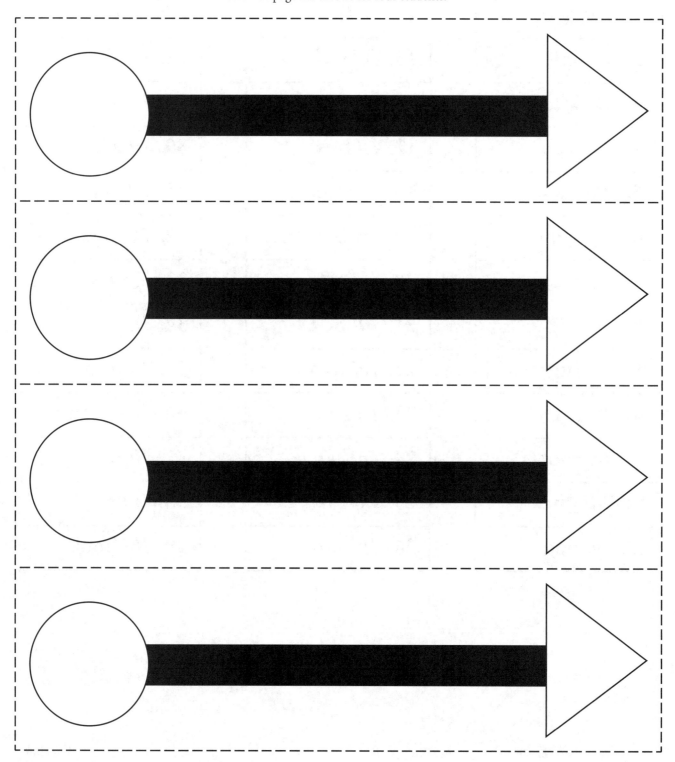

Beginning/Ending Consonant Sounds
Showdown (Teacher Set)

Instructions: Make into a transparency and cut apart. The teacher (Showdown Captain) shows these pictures one at a time. Students individually in teams slide a pointer finger along the arrow on the student card while repeating the word. If the identified letter sound on the card is heard at the beginning of the word, a clothespin is clipped to the green circle. If the identified sound is heard at the end of the word, the clothespin is clipped to the red triangle at the end of the arrow. Students hold up their arrows when the teacher calls, "Showdown."

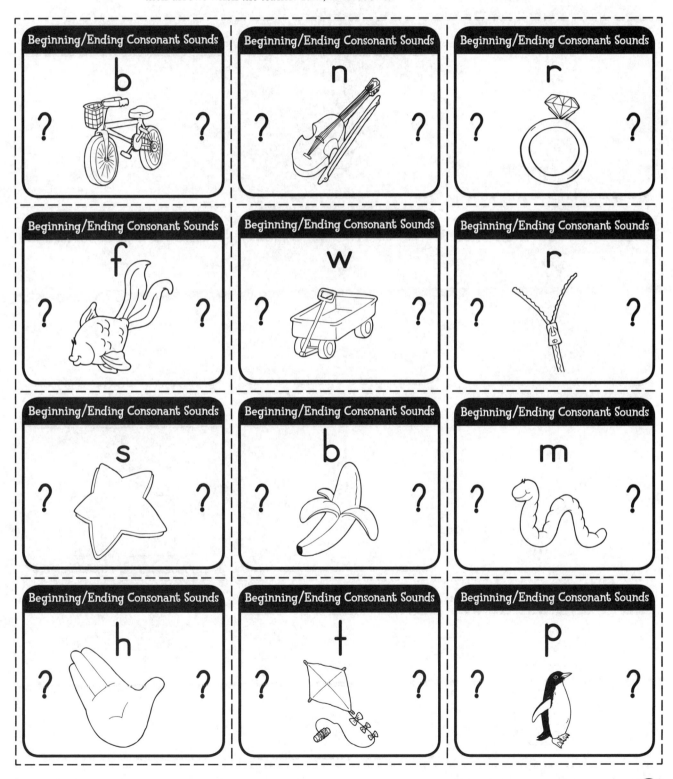

Beginning/Ending Consonant Sounds
Showdown (Teacher Set)

Instructions: Make into a transparency and cut apart. The teacher (Showdown Captain) shows these pictures one at a time. Students individually in teams slide a pointer finger along the arrow on the student card while repeating the word. If the identified letter sound on the card is heard at the beginning of the word, a clothespin is clipped to the green circle. If the identified sound is heard at the end of the word, the clothespin is clipped to the red triangle at the end of the arrow. Students hold up their arrows when the teacher calls, "Showdown."

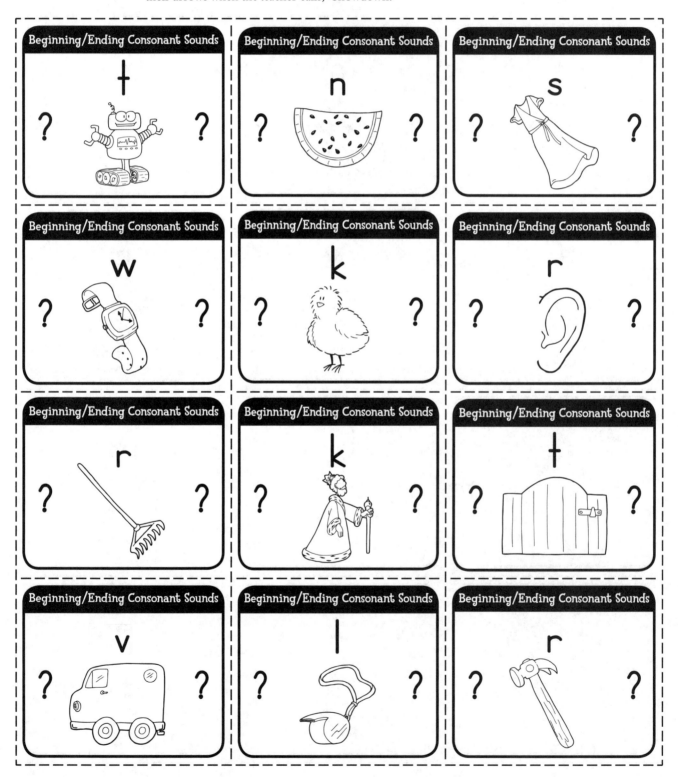

Beginning/Ending Consonant Sounds
Showdown (Teacher Set)

Instructions: Make into a transparency and cut apart. The teacher (Showdown Captain) shows these pictures one at a time. Students individually in teams slide a pointer finger along the arrow on the student card while repeating the word. If the identified letter sound on the card is heard at the beginning of the word, a clothespin is clipped to the green circle. If the identified sound is heard at the end of the word, the clothespin is clipped to the red triangle at the end of the arrow. Students hold up their arrows when the teacher calls, "Showdown."

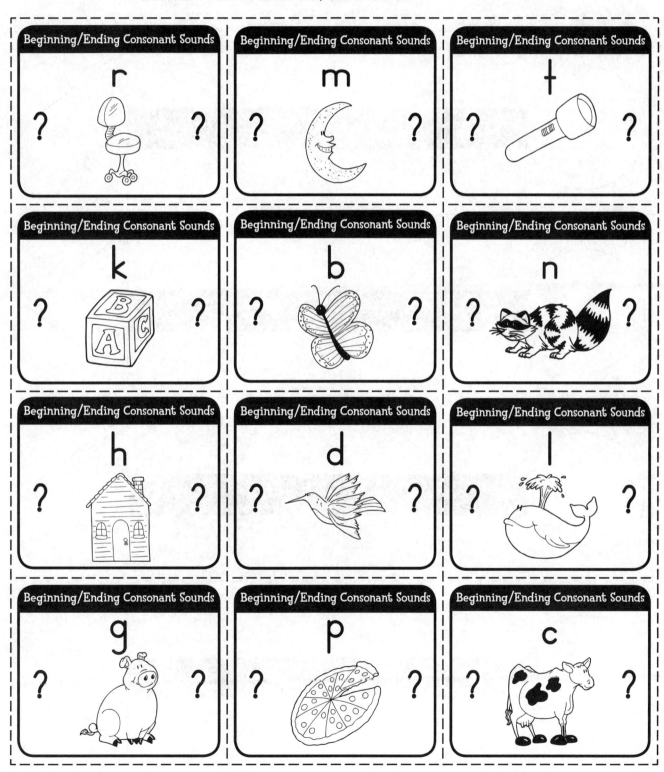

Beginning/Ending Consonant Sounds

Showdown (Student Set)

Instructions: Copy and cut out an arrow for each student. On the arrow, color the circle green and the triangle red. Each student will slide a pointer finger along the arrow as he or she says the word represented by the teacher's picture card. If the indicated sound is located at the beginning of the word, a clothespin is clipped to the green circle. If the indicated sound is located at the end of the word, a clothespin is clipped to the red triangle part of the arrow. Students hold up their arrows when the teacher calls, "Showdown." **Note:** This page has arrows for four students.

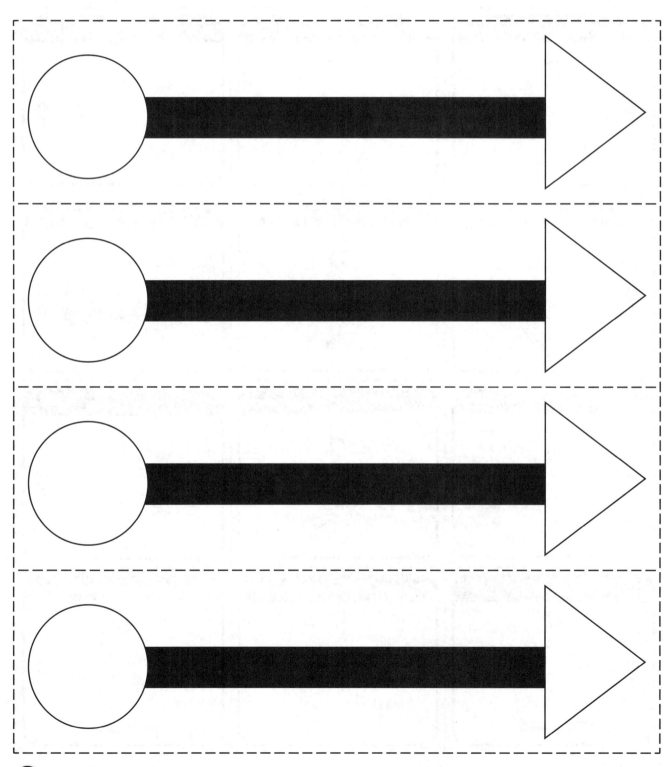

Phoneme Identification Strips

Showdown (Teacher Set)

Instructions: Showdown Captain (Teacher) shows a strip of three pictures all beginning with the same sound. Students write the common beginning letter on dry-erase boards. On the teacher's signal, students turn to a partner, show the written letter, and tell their partner the sound it makes. Teacher then leads a discussion.

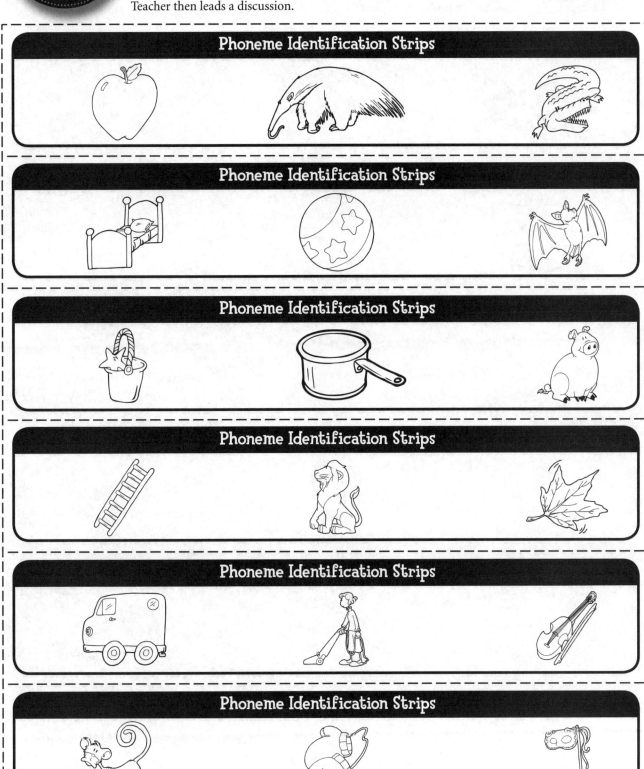

Phoneme Identification Strips
Showdown (Teacher Set)

Instructions: Showdown Captain (Teacher) shows a strip of three pictures all beginning with the same sound. Students write the common beginning letter on dry-erase boards. On the teacher's signal, students turn to a partner, show the written letter and tell their partner the sound it makes. Teacher then leads a discussion.

Phoneme Identification Strips

Phoneme Identification Strips

Phoneme Identification Strips

Phoneme Identification Strips

Phoneme Identification Strips

Phoneme Identification Strips

Phoneme Identification Strips
Showdown (Teacher Set)

Instructions: Showdown Captain (Teacher) shows a strip of three pictures all beginning with the same sound. Students write the common beginning letter on dry-erase boards. On the teacher's signal, students turn to a partner, show the written letter and tell their partner the sound it makes. Teacher then leads a discussion.

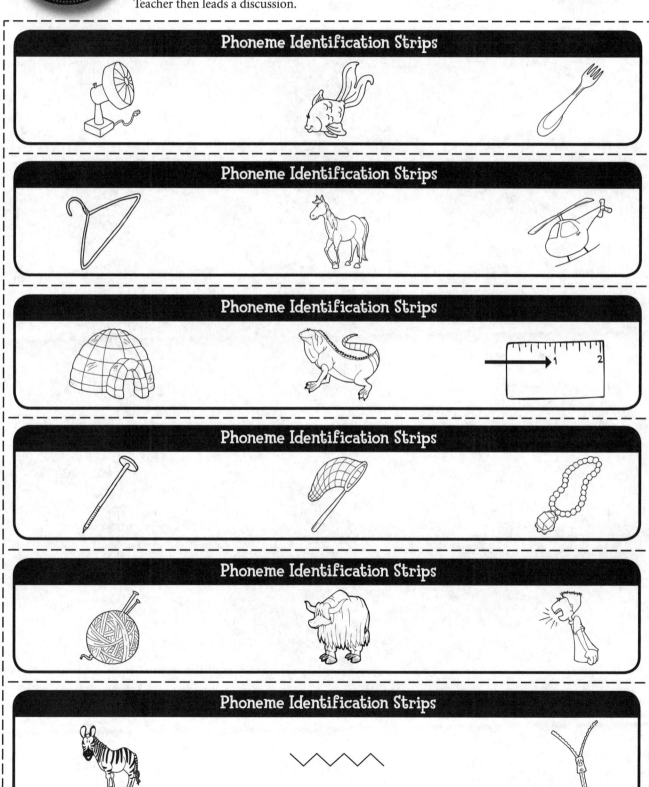

Phoneme Identification Strips

Phoneme Identification Strips

Phoneme Identification Strips

Phoneme Identification Strips

Phoneme Identification Strips

Phoneme Identification Strips

Phoneme Categorization Strips
Showdown (Teacher Set)

Instructions: Make a transparency for the teacher, who is the Showdown Captain. The teacher shows a strip with three numbered pictures. Students use the numbered student cards to indicate the picture that does not begin like the others.

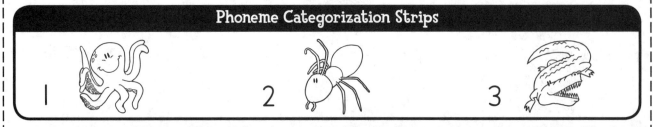

Phoneme Categorization Strips

1   2   3

Phoneme Categorization Strips

1   2   3

Phoneme Categorization Strips

1   2   3

Phoneme Categorization Strips

1   2   3

Phoneme Categorization Strips

1   2   3

Phoneme Categorization Strips

1   2   3

Phoneme Categorization Strips
Showdown (Teacher Set)

Instructions: Make a transparency for the teacher, who is the Showdown Captain. The teacher shows a strip with three numbered pictures. Students use the numbered student cards to indicate the picture that does not begin like the others.

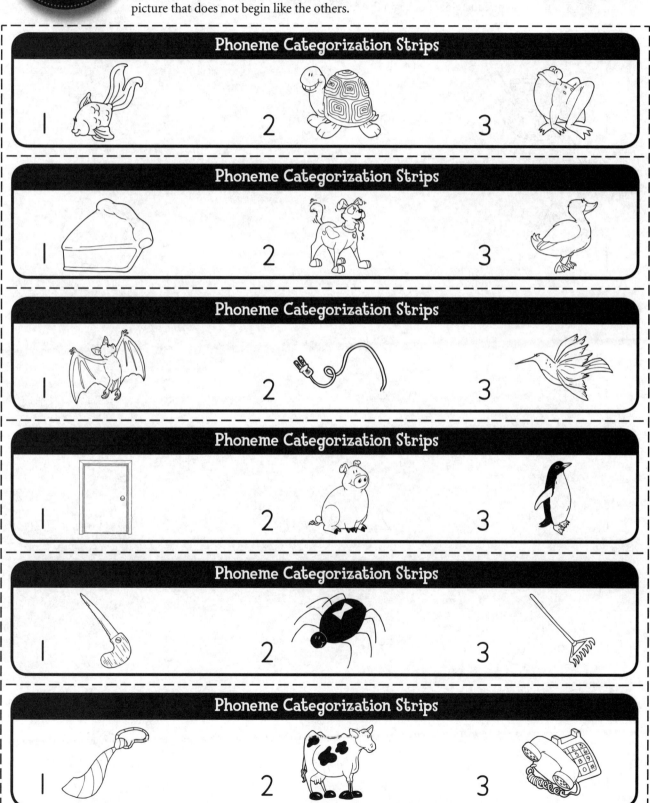

Phoneme Categorization Strips

Showdown (Teacher Set)

Instructions: Make a transparency for the teacher, who is the Showdown Captain. The teacher shows a strip with three numbered pictures. Students use the numbered student cards to indicate the picture that does not begin like the others.

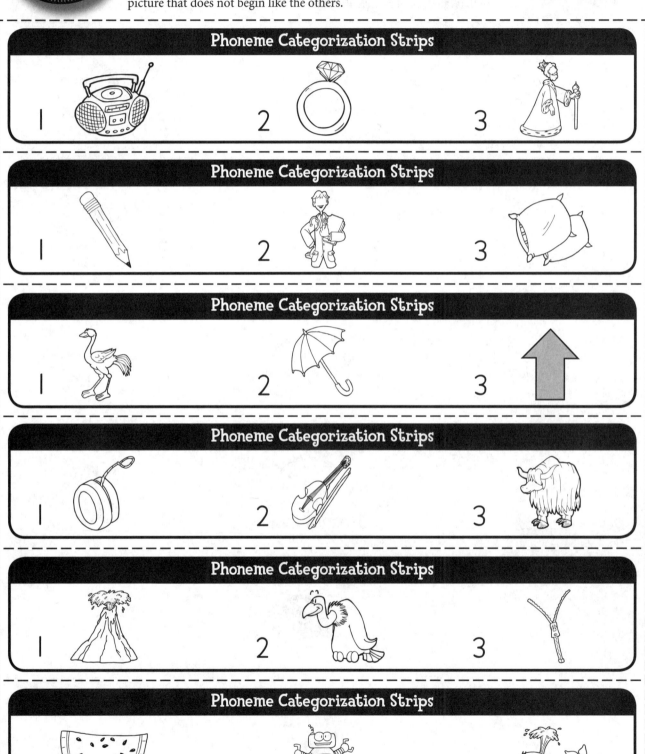

Phoneme Categorization Strips
Showdown (Student Set)

Instructions: Copy a set of cards 1–3 for each student. This page has cards for two students. The teacher is the Showdown Captain and shows three numbered pictures. Students use the numbered cards to indicate the picture that does not begin like the others.

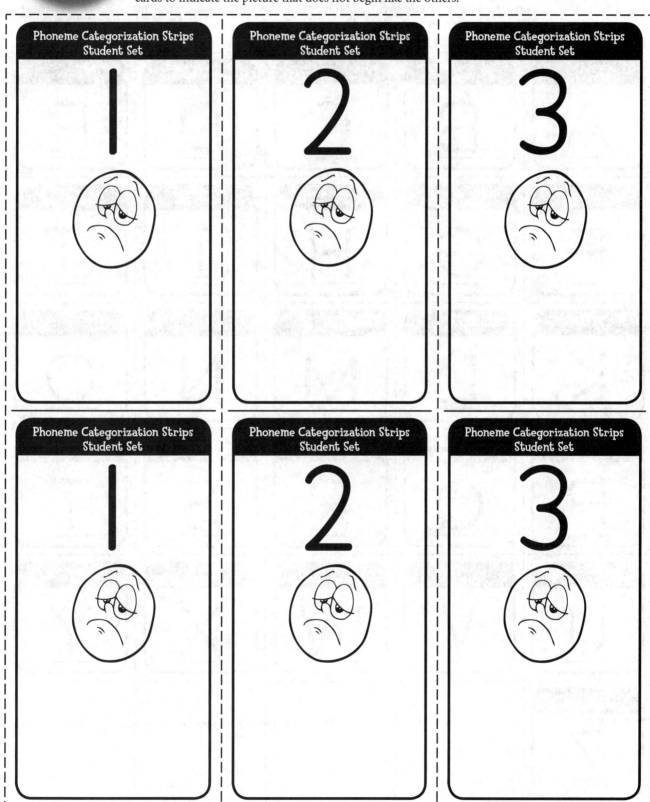

Matching Partner Letters
Showdown

Instructions: Make one set of lower case and capital letters for students. Make one set of lower case and capital letters as a transparency for teacher use. As Showdown Captain, the teacher places a letter card transparency on the overhead projector. Students find either the matching letter or the partner letter, depending on the teacher's directions.

Matching Partner Letter Cards **A**	Matching Partner Letter Cards **B**	Matching Partner Letter Cards **C**	Matching Partner Letter Cards **D**	Matching Partner Letter Cards **E**
Matching Partner Letter Cards **F**	Matching Partner Letter Cards **G**	Matching Partner Letter Cards **H**	Matching Partner Letter Cards **I**	Matching Partner Letter Cards **J**
Matching Partner Letter Cards **K**	Matching Partner Letter Cards **L**	Matching Partner Letter Cards **M**	Matching Partner Letter Cards **N**	Matching Partner Letter Cards **O**
Matching Partner Letter Cards **P**	Matching Partner Letter Cards **Q**	Matching Partner Letter Cards **R**	Matching Partner Letter Cards **S**	Matching Partner Letter Cards **T**
Matching Partner Letter Cards **U**	Matching Partner Letter Cards **V**	Matching Partner Letter Cards **W**	Matching Partner Letter Cards **X**	Matching Partner Letter Cards **Y**
Matching Partner Letter Cards **Z**				

Matching Partner Letters
Showdown

Instructions: Make one set of lower case and capital letters for students. Make one set of lower case and capital letters as a transparency for teacher use. As Showdown Captain, the teacher places a letter card transparency on the overhead projector. Students find either the matching letter or the partner letter, depending on the teacher's directions.

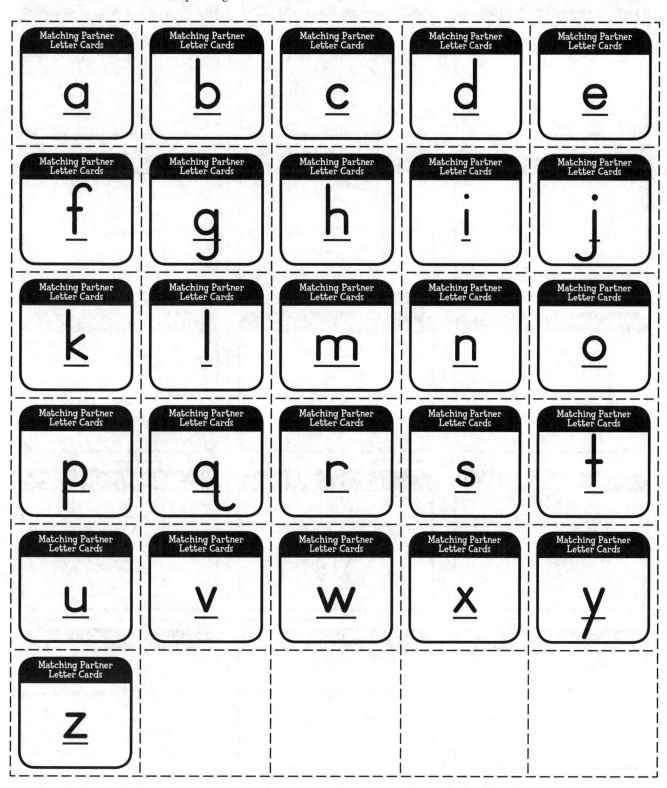

Matching Partner Letter Cards	Matching Partner Letter Cards	Matching Partner Letter Cards	Matching Partner Letter Cards	Matching Partner Letter Cards
a	b	c	d	e
f	g	h	i	j
k	l	m	n	o
p	q	r	s	t
u	v	w	x	y
z				

Beginning Sounds #1
Showdown (Teacher Set)

Instructions: Make a transparency for teacher use and cut apart. The teacher (Showdown Captain) shows one picture at a time. Students individually choose the beginning sound of the picture from their Student Set of letter cards. Students hold up their letter choice when the teacher calls, "Showdown."

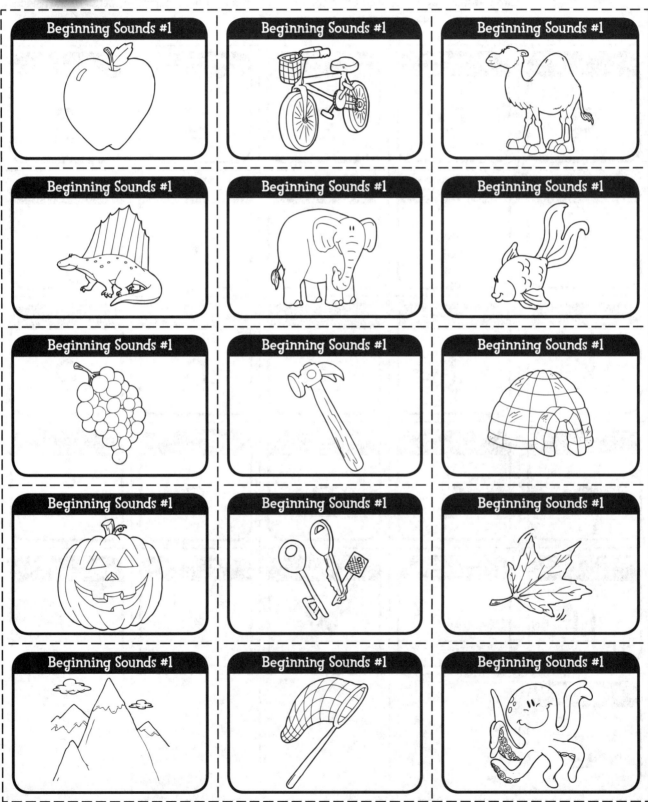

Beginning Sounds #1

Showdown (Teacher Set)

Instructions: Make a transparency for teacher use and cut apart. The teacher (Showdown Captain) shows one picture at a time. Students individually choose the beginning sound of the picture from their Student Set of letter cards. Students hold up their letter choice when the teacher calls, "Showdown."

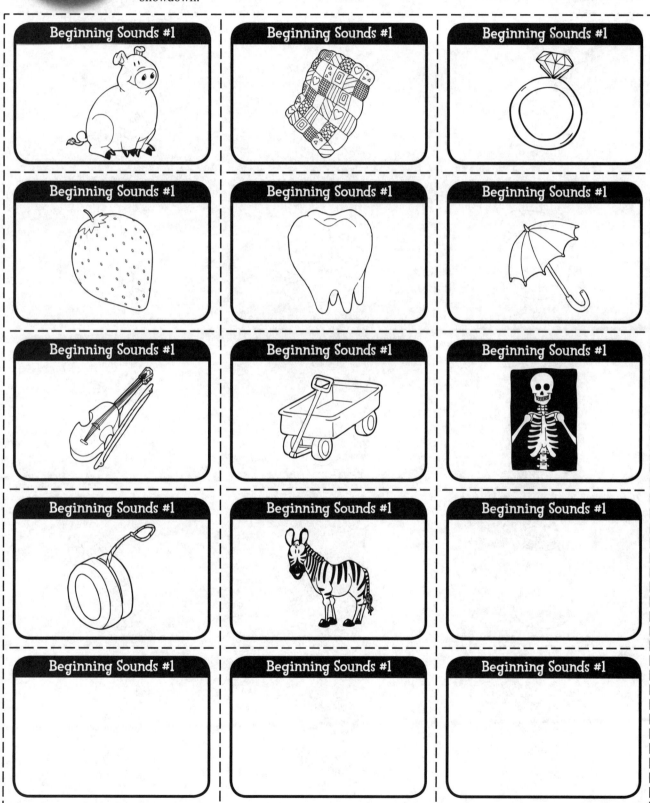

Beginning Sounds #2
Showdown (Teacher Set)

Instructions: Make a transparency for teacher use and cut apart. The teacher (Showdown Captain) shows one picture at a time. Students individually choose the beginning sound of the picture from their Student Set of letter cards. Students hold up their letter choice when the teacher calls, "Showdown."

Beginning Sounds #2	Beginning Sounds #2	Beginning Sounds #2
Beginning Sounds #2	Beginning Sounds #2	Beginning Sounds #2
Beginning Sounds #2	Beginning Sounds #2	Beginning Sounds #2
Beginning Sounds #2	Beginning Sounds #2	Beginning Sounds #2
Beginning Sounds #2	Beginning Sounds #2	Beginning Sounds #2

Beginning Sounds #2

Showdown (Teacher Set)

Instructions: Make a transparency for teacher use and cut apart. The teacher (Showdown Captain) shows one picture at a time. Students individually choose the beginning sound of the picture from their Student Set of letter cards. Students hold up their letter choice when the teacher calls, "Showdown."

Beginning Sounds
Showdown (Student Set)

Instructions: Use with Beginning Sounds #1 and #2.

Beginning Sounds	Beginning Sounds	Beginning Sounds	Beginning Sounds	Beginning Sounds
a	b	c	d	e
f	g	h	i	j
k	l	m	n	o
p	q	r	s	t
u	v	w	x	y
z				

Ending Sounds
Showdown (Teacher Set)

Instructions: Make a transparency for teacher use and cut apart. The teacher (Showdown Captain) shows one picture at a time. Students individually choose the ending sound of the picture from their Student Set of letter cards. Students hold up their letter choice when the teacher calls, "Showdown."

Ending Sounds
Showdown (Teacher Set)

Instructions: Make a transparency for teacher use and cut apart. The teacher (Showdown Captain) shows one picture at a time. Students individually choose the ending sound of the picture from their Student Set of letter cards. Students hold up their letter choice when the teacher calls, "Showdown."

Balanced Literacy • Kindergarten • Skidmore & Graber
Kagan Publishing • 1 (800) 933-2667 • www.KaganOnline.com

Ending Sounds
Showdown (Student Set)

Instructions: Use with Ending Sounds #1 and #2. **Note:** This page has cards for two students.

Ending Sounds Cards	Ending Sounds Cards	Ending Sounds Cards	Ending Sounds Cards	Ending Sounds Cards
b	d	f	g	k
l	m	n	p	r
s	t	x	z	
b	d	f	g	k
l	m	n	p	r
s	t	x	z	

Beginning Letter–
Sound Identification (b, p, t, d)
Showdown (Teacher Set)

Instructions: Teacher shows a picture on the overhead. Students choose a letter card representing the beginning sound of the picture from their individual student cards.

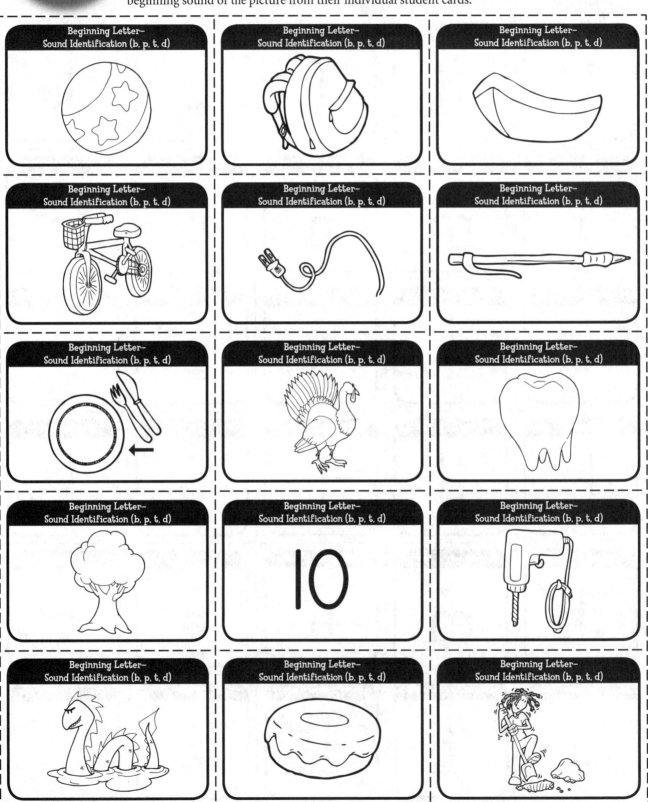

Balanced Literacy • Kindergarten • Skidmore & Graber
Kagan Publishing • 1 (800) 933-2667 • www.KaganOnline.com

Beginning Letter–Sound Identification (b, p, t, d)
Showdown (Student Set)

Instructions: Teacher shows a picture card on the overhead. Students choose a letter card representing the beginning sound of the picture. **Note:** This page contains cards for two students.

b, p, t, d Cards Student Set	b, p, t, d Cards Student Set	b, p, t, d Cards Student Set	b, p, t, d Cards Student Set
b	p	t	d

b, p, t, d Cards Student Set	b, p, t, d Cards Student Set	b, p, t, d Cards Student Set	b, p, t, d Cards Student Set
b	p	t	d

Beginning Letter– Sound Identification (v, w, q, y)

WORD STUDY
Blackline

Showdown (Teacher Set)

Instructions: Teacher shows a picture on the overhead. Students choose a letter card representing the beginning sound of the picture from their individual student cards.

Beginning Letter–
Sound Identification (v, w, q, y)
Showdown (Student Set)

Instructions: Teacher shows a picture card on the overhead. Students choose a letter card representing the beginning sound of the picture. **Note:** This page contains cards for two students.

v, w, q, y Cards Student Set	v, w, q, y Cards Student Set	v, w, q, y Cards Student Set	v, w, q, y Cards Student Set
v̲	w̲	q	y

v, w, q, y Cards Student Set	v, w, q, y Cards Student Set	v, w, q, y Cards Student Set	v, w, q, y Cards Student Set
v̲	w̲	q	y

Beginning Sounds (b, p, t, d)
Showdown (Teacher Set)

Instructions: The teacher reads the words on the list orally, one at a time, as individual students in teams choose the Showdown Card, that shows the beginning consonant sound. Follow the Showdown structure directions.

1. **p**up	14. **b**ank
2. **b**ell	15. **p**enny
3. **t**op	16. **b**all
4. **d**ime	17. **p**ick
5. **b**aby	18. **t**ail
6. **t**ag	19. **b**at
7. **p**enguin	20. **p**izza
8. **d**ig	21. **t**oe
9. **b**ath	22. **b**asket
10. **d**ive	23. **d**irt
11. **p**urse	24. **t**ruck
12. **b**oot	25. **d**octor
13. **d**rum	26. **b**one

Beginning Sounds (b, p, t, d)
Showdown (Student Set)

Instructions: This page contains cards for two students. Copy, cut apart, and give each student one set of cards. The Showdown Captain (teacher) says a word orally. Students choose a letter card representing the beginning sound of the word. Follow the Showdown structure directions.

b, p, t, d Cards Student Set	b, p, t, d Cards Student Set	b, p, t, d Cards Student Set	b, p, t, d Cards Student Set
b	p	t	d

b, p, t, d Cards Student Set	b, p, t, d Cards Student Set	b, p, t, d Cards Student Set	b, p, t, d Cards Student Set
b	p	t	d

ch, sh, th, wh

Showdown (Teacher Set)

Instructions: Make into a transparency and cut apart. Showdown Captain (teacher) shows a picture on the overhead. Students choose a letter card representing the beginning sound of the picture from their individual student cards. Follow the Showdown structure directions.

ch, sh, th, wh cards	ch, sh, th, wh cards	ch, sh, th, wh cards
ch, sh, th, wh cards	ch, sh, th, wh cards	ch, sh, th, wh cards
ch, sh, th, wh cards	ch, sh, th, wh cards	ch, sh, th, wh cards
ch, sh, th, wh cards	ch, sh, th, wh cards	ch, sh, th, wh cards

 Balanced Literacy • Kindergarten • Skidmore & Graber
Kagan Publishing • 1 (800) 933-2667 • www.KaganOnline.com

ch, sh, th, wh
Showdown (Teacher Set)

Instructions: Make into a transparency and cut apart. Showdown Captain (teacher) shows a picture on the overhead. Students choose a letter card representing the beginning sound of the picture from their individual student cards. Follow the Showdown structure directions.

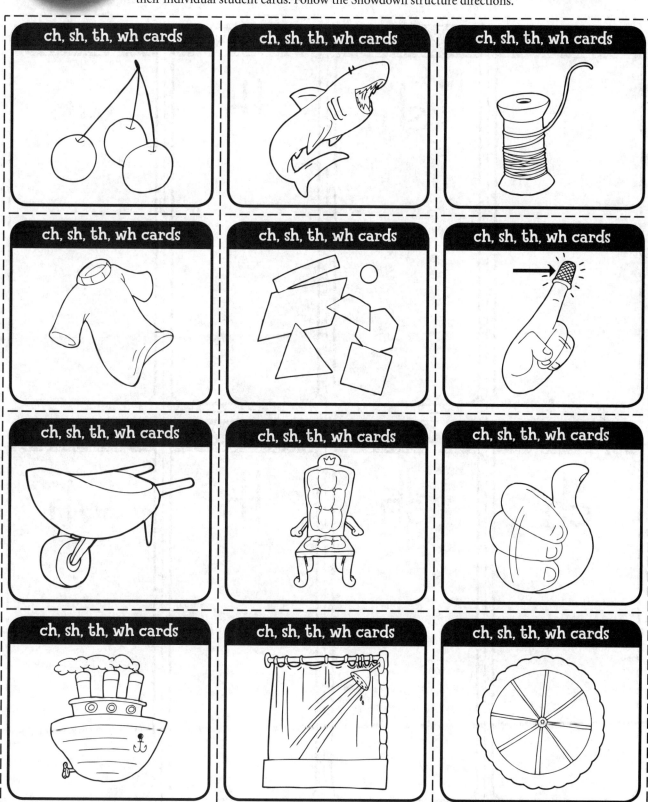

ch, sh, th, wh
Showdown (Student Set)

Instructions: This page has cards for two students. Copy, cut apart, and give each student one set of cards. Students choose a card representing the beginning sound of the picture card.

ch, sh, th, wh Student Set	ch, sh, th, wh Student Set	ch, sh, th, wh Student Set	ch, sh, th, wh Student Set
ch	sh	th	wh

ch, sh, th, wh Student Set	ch, sh, th, wh Student Set	ch, sh, th, wh Student Set	ch, sh, th, wh Student Set
ch	sh	th	wh

Letter ID/Word Patterns

In pairs, students alternate choosing letters or adding words.

STRUCTURE

Simultaneous RallyTable or CenterPiece

Activity Steps

1. Teacher assigns the letter identification strips or word pattern strips to be used from pages 348–353.

2. In pairs students each have a letter identification or word pattern strip. Each circles one letter or writes one word at a time. They trade papers at the same time.

3. Continue circling/writing and trading paper strips until time is called.

CenterPiece

Students brainstorm words to add to the list, always trading their paper with the centerpiece.

Activity Steps

1. Teacher assigns the letter identification strips/word pattern strips to be used from 348–353 pages.

2. Students circle one letter at a time on the letter identification strip or generate and add one word at a time on the word pattern strip. They say the letter/word, circle/write it, and trade their paper with the one in the center.

3. Students continue circling letters or brainstorming words, each time trading their paper with the centerpiece.

Blacklines

Letter Identification Strips
Simultaneous RallyTable or CenterPiece

Instructions: <u>Simultaneous RallyTable</u>: For each pair of students, copy and cut apart two different Letter Identification Strips for them to exchange back and forth as they circle letters that match the letters at the top of the strip. <u>CenterPiece</u>: Copy and cut apart a different Letter Identification Strip for each student in the team or pair, plus one extra, so during the activity there is always one in the center to trade with.

M m — M n H M N m M M M b m H m K w N H m N M

P p — b q P B d p P P p D P p B b P d p D P p

D d — d d b D P d D D b B B D d D d a D D b D B d D

B b — b b d B B P B b d b B b D B P d b B b D B

Letter Identification Strips
Simultaneous RallyTable or CenterPiece

Instructions: <u>Simultaneous RallyTable</u>: For each pair of students, copy and cut apart two different Letter Identification Strips for them to exchange back and forth as they circle letters that match the letters at the top of the strip. <u>CenterPiece</u>: Copy and cut apart a different Letter Identification Strip for each student in the team or pair, plus one extra, so during the activity there is always one in the center to trade with.

Word Pattern Strips

Simultaneous RallyTable or Centerpiece

Instructions: <u>Simultaneous RallyTable</u>: For each pair of students, copy and cut apart two different Word Pattern Strips for them to exchange back and forth as they write words that end with the same word pattern by adding a single consonant (or blend). <u>CenterPiece</u>: Copy and cut apart a different Word Pattern Strip for each student in the team or pair, plus one extra, so during the activity there is always one in the center to trade with.

___ ot

___ an

___ en

___ at

Balanced Literacy • Kindergarten • Skidmore & Graber
Kagan Publishing • 1 (800) 933-2667 • www.KaganOnline.com

Word Pattern Strips

Simultaneous RallyTable or Centerpiece

Instructions: <u>Simultaneous RallyTable</u>: For each pair of students, copy and cut apart two different Word Pattern Strips for them to exchange back and forth as they write words that end with the same word pattern by adding a single consonant (or blend). <u>CenterPiece</u>: Copy and cut apart a different Word Pattern Strip for each student in the team or pair, plus one extra, so during the activity there is always one in the center to trade with.

op ____

op ____

it ____

ug ____

Blank Word Pattern Strips
Simultaneous RallyTable or Centerpiece

Instructions: Fill in top space on strips with desired word patterns. <u>Simultaneous RallyTable</u>: For each pair of students, copy and cut apart two different word pattern strips for them to exchange back and forth as they write words that have the same word pattern by adding a single consonant or blend. <u>CenterPiece</u>: Copy and cut apart a different word pattern strip for each student in the team or pair, plus one extra, so during the activity there is always one in the center to trade with.

Alphabet Strips
Simultaneous RallyTable or Centerpiece

Instructions: These alphabet strips are a tool for students to use as they generate words with the same word patterns on their word pattern strips. Copy and cut out one alphabet strip for each pair of students. **Note:** This page includes alphabet strips for four pairs of students.

z	z	z	z
y	y	y	y
x	x	x	x
w	w	w	w
v	v	v	v
u	u	u	u
t	t	t	t
s	s	s	s
r	r	r	r
q	q	q	q
p	p	p	p
o	o	o	o
n	n	n	n
m	m	m	m
l	l	l	l
k	k	k	k
j	j	j	j
i	i	i	i
h	h	h	h
g	g	g	g
f	f	f	f
e	e	e	e
d	d	d	d
c	c	c	c
b	b	b	b
a	a	a	a

Activity

Write the Sound

After writing their own answer to a question, teammates put their "heads together" to make certain all members can answer. The teacher then calls a number and students with that number share their answers simultaneously.

Activity Steps

1. Students number off in small groups.

2. The teacher displays a picture card on the overhead.

3. Students privately write the beginning or ending letter of the picture word on a markerboard or on a piece of paper.

4. The teacher says "Heads Together!" and students lift up from their chairs to put their heads together, show their answers, and discuss until they can come up with an answer. Everyone sits down when they agree on a letter. Clear boards.

5. The teacher calls out a number. The student with that number writes the agreed upon letter on the markerboard.

6. The students with the called number hold up their boards and call out the letter sound simultaneously. The teacher writes each group's letter on the overhead.

7. The teacher leads the class in a discussion of the answer.

8. Teammates celebrate or correct spelling on boards.

9. Repeat.

STRUCTURE
Numbered Heads Together

Variation

Students follow the same steps as above but work in pairs instead of teams.

Blacklines

Beginning Word Sounds
Numbered Heads Together

Instructions: Make a transparency for teacher use and cut apart. The teacher displays a picture card. Students write the beginning sound of the picture word on a markerboard or paper. Follow Numbered Heads Together directions.

Beginning Word Sounds

Numbered Heads Together

Instructions: Make a transparency for teacher use and cut apart. The teacher displays a picture card. Students write the beginning sound of the picture word on a markerboard or paper. Follow Numbered Heads Together directions.

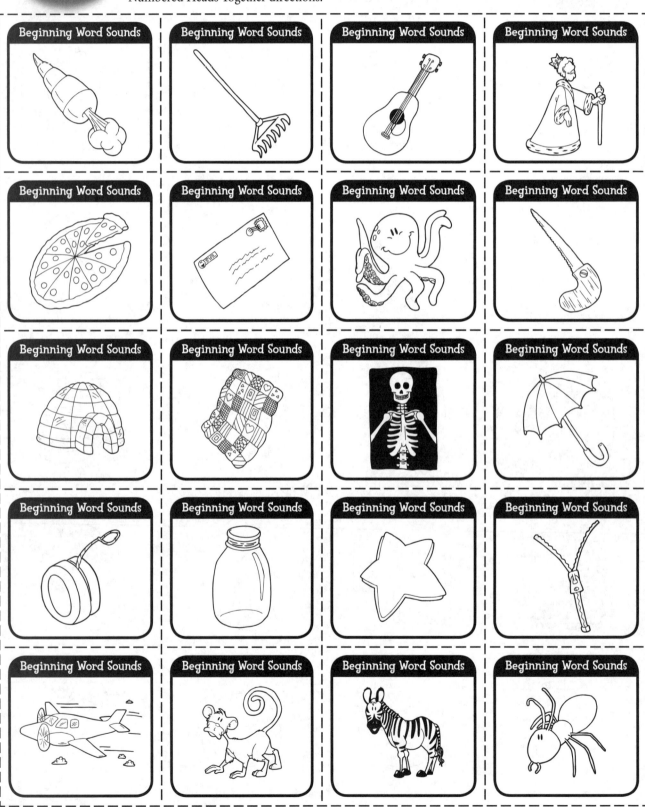

Balanced Literacy • Kindergarten • Skidmore & Graber
Kagan Publishing • 1 (800) 933-2667 • www.KaganOnline.com

Ending Word Sounds
Numbered Heads Together

Instructions: Make a transparency for teacher use and cut apart. The teacher displays a picture card. Students write the ending sound of the picture word on a markerboard or paper. Follow Numbered Heads Together directions.

Ending Word Sounds
Numbered Heads Together

Instructions: Make a transparency for teacher use and cut apart. The teacher displays a picture card. Students write the ending sound of the picture word on a markerboard or paper. Follow Numbered Heads Together directions.

Activity

Word Wall Spelling

After spelling the word themselves, teammates put their "heads together" to make certain all members can correctly spell the word wall word. The teacher then calls a number and all students with that number share their team's spelling.

STRUCTURE

Numbered Heads Together

Note:
The Word Wall Cards on the following pages are not used for this activity. They are provided for your convenience to post on your word wall. However, before you begin this activity, make sure you take down word wall words students will spell.

Activity Steps

1. Students number off in small groups.

2. The teacher reads a selected word from the Word List.

3. Students privately write the word on a markerboard or on a piece of paper.

4. The teacher says, "Heads Together!" and students lift up from their chairs to put their heads together, show their answers, and discuss until they reach consensus on the word spelling.

5. Everyone clears their boards and sits down when they agree.

6. The teacher calls out a number. All students with that number write the agreed-upon spelling of the word on their markerboards.

7. All students with their number selected hold up their boards simultaneously. The teacher writes each group's spelling on the overhead.

8. The teacher leads the class in a discussion of each spelling by asking questions such as "Which way looks right?" "How do you know?" or "What was the tricky part or familiar part?"

9. Teammates celebrate or correct spelling on boards.

10. The process is repeated for each new word.

Blacklines

Kindergarten Word List

Instructions: Words to be used with Word Wall Spelling.

a	he	no
am	I	see
an	in	she
and	is	so
at	it	the
can	like	to
do	me	up
go	my	we

Kindergarten
Word Wall Cards

Instructions: Use the cards provided to create a Word Wall.

Kindergarten Word Wall Cards

at

Kindergarten Word Wall Cards

can

Kindergarten Word Wall Cards

do

Kindergarten Word Wall Cards

go

Kindergarten Word Wall Cards

a

Kindergarten Word Wall Cards

am

Kindergarten Word Wall Cards

an

Kindergarten Word Wall Cards

and

Kindergarten
Word Wall Cards

Instructions: Use the cards provided to create a Word Wall.

Kindergarten Word Wall Cards	Kindergarten Word Wall Cards	Kindergarten Word Wall Cards	Kindergarten Word Wall Cards
it	like	me	my
he	I	in	is

Kindergarten
Word Wall Cards

Instructions: Use the cards provided to create a Word Wall.

Kindergarten Word Wall Cards

the

Kindergarten Word Wall Cards

to

Kindergarten Word Wall Cards

up

Kindergarten Word Wall Cards

we

Kindergarten Word Wall Cards

no

Kindergarten Word Wall Cards

see

Kindergarten Word Wall Cards

she

Kindergarten Word Wall Cards

so

Kindergarten Blank
Word Wall Cards

Instructions: Add additional words to these cards for the Word Wall.

Kindergarten Word Wall Cards

Kindergarten Word Wall Cards

Kindergarten Word Wall Cards

Kindergarten Word Wall Cards

Kindergarten Word Wall Cards

Kindergarten Word Wall Cards

Kindergarten Word Wall Cards

Kindergarten Word Wall Cards

Balanced Literacy

Comprehension

Word Study

Fluency

Writing

Fluency

Fluency Overview

Fluency is a part of an effective reading program. When a reader is fluent, energies are automatically channeled into comprehending the text instead of decoding words.

Reading fluency includes the following components:
- expression (stress, pitch, volume, clarity)
- phrasing (pauses, word groups)
- rate (just the right speed)
- accuracy (correct words and punctuation)

The fluency resources and materials at the beginning of this section are designed to be used in the suggested order to scaffold the learner and ensure understanding (*aloud* and *shared*). The remainder of the activities in this section are designed to provide fluency practice (*guided* and *independent*).

Table of Fluency Resources

Page(s)	Resources	Balanced Literacy				
		Aloud	Shared	Guided	Independent	Literature Circles
370	Fluency Resource/Materials Descriptions					
372	Decoding Strategy Posters	●	●	●	●	
378	Decoding Flashcards	●	●	●	●	
380	Decoding Strategy Bookmarks	●	●	●	●	

Table of Fluency Activities

Page(s)	Activities/Lessons	Blacklines	Balanced Literacy				
			Aloud	Shared	Guided	Independent	Literature Circles
382	**Poems for Two Voices Activities**						
383	The Zoo	• Copy of Poem		●	●		
384	The Farm	• Copy of Poem		●	●		
385	Blank Form	• Blank Worksheet		●	●		
386	**Quiz-Quiz-Trade Activities**						
387	Fluency Practice	• Sentence Cards		●	●	●	
392	Fluency Sentences	• Sentence Cards		●	●	●	
400	Sight Words	• Cards		●	●	●	

Balanced Literacy • Kindergarten • Skidmore & Graber
Kagan Publishing • 1 (800) 933-2667 • www.KaganOnline.com

Fluency Resources

Fluency Resources

Resources/Materials Descriptions

Decoding Strategy Posters (pp. 372-377)
• Shared Reading

The teacher can hold up a decoding strategy poster, as the strategy(ies) is being modeled during shared reading. This introduction to the use of decoding strategies is the beginning scaffolding to learning what good readers do when they have difficulty with a word. The teacher will model trying several different strategies until one works.

• Guided Reading

The decoding posters can be used during guided reading, as the implementation of a specific decoding strategy(ies) is practiced.

Decoding Flashcards (pp. 378-379)
Students will have all of the Decoding Flashcards available to them in an envelope or small plastic bag. The teacher may choose to focus on a few strategies at a time and have students work with only those particular cards until all the strategies have been introduced.

The Decoding Flashcards can be used in various ways:

• Shared Reading

As the teacher models a strategy(ies), the students can each identify the modeled strategy and hold up the appropriate flashcard(s). To help the students realize that good readers use multiple strategies, the teacher will model trying several different strategies until one works.

• Guided Reading

Periodically, the teacher may ask the students to locate a place in their text where they needed to use a decoding strategy. Each student demonstrates and explains to the group the strategy(ies) attempted. The Decoding Flashcards are used to identify the strategy(ies) as the group listens and coaches.

• Partner Reading

The above practice may also be used with partners using the RallyCoach structure.

Fluency Resources

Resources/Materials Descriptions (continued)

Decoding Strategy Bookmarks (p. 380)

Learning to read requires that we guide each student in becoming an independent reader. Successful readers are able to pull appropriate strategies from a repertoire of choices when they come to a word they do not know. It is important to scaffold the instruction to help the students move from observation, to understanding, to practice, and finally to independent implementation. As the teacher models decoding strategies during shared reading and interacts with students during guided reading, the Decoding Strategy Bookmark becomes a visual reference. The Decoding Strategy Bookmark will be a helpful tool for individual students during guided reading and independent reading.

The three questions listed at the top of the bookmark are to help students self-monitor their reading and to help them know when to apply a strategy(ies). Students should ask themselves the three questions. If they answer "No" to one of the questions, they need to try various strategies until they can answer "Yes" to all three questions. Eight decoding strategies are listed below the questions to serve as prompts.

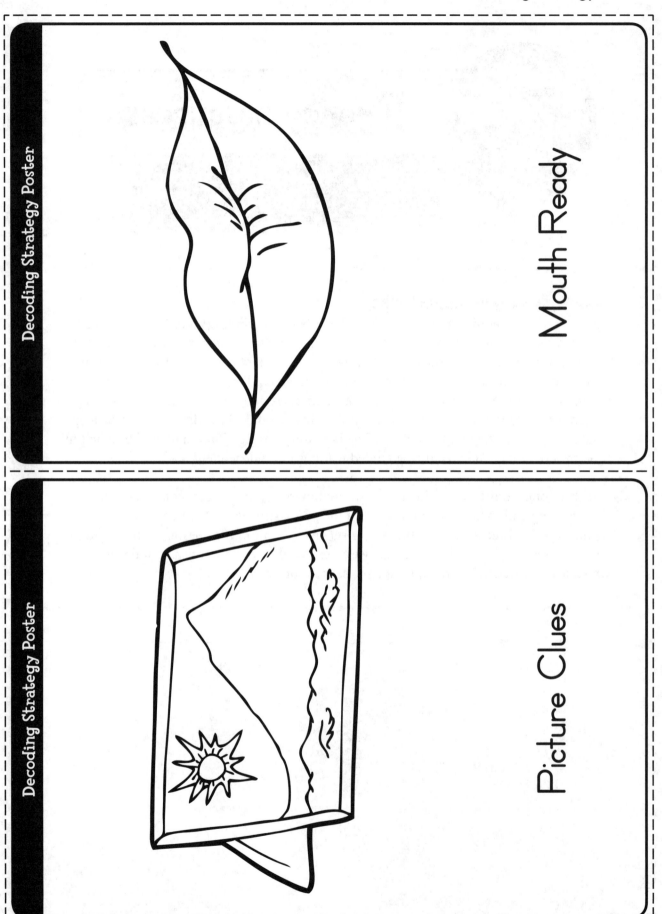

Decoding Strategy Poster

Mouth Ready

Decoding Strategy Poster

Picture Clues

Decoding Strategy Poster

Reread.
Fix.

Decoding Strategy Poster

Pattern (Chunk)

Decoding Strategy Poster

Think about what word makes sense.

Decoding Strategy Poster

Skip word. Get clues. Reread.

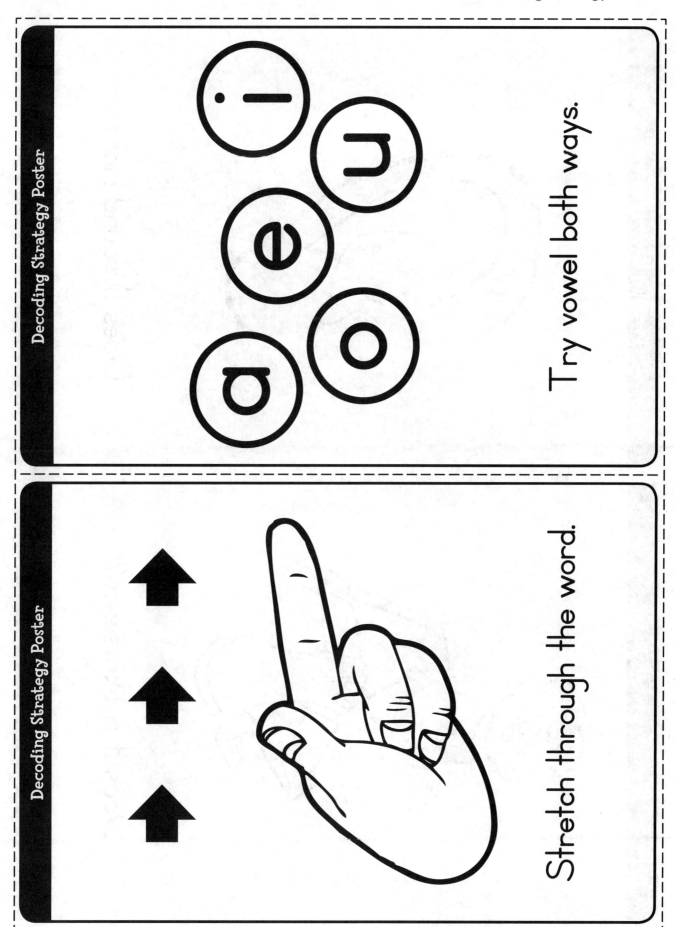

Decoding Strategy Poster

Try vowel both ways.

Decoding Strategy Poster

Stretch through the word.

Decoding Strategy Poster

Does it sound right?

Decoding Strategy Poster

Does it make sense?

Balanced Literacy • Kindergarten • Skidmore & Graber
Kagan Publishing • 1 (800) 933-2667 • www.KaganOnline.com

Decoding Strategy Poster

Decoding Strategy Poster

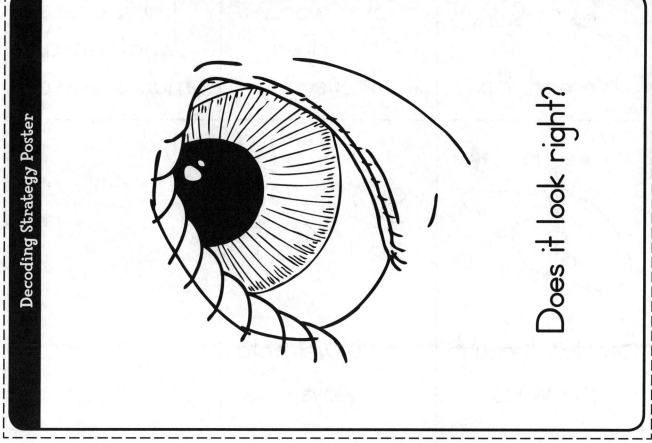

Does it look right?

Picture Clues

Mouth Ready

Pattern (Chunk)

Reread. Fix.

Skip word.
Get clues.
Reread.

Think about
what word
makes sense.

Stretch through
the word.

Try vowel both
ways.

Does it make sense?	Does it sound right?	Does it look right?

Decoding Strategy Bookmark	Decoding Strategy Bookmark
Does it make sense? Does it sound right? Does it look right?	Does it make sense? Does it sound right? Does it look right?
Picture Clues	Picture Clues
Mouth Ready	Mouth Ready
Pattern (Chunk)	Pattern (Chunk)
Reread. Fix.	Reread. Fix.
Skip word. Get clues. Reread.	Skip word. Get clues. Reread.
Think about what word makes sense.	Think about what word makes sense.
Stretch through word.	Stretch through word.
Try vowel both ways. a e i o u	Try vowel both ways. a e i o u

Balanced Literacy • Kindergarten • Skidmore & Graber
Kagan Publishing • 1 (800) 933-2667 • www.KaganOnline.com

Fluency Activities

Activity

Fluency Poems

Partners present a poem—recited at times by one partner, the other partner, or both.

Activity Steps

1 The teacher provides students a poem. The poem has some lines labeled "A," some lines labeled "B," and some lines labeled "AB." The teacher assigns pairs.

2 Pairs practice their poems. Partner A reads the A lines. Partner B reads the B lines. They read the AB lines in unison. Students listen carefully to their partners to keep the flow.

3 When ready, pairs read their poem to another pair.

STRUCTURE
Poems for Two Voices

Blacklines

The Zoo

Poems for Two Voices

Instructions: Copy for each student or pair.

A I see an  .

B I see an  .

AB Let's go see the  .

A I love  s.

B Do you see the big brown  ?

AB The zoo is fun!

The Farm

Poems for Two Voices

Instructions: Copy for each student or pair.

A The has  for the .

B The has an  for the .

A The has a for the .

B The has a for the  .

AB Oh, no! The eats the  .

Blank Form

Poems for Two Voices

Names: _____

_____

Our Poem Is About: _____

Instructions: Copy for each pair of students.

A _____

B _____

A _____

B _____

AB _____

QUIZ-QUIZ-TRADE
Activity

Reading with Fluency

Students quiz a partner, get quizzed by a partner, and then trade cards to repeat the process with a new partner.

Activity Steps

1 StandUp–HandUp–PairUp.

2 Partner A quizzes.

3 Partner B answers.

4 Partner A praises or coaches.

5 Switch roles.

6 Partners trade cards.

7 Repeat Steps 1–6 a number of times.

STRUCTURE
Quiz-Quiz-Trade

Front

Fluency Sentences
Practice reading this sentence 3 times.

He was **so** sad!

Back

Fluency Sentences
Answer: (Read 3 times.)

He was **so** sad!

Blacklines

Fluency Practice
Quiz-Quiz-Trade

Instructions: Copy enough cards so each student has one card. Cut on dotted lines and fold in half.

Fluency Practice	Fluency Practice
Read:	Answer:
She can see a dog.	She can see a dog.

Fluency Practice	Fluency Practice
Read:	Answer:
He can go to the vet.	He can go to the vet.

Fluency Practice	Fluency Practice
Read:	Answer:
I met a cat.	I met a cat.

Fluency Practice	Fluency Practice
Read:	Answer:
Is it in the pit?	Is it in the pit?

Fluency Practice
Quiz-Quiz-Trade

Instructions: Copy enough cards so each student has one card. Cut on dotted lines and fold in half.

Fluency Practice	Fluency Practice
Read:	Answer:
The cat is on the rug.	The cat is on the rug.
Read:	Answer:
The pan is so hot!	The pan is so hot!
Read:	Answer:
We ran to win!	We ran to win!
Read:	Answer:
She sees west on the map.	She sees west on the map.

Balanced Literacy • Kindergarten • Skidmore & Graber
Kagan Publishing • 1 (800) 933-2667 • www.KaganOnline.com

Fluency Practice
Quiz-Quiz-Trade

Instructions: Copy enough cards so each student has one card. Cut on dotted lines and fold in half.

Fluency Practice	Fluency Practice
Read:	Answer:
I like to pet the fat cat.	I like to pet the fat cat.

Fluency Practice	Fluency Practice
Read:	Answer:
See me sit and rest.	See me sit and rest.

Fluency Practice	Fluency Practice
Read:	Answer:
I met the man in the hat.	I met the man in the hat.

Fluency Practice	Fluency Practice
Read:	Answer:
I do not like bugs.	I do not like bugs.

Fluency Practice
Quiz-Quiz-Trade

Instructions: Copy enough cards so each student has one card. Cut on dotted lines and fold in half.

Fluency Practice Read: Go to the van.	**Fluency Practice** Answer: Go to the van.
Fluency Practice Read: I like hugs.	**Fluency Practice** Answer: I like hugs.
Fluency Practice Read: The pin fit in the can.	**Fluency Practice** Answer: The pin fit in the can.
Fluency Practice Read: I do like to nap on the mat.	**Fluency Practice** Answer: I do like to nap on the mat.

Balanced Literacy • Kindergarten • Skidmore & Graber
Kagan Publishing • 1 (800) 933-2667 • www.KaganOnline.com

Fluency Practice
Quiz-Quiz-Trade

Instructions: Copy enough cards so each student has one card. Cut on dotted lines and fold in half.

Fluency Practice	Fluency Practice
Read:	Answer:
My fat cat is at the vet.	My fat cat is at the vet.

Fluency Practice	Fluency Practice
Read:	Answer:
We go to see the man.	We go to see the man.

Fluency Practice	Fluency Practice
Read:	Answer:
Set the fan on the mat.	Set the fan on the mat.

Fluency Practice	Fluency Practice
Read:	Answer:
He sat on the bug.	He sat on the bug.

Fluency Sentences
Quiz-Quiz-Trade

Instructions: Copy enough cards so each student has one card. Cut on dotted lines and fold in half.

Fluency Sentences	Fluency Sentences
Practice reading this sentence 3 times. I can see my cat.	Answer: (Read 3 times.) I can see my cat.
Practice reading this sentence 3 times. Do you like bugs?	Answer: (Read 3 times.) Do you like bugs?
Practice reading this sentence 3 times. It is HOT!	Answer: (Read 3 times.) It is HOT!
Practice reading this sentence 3 times. I see Mom and Dad in the van.	Answer: (Read 3 times.) I see Mom and Dad in the van.

Fluency Sentences
Quiz-Quiz-Trade

Instructions: Copy enough cards so each student has one card. Cut on dotted lines and fold in half.

Fluency Sentences	Fluency Sentences
Practice reading this sentence 3 times.	Answer: (Read 3 times.)
She got me wet!	**She got me wet!**
Fluency Sentences	Fluency Sentences
Practice reading this sentence 3 times.	Answer: (Read 3 times.)
The dog is so fat.	**The dog is so fat.**
Fluency Sentences	Fluency Sentences
Practice reading this sentence 3 times.	Answer: (Read 3 times.)
He cannot go.	**He cannot go.**
Fluency Sentences	Fluency Sentences
Practice reading this sentence 3 times.	Answer: (Read 3 times.)
The cap is red.	**The cap is red.**

Fluency Sentences
Quiz-Quiz-Trade

Instructions: Copy enough cards so each student has one card. Cut on dotted lines and fold in half.

Fluency Sentences Practice reading this sentence 3 times. My pet is BEST!	**Fluency Sentences** Answer: (Read 3 times.) My pet is BEST!
Fluency Sentences Practice reading this sentence 3 times. The cat is on a rug.	**Fluency Sentences** Answer: (Read 3 times.) The cat is on a rug.
Fluency Sentences Practice reading this sentence 3 times. He can nap.	**Fluency Sentences** Answer: (Read 3 times.) He can nap.
Fluency Sentences Practice reading this sentence 3 times. Are you going in or out?	**Fluency Sentences** Answer: (Read 3 times.) Are you going in or out?

Fluency Sentences
Quiz-Quiz-Trade

Instructions: Copy enough cards so each student has one card. Cut on dotted lines and fold in half.

Fluency Sentences	Fluency Sentences
Practice reading this sentence 3 times.	Answer: (Read 3 times.)
Can I go with you?	Can I go with you?

Fluency Sentences	Fluency Sentences
Practice reading this sentence 3 times.	Answer: (Read 3 times.)
He was **so** sad!	He was **so** sad!

Fluency Sentences	Fluency Sentences
Practice reading this sentence 3 times.	Answer: (Read 3 times.)
What do you like to play?	What do you like to play?

Fluency Sentences	Fluency Sentences
Practice reading this sentence 3 times.	Answer: (Read 3 times.)
I like to sit up in a tree.	I like to sit up in a tree.

Fluency Sentences
Quiz-Quiz-Trade

Instructions: Copy enough cards so each student has one card. Cut on dotted lines and fold in half.

Fluency Sentences	Fluency Sentences
Practice reading this sentence 3 times. I can see Ben's dog.	Answer: (Read 3 times.) I can see Ben's dog.
Practice reading this sentence 3 times. It was NOT from me!	Answer: (Read 3 times.) It was NOT from me!
Practice reading this sentence 3 times. I <u>like</u> that plan!	Answer: (Read 3 times.) I <u>like</u> that plan!
Practice reading this sentence 3 times. He likes to get the red ball.	Answer: (Read 3 times.) He likes to get the red ball.

Fluency Sentences
Quiz-Quiz-Trade

Instructions: Copy enough cards so each student has one card. Cut on dotted lines and fold in half.

Fluency Sentences	Fluency Sentences
Practice reading this sentence 3 times. **All her bugs were BIG.**	Answer: (Read 3 times.) **All her bugs were BIG.**
Practice reading this sentence 3 times. **We have to go play!**	Answer: (Read 3 times.) **We have to go play!**
Practice reading this sentence 3 times. **It will be FUN!**	Answer: (Read 3 times.) **It will be FUN!**
Practice reading this sentence 3 times. **Is it an ant or a slug?**	Answer: (Read 3 times.) **Is it an ant or a slug?**

Fluency Sentences
Quiz-Quiz-Trade

Instructions: Copy enough cards so each student has one card. Cut on dotted lines and fold in half.

Fluency Sentences	Fluency Sentences
Practice reading this sentence 3 times.	Answer: (Read 3 times.)
They are by the car.	**They are by the car.**
Fluency Sentences	Fluency Sentences
Practice reading this sentence 3 times.	Answer: (Read 3 times.)
Do you see the bug on the wall?	**Do you see the bug on the wall?**
Fluency Sentences	Fluency Sentences
Practice reading this sentence 3 times.	Answer: (Read 3 times.)
I will be back!	**I will be back!**
Fluency Sentences	Fluency Sentences
Practice reading this sentence 3 times.	Answer: (Read 3 times.)
She sees my hat.	**She sees my hat.**

Balanced Literacy • Kindergarten • Skidmore & Graber
Kagan Publishing • 1 (800) 933-2667 • www.KaganOnline.com

Fluency Sentences
Quiz-Quiz-Trade

Instructions: Copy enough cards so each student has one card. Cut on dotted lines and fold in half.

Fluency Sentences	Fluency Sentences
Practice reading this sentence 3 times.	Answer: (Read 3 times.)
He likes to go up the hill.	He likes to go up the hill.

Fluency Sentences	Fluency Sentences
Practice reading this sentence 3 times.	Answer: (Read 3 times.)
What will you do?	What will you do?

Fluency Sentences	Fluency Sentences
Practice reading this sentence 3 times.	Answer: (Read 3 times.)
When can we go?	When can we go?

Fluency Sentences	Fluency Sentences
Practice reading this sentence 3 times.	Answer: (Read 3 times.)
She can see me on the sled.	She can see me on the sled.

Sight Words
Quiz-Quiz-Trade

Instructions: Copy enough cards so each student has one card. Cut on dotted lines and fold in half.

Sight Words	Sight Words
Question: Can you read this word?	Answer:
yes	**yes**

Sight Words	Sight Words
Question: Can you read this word?	Answer:
up	**up**

Sight Words	Sight Words
Question: Can you read this word?	Answer:
you	**you**

Sight Words	Sight Words
Question: Can you read this word?	Answer:
us	**us**

Sight Words	Sight Words
Question: Can you read this word?	Answer:
not	**not**

Sight Words
Quiz-Quiz-Trade

Instructions: Copy enough cards so each student has one card. Cut on dotted lines and fold in half.

Sight Words	Sight Words
Question: Can you read this word?	Answer:
no	**no**

Sight Words	Sight Words
Question: Can you read this word?	Answer:
she	**she**

Sight Words	Sight Words
Question: Can you read this word?	Answer:
so	**so**

Sight Words	Sight Words
Question: Can you read this word?	Answer:
we	**we**

Sight Words	Sight Words
Question: Can you read this word?	Answer:
to	**to**

Sight Words
Quiz-Quiz-Trade

Instructions: Copy enough cards so each student has one card. Cut on dotted lines and fold in half.

Sight Words	Sight Words
Question: Can you read this word?	Answer:
is	**is**

Sight Words	Sight Words
Question: Can you read this word?	Answer:
my	**my**

Sight Words	Sight Words
Question: Can you read this word?	Answer:
me	**me**

Sight Words	Sight Words
Question: Can you read this word?	Answer:
said	**said**

Sight Words	Sight Words
Question: Can you read this word?	Answer:
it	**it**

Sight Words
Quiz-Quiz-Trade

Instructions: Copy enough cards so each student has one card. Cut on dotted lines and fold in half.

Sight Words	Sight Words
Question: Can you read this word?	Answer:
do	**do**

Sight Words	Sight Words
Question: Can you read this word?	Answer:
go	**go**

Sight Words	Sight Words
Question: Can you read this word?	Answer:
like	**like**

Sight Words	Sight Words
Question: Can you read this word?	Answer:
he	**he**

Sight Words	Sight Words
Question: Can you read this word?	Answer:
in	**in**

Sight Words

Quiz-Quiz-Trade

Instructions: Copy enough cards so each student has one card. Cut on dotted lines and fold in half.

Sight Words	Sight Words
Question: Can you read this word?	Answer:
at	**at**

Sight Words	Sight Words
Question: Can you read this word?	Answer:
and	**and**

Sight Words	Sight Words
Question: Can you read this word?	Answer:
you	**you**

Sight Words	Sight Words
Question: Can you read this word?	Answer:
see	**see**

Sight Words	Sight Words
Question: Can you read this word?	Answer:
am	**am**

Sight Words
Quiz-Quiz-Trade

Instructions: Copy enough cards so each student has one card. Cut on dotted lines and fold in half.

Sight Words	Sight Words
Question: Can you read this word?	Answer:
can	**can**

Sight Words	Sight Words
Question: Can you read this word?	Answer:
the	**the**

Sight Words	Sight Words
Question: Can you read this word?	Answer:
is	**is**

Sight Words	Sight Words
Question: Can you read this word?	Answer:
big	**big**

Sight Words	Sight Words
Question: Can you read this word?	Answer:
look	**look**

Writing

Writing Overview

Authors use four main text types to convey meaning in print:

- **Narrative**—to entertain
- **Expository**—to inform
- **Technical**—to tell how to...
- **Persuasive**—to convince

Expository writing is a great starting place for students. Children naturally write in expository form, informing us of what they know or are learning from their experiences. Writing and reading are reciprocal processes, each supporting the other.

This writing section is organized in sequential lessons that will produce an expository piece of writing through a cooperative group learning process. The goal is for students to apply what they have learned through group work to their individual writing.

Note:

The teacher should have his or her own photograph/picture and an ongoing piece of writing that is used for modeling in each lesson.

Table of Writing Resources

Page(s)	Resources	Balanced Literacy				
		Aloud	Shared	Guided	Independent	Literature Circles
412	Expository Writing Resources/Materials Descriptions					
413	Types of Words • Action Words • Naming Words • Describing Words	●	●	●	●	
416	Six Trait Questions	●	●			
417	Six Trait Question Strips	●	●	●	●	

Table of Writing Activities and Lessons

Page(s)	Six Traits	Structures	Activities	Resources
426–428	**Ideas**			
428		Timed Pair Share	Emotion Words	
429–452	**Word Choice**			
430		RallyRobin	Creating Description Chart • Day 1 • Day 2	
431–432		RallyRobin and **Timed Pair Share**	Writing Descriptions	
433–435		StandUp-HandUp-PairUp, Timed Pair Share, and RallyCoach	Listing and Writing Action Words	• Six Trait Question Strips—Word Choice • Shared Writing Example
436–449		RallyCoach	Word Sort (action, naming, describing words)	• Sorting Mat • Word Cards • Word Choice Picture Cards
450–452		RallyCoach	Adding Describing Words	• Naming and Action Phrase Cards
453–487	**Conventions**			
454–468		Simultaneous RallyTable and Centerpiece	Letter Writing	• Conventions Cards • Blank Form
469–475		RallyCoach	• Capital Letters • Capitalization and Punctuation	• Worksheet • Capitalization and Punctuation Strips
476–479		Showdown	Ending Punctuation	• Ending Punctuation Strips
480–487		Quiz-Quiz-Trade	Capitalization and Punctuation	• Capitalization and Punctuation Cards

Balanced Literacy • Kindergarten • Skidmore & Graber
Kagan Publishing • 1 (800) 933-2667 • www.KaganOnline.com

Writing Resources

Expository Writing Resources

Writing Resources/Materials Descriptions

Students choose a photograph to use as the focus for their writing. Each student has his or her own photograph. Photographs could be of individual students engaged in an activity that they would like to write about (playing soccer at recess, reading, climbing on a jungle gym, eating lunch, getting on the bus, etc.). The photographs need to show action and details, which will allow for more powerful writing.

One key to scaffolding instruction is the inclusion of modeling. **The teacher should have his or her own photograph and ongoing piece of writing that are used for modeling in each lesson.** This permits the students to see the skill being used, creates a better understanding of what is expected, and allows for more effective application of the skill.

Types of Words (pp. 413–415)
These three pages give examples of action words, naming words, and describing words. They are a resource that can be made into overhead transparencies or enlarged and used as posters.

Six Trait Questions (p. 416)
This page is a teacher resource listing the six traits and questions for each trait to help students focus as they are writing.

Six Trait Question Strips (pp. 417–422)
Each trait and two easy-to-understand questions that reinforce the trait have been made into question strips that can be used for classroom wall displays, overhead transparencies, and/or individually held up next to the teacher's enlarged writing text. During this shared writing time, the students can focus their attention on the teacher as she or he writes, answers the questions, and makes additions to the text. The individual question strips allow the teacher to scaffold the instruction by concentrating on one or two traits at a time. Students will soon understand that answering "yes" to the questions given for each trait will not only strengthen the writer's skill, but will also increase the reader's engagement as he or she reads the piece.

Balanced Literacy • Kindergarten • Skidmore & Graber
Kagan Publishing • 1 (800) 933-2667 • www.KaganOnline.com

Action Words
Types of Words

Action words are words telling what someone or something is doing.

push

run

hit

read

hop

buzz

pull

nap

skate

Naming Words
Types of Words

Naming words are words given to people, things, animals, or places.

house	girl	sun
umbrella	friends	butterfly
books	playground	

Describing Words
Types of Words

Describing words are words telling something about the naming word.

size (tall, short)

color (gray)

shape (round)

texture-feel (prickly)

number (three)

Six Trait Questions
Teacher Resources

Trait	Question
Ideas	• Do I like my topic? • Does my writing make sense when I read it?
Organization	• Did I use a hook at the beginning? • Does my writing have a good ending?
Voice	• Does my writing tell the reader how I feel? • Did I use some sentences that can be read with expression?
Word Choice	• Did I use strong action words? • Did I use describing words?
Sentence Fluency	• Is my paper easy to read? • Do my sentences start with different words?
Conventions	• Does each sentence begin with a capital? • Does each sentence end with punctuation?

Six Trait Question Strips

Ideas

Adapted from Six Trait Writing Model: NWREL (Northwest Regional Educational Lab)

Ideas

Do I like my topic?

Ideas

Does my writing make sense when I read it?

Six Trait Question Strips
Organization

Adapted from Six Trait Writing Model: NWREL (Northwest Regional Educational Lab)

Organization

Did I use a hook at the beginning?

Organization

Does my writing have a good ending?

Six Trait Question Strips
Voice

Adapted from Six Trait Writing Model: NWREL (Northwest Regional Educational Lab)

Voice

Does my writing tell the reader how I feel?

Voice

Did I use some sentences that can be read with expression?

Six Trait Question Strips
Word Choice

Adapted from Six Trait Writing Model: NWREL (Northwest Regional Educational Lab)

Word Choice

Did I use strong action words?

Word Choice

Did I use describing words?

☐ color ☐ size ☐ shape

☐ texture ☐ number

Balanced Literacy • Kindergarten • Skidmore & Graber
Kagan Publishing • 1 (800) 933-2667 • www.KaganOnline.com

Six Trait Question Strips
Sentence Fluency

Adapted from Six Trait Writing Model: NWREL (Northwest Regional Educational Lab)

Sentence Fluency

Is my paper easy to read?

Sentence Fluency

Do my sentences start with different words?

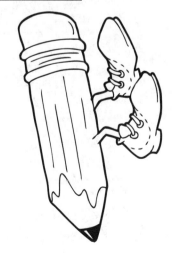

Six Trait Question Strips
Conventions

Adapted from Six Trait Writing Model: NWREL (Northwest Regional Educational Lab)

Conventions

Does each sentence begin with a capital?

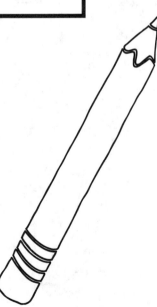

Conventions

Does each sentence end with punctuation?

Writing
Activities

Writing Activities

Shared writing is a powerful instructional component of balanced literacy. The following lessons are guides for the teacher to use to introduce the skill. Shared writing lets the students observe the skill being implemented into authentic writing. With this understanding and the practice opportunities provided in the lessons, students will be better equipped to integrate the skills into their own writing.

Page(s)	Six Traits	Structures	Activities	Resources
426–428	Ideas			
428		Timed Pair Share	Ideas Emotion Words	
429–452	Word Choice			
430		RallyRobin	Creating Description Chart • Day 1 • Day 2	
431–432		RallyRobin and Timed Pair Share	Writing Descriptions	
433–435		StandUp–HandUp–PairUp, Timed Pair Share, and RallyCoach	Listing and Writing Action Words in Sentences	• Six Trait Question Strips • Shared Writing Example
436–449		RallyCoach	Word Sort (Action, Naming, Describing Words)	• Sorting Mat • Picture/Word Cards
450–452		RallyCoach	Adding Describing Words	• Naming and Action Phrase Cards

Writing Activities

(continued)

Page(s)	Six Traits	Structures	Activities	Resources
453–487	Conventions			
454–468		Simultaneous RallyTable and CenterPiece	Letter Writing	• Conventions Cards • Conventions Cards Blank Form
469–475		RallyCoach	• Capital Letters • Capitalization and Punctuation	• Conventions Worksheet • Conventions Strips • Blank Form
476–479		Showdown	Ending Punctuation	• Ending Punctuation Strips
480–487		Quiz-Quiz-Trade	Capitalization and Punctuation	• Conventions Cards

Ideas

- Do I like my topic?

- Does my writing make sense when I read it?

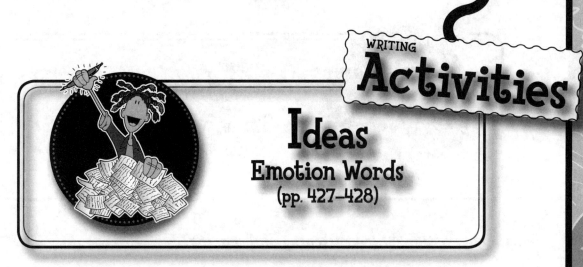

Ideas
Emotion Words
(pp. 427–428)

Students generate a list of writing possibilities for future reference.

Setup

- *Poster labeled with magazine cutout pictures of facial expressions or photographs of students depicting each emotion*

A class discussion is held about situations for each emotion. The teacher writes a few example statements under each emotion. The students can use this class chart to help them choose ideas to write about when they are stuck. Another option is to have each student create an individual chart for his or her own use.

happy	sad	surprised	angry	puzzled
-a new puppy	-fell at recess	-birthday party	-stolen bike	-wrapped present
-spend a night at a friend's house	-toy broke	-new pet	-name calling	-lost backpack
	-no TV			

Ideas
Emotion Words
(pp. 427-428)

Partners take timed turns listening and sharing.

Students generate a list of writing possibilities for future reference. A class discussion is held about situations for each emotion.

Setup

- *Poster labeled with magazine cutout pictures of facial expressions or photographs of students depicting each emotion*
- *Writing paper*

STRUCTURE
Timed Pair Share

Activity Steps

1. Teacher identifies an emotion from the chart and states how long each student will have to share about his or her personal experience.

2. Teacher provides think time.

3. In pairs, Partner A shares; Partner B listens.

4. Partner B responds.

5. Partners switch roles.

   * *Students return to their seats to write.*

Variations

- *The teacher may repeat Steps 3 through 5 to allow students to generate more than one idea for the chosen emotion. Students will then choose one of the situations to write about.*
- *After going through all the emotions, the teacher may choose two different emotions for Timed Pair Share allowing more writing choices for students.*
- *As the year progresses, the teacher may add additional emotions to the chart.*

Word Choice

- Did I use strong action words?

- Did I use describing words?

  ☐ color   ☐ size   ☐ shape

  ☐ texture   ☐ number

Word Choice
Creating Description Chart
(p. 430)

In pairs, students alternate generating oral responses.

The teacher and students create a Description Chart to be used as a classroom reference to reinforce word choice.

Activity Steps: Day 1

1. Teacher holds up and passes around an object.

2. In pairs, students take turns orally listing describing words for the object.

• *The teacher makes a list on chart paper as the class orally shares words.*

3. Repeat Steps 1 and 2 for several more objects.

Activity Steps: Day 2

1. Prior to this lesson, the teacher writes each word from the list on a separate card.

2. Display all word cards (tape to chalkboard).

3. Students help group words.

4. Generate headings for categories.

5. Explain that these words are describing words. The purpose of describing words is to create a picture in the mind of the reader.

6. The chart is displayed in the room as a writing reference.

STRUCTURE
RallyRobin

Setup: Day 1

• *Two or three objects*
• *Chart paper*

Setup: Day 2

• *Blank word cards or index cards*
• *Chart paper*

size	color	shape	texture (feels like)	number
big short	blue green	round flat	smooth fluffy	four ten
_____	_____	_____	_____	_____

Word Choice
Writing Descriptions
(pp. 431–432)

In pairs, students alternate generating oral responses.

Students generate describing words for a stuffed animal.

Setup

- **One stuffed animal**
- **Chart paper**

STRUCTURE
RallyRobin

Activity Steps

- *Teacher uses a stuffed animal (zebra) for her modeled writing.*

1 Students turn to their partner and orally take turns listing describing words about the animal.

- *The teacher writes a few sentences about the animal with minimal description.*

> The zebra has eyes.
> It has stripes.
> It has a tail.

- *The teacher has students follow along as she reads aloud sentences. She then asks them to close their eyes and think about the picture formed in their minds as she reads the sentences again.*

Word Choice
Writing Descriptions
(pp. 431–432)

Partners take timed turns listening and sharing.

Students generate describing words to add to sentences.

Activity Steps

1. Teacher asks students to find one or two places to add a describing word in the zebra sentences and states how long each student will have to share. *(Refer to the description chart made on Day 2 of the previous word choice activity for examples of describing words, if needed.)*

2. Teacher provides think time.

3. In pairs Partner A shares; Partner B listens.

4. Partner B responds.

5. Partners switch roles.

• *The teacher adds describing words to the sentences.*

> The zebra has **two round** eyes.
> It has **black** and **white** stripes.
> It has a **long** tail.

• *The teacher reads aloud the sentences.*

• *The teacher has the students close their eyes as she rereads.*

• *Students discuss how a description created a more detailed picture in their minds.*

* *Repeat the activity with each team having a different animal.*

STRUCTURE
Timed
Pair Share

Word Choice
Listing Action Words
(pp. 433-435)

Students stand up, put their hands up, and quickly find a partner.

Action words reinforce descriptive writing, as well as keep the reader actively involved.

STRUCTURE
StandUp-HandUp-PairUp

Setup

- *The teacher takes a digital photograph of each student doing something (going down a slide, jumping rope, reading, talking to a friend, etc.) or has each child bring a home photo with him or her in it.*
- *This photograph will be used for the lessons on page 433–435.*

Activity Steps

- *Teacher models generating action words by showing his or her photograph and orally listing action words (pushing, holding, sitting).*

1. Teacher says, "Stand up, hand up, pair up!" Students take their individual photographs with them.

2. Students stand up and keep one hand in the air until they find the closest partner who's not a teammate.

3. Teacher states that students will be sharing action words about their individual photographs.

4. Teacher provides think time.

5. Partners share using **Timed Pair Share**.

Activity Steps

STRUCTURE
Timed Pair Share

1. Teacher states how long partners have to share.

2. In Pairs, Partner A shares; Partner B listens.

3. Partner B responds.

4. Partners switch roles.

Word Choice
Listing Action Words
(pp. 433-435)

Partners take turns reading their writing and coaching.

Action words reinforce descriptive writing, as well as keep the reader actively involved.

Setup

- *Chart paper with photograph attached for modeling*
- *Six Trait Question Strip for Word Choice (Did I use strong action words?)*
- *Individual student photographs attached to writing paper*

Activity Steps

- *Teacher models several complete thoughts about the actions she sees in her photograph and uses the Six Trait Question Strips for Word Choice (Did I use strong action words?) to model checking and revising writing. The teacher rereads the sentences. Using class consensus, the action words are identified and underlined on the chart example. (See the Shared Writing Example on the following page.)*

- *The students write several complete thoughts about the action that is taking place in their photographs.*

1. Partner A reads his or her writing underlining the action words.

2. Partner B watches, listens, checks for action words, and praises.

3. Partner B reads his or her writing underlining the action words.

4. Partner A watches, listens, checks for action words, and praises.

STRUCTURE
RallyCoach

Blacklines

Shared Writing Example
Word Choice–Action
RallyCoach

The boy is <u>sitting</u> in his pool.

He is in the water. He is <u>splashing</u> the water.

His hair is all <u>wet</u>.

He is <u>smiling</u>.

Word Choice
Word Sort
(pp. 436-449)

Partners take turns, one sorting a picture/word card while the other checks, coaches, and praises.

Setup

- *Picture/word cards for each pair*
- *Sorting mat for each pair*

STRUCTURE
RallyCoach

Activity Steps

1. Partner A puts the picture/word card in the correct column on the sorting mat.

2. Partner B watches and listens, checks, and praises.

3. Partner B puts the picture/word card in the correct column on the sorting mat.

4. Partner A watches and listens, checks, and praises.

5. Repeat starting at Step 1.

Blacklines

Word Choice Sorting Mat

Action, Naming, Describing Words

RallyCoach

Action	Naming	Describing

Word Choice Picture Cards

Action, Naming, and Describing Words
RallyCoach

kick	swing	sled	hide
eat	blow	slide	cry
push	run	drink	throw
jump	dig	sweep	wash

 Balanced Literacy • Kindergarten • Skidmore & Graber
Kagan Publishing • 1 (800) 933-2667 • www.KaganOnline.com

Word Choice Picture Cards
Action, Naming, and Describing Words
RallyCoach

cut	fall	crawl	paint
sew	carry	watch	build
fight	sit	talk	swim
fish	pull	dive	break

Balanced Literacy • Kindergarten • Skidmore & Graber
Kagan Publishing • 1 (800) 933-2667 • www.KaganOnline.com 439

Word Choice Picture Cards

Action, Naming, and Describing Words
RallyCoach

 # Word Choice Picture Cards
Action, Naming, and Describing Words
RallyCoach

sleep	cook	read	snore
write	dance	laugh	bounce
draw	roll	listen	play
skip	spin	flip	scratch

Word Choice Picture Cards

Action, Naming, and Describing Words
RallyCoach

man	lady	table	telephone
pan	tree	ladder	web
store	playground	blocks	shirt
ring	keys	button	chair

Word Choice Picture Cards
Action, Naming, and Describing Words
RallyCoach

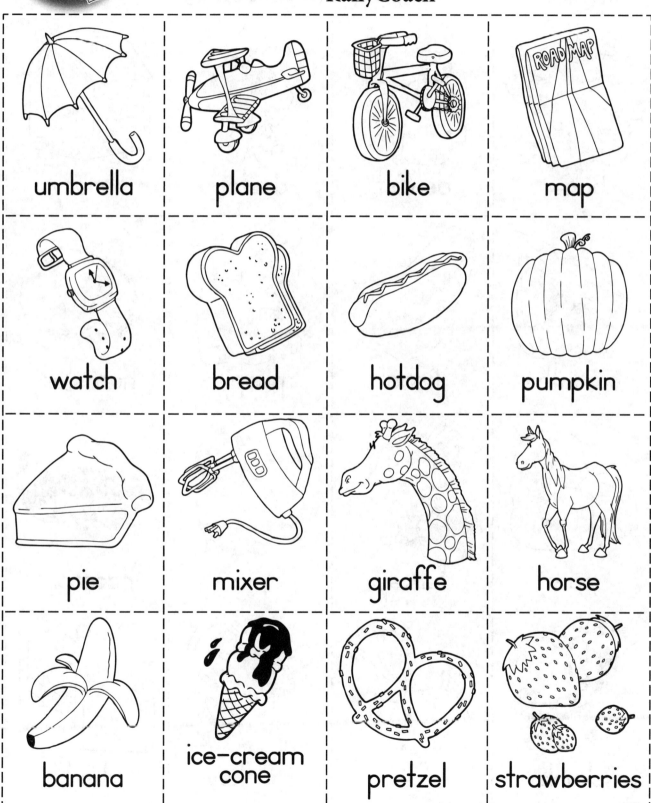

umbrella	plane	bike	map
watch	bread	hotdog	pumpkin
pie	mixer	giraffe	horse
banana	ice-cream cone	pretzel	strawberries

Word Choice Picture Cards
Action, Naming, and Describing Words
RallyCoach

baker	dentist	doctor	library
mouth	hand	puppy	hamster
paw	turkey	pig	raccoon
skunk	fish	monkey	bed

 Balanced Literacy • Kindergarten • Skidmore & Graber
Kagan Publishing • 1 (800) 933-2667 • www.KaganOnline.com

Word Choice Picture Cards

Action, Naming, and Describing Words
RallyCoach

zebra	school	city	bus
flowers	wagon	bottle	letter
box	window	flag	shoe
ship	shell	snowflake	baby

Word Choice Picture Cards
Action, Naming, and Describing Words
RallyCoach

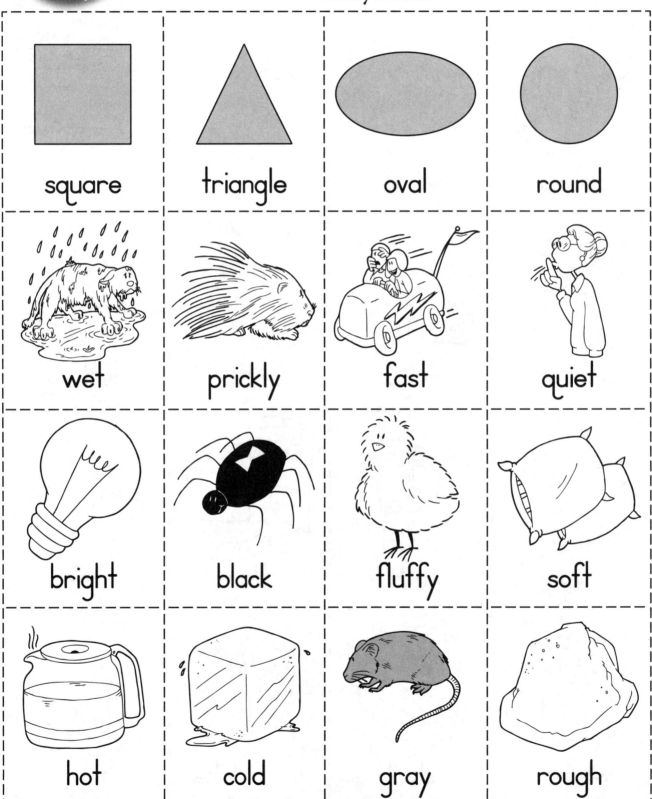

square	triangle	oval	round
wet	prickly	fast	quiet
bright	black	fluffy	soft
hot	cold	gray	rough

Balanced Literacy • Kindergarten • Skidmore & Graber
Kagan Publishing • 1 (800) 933-2667 • www.KaganOnline.com

Word Choice Picture Cards
Action, Naming, and Describing Words
RallyCoach

surprised	hard	huge	bumpy
sad	angry	happy	sunny
rainy	smoky	old	windy
shiny	spiny	dry	noisy

Word Choice Picture Cards
Action, Naming, and Describing Words
RallyCoach

new	striped	spotted	itchy
curvy	friendly	sweet	salty
sour	checked	loud	straight
little	excited	smelly	tall

Balanced Literacy • Kindergarten • Skidmore & Graber
Kagan Publishing • 1 (800) 933-2667 • www.KaganOnline.com

Word Choice Picture Cards
Action, Naming, and Describing Words
RallyCoach

white	many	five	spicy
one	two	strong	kind
many	chilly	warm	dark
cloudy	stormy	fuzzy	funny

Word Choice
Adding Describing Words
(pp. 450–452)

Partners take turns reading their writing and coaching.

Action words reinforce descriptive writing, as well as keep the reader actively involved.

Setup

• *One set of naming phrase cards and one set of action phrase cards per pair* (each set copied on a different color of paper and stacked upside down on two piles)

Activity Steps

1. Partner A takes one phrase card from each stack and reads the sentence they make when put together.

2. Partner A adds a describing word to the sentence and rereads it.

3. Partner B watches and listens, checks, and praises.

4. Partner B takes one phrase card from each stack and reads the sentence they make when put together.

5. Partner B adds a describing word to the sentence and rereads it.

6. Partner A watches and listens, checks, and praises.

7. Repeat starting at Step 1.

8. Individuals may return to their writing project and add several describing words.

Option: Partners may add two describing words to each sentence.

STRUCTURE
RallyCoach

Blacklines

Word Choice Cards
Adding Describing Words
RallyCoach

The cat

A pig

A hen

The fox

The dog

A man

A frog

The rat

Word Choice Picture Cards
Action, Naming, and Describing Words
RallyCoach

can run

can sit

can see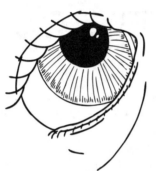

can look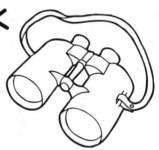

can go

walks

likes me

calls

 Balanced Literacy • Kindergarten • Skidmore & Graber
Kagan Publishing • 1 (800) 933-2667 • www.KaganOnline.com

Conventions

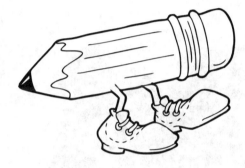

- Does each sentence begin with a capital?

- Does each sentence end with punctuation?

Conventions
Letter Writing
(pp. 454–468)

In pairs, students alternate generating written responses or solving problems.

Setup

- *Two letter writing strips per pair (any combination of strips may be chosen from the following pages)*
- *A different colored pencil for each student*

STRUCTURE
Simultaneous RallyTable

Activity Steps

1. Teacher assigns the letter writing strips to be used from the following pages.

2. In pairs, students each have a strip. Each writes one letter at the same time. Pairs then trade at the same time.

3. Continue writing and trading strips until time is called.

Blacklines

Conventions
Letter Writing
(pp. 454–468)

Students add one letter at a time to the list, always trading their paper with the centerpiece.

- *Five letter writing strips per teams of four, one per person and one in the center (any combination of letter writing strips may be used from the following pages)*
- *A different colored pencil for each student*

STRUCTURE
CenterPiece

Activity Steps

1. Teacher assigns the letter writing strips to be used from the following pages.

2. Students practice writing one letter at a time on the strips. They say the letter, write it, and trade their paper with the one in the center. Students continue practicing writing letters, each time trading their paper with the centerpiece.

Blacklines

Conventions Cards
Letter Writing (curved line letters)
Simultaneous RallyTable or CenterPiece

a

b

Balanced Literacy • Kindergarten • Skidmore & Graber
Kagan Publishing • 1 (800) 933-2667 • www.KaganOnline.com

Conventions Cards
Letter Writing (curved line letters)
Simultaneous RallyTable or CenterPiece

d

c

Conventions Cards

Letter Writing (curved line letters)
Simultaneous RallyTable or CenterPiece

e

o

Conventions Cards

Letter Writing (stick/curved letters)

Simultaneous RallyTable or CenterPiece

u

f

Conventions Cards

Letter Writing (stick/curved letters)
Simultaneous RallyTable or CenterPiece

h

r

Conventions Cards

Letter Writing (stick/curved letters)
Simultaneous RallyTable or CenterPiece

m

n

Conventions Cards
Letter Writing (straight line letters)
Simultaneous RallyTable or CenterPiece

I

k

Conventions Cards

Letter Writing (straight line letters)
Simultaneous RallyTable or CenterPiece

V

W

Conventions Cards
Letter Writing (straight line letters)
Simultaneous RallyTable or CenterPiece

X

Z

Conventions Cards
Letter Writing (tail letters)
Simultaneous RallyTable or CenterPiece

j

p

Conventions Cards
Letter Writing (tail letters)
Simultaneous RallyTable or CenterPiece

g

q

Conventions Cards
Letter Writing (tail letters)
Simultaneous RallyTable or CenterPiece

y

Conventions Cards

Blank Letter Writing Form
Simultaneous RallyTable or CenterPiece

 Balanced Literacy • Kindergarten • Skidmore & Graber
Kagan Publishing • 1 (800) 933-2667 • www.KaganOnline.com

Conventions
Capital Letters
(pp. 469–475)

Partners take turns, one solving a problem while the other coaches.

Setup

- *One letter worksheet per pair (Boxes may be cut down the middle before activity to help students focus on fewer letters at a time.)*

  or

- *Set of cut apart sentence strips per pair*
- *One pencil per pair*

STRUCTURE

RallyCoach

Activity Steps

1. Partner A says the letter name of the letters in Box 1 and circles the capital letter (or reads the sentence on the first sentence strip) and makes one capitalization or punctuation correction telling why the correction was made.

2. Partner B watches and listens, checks, and praises.

3. Partner B says the letter name of the letters in Box 2 and circles the capital letter (or rereads the previous sentence) and makes another capitalization or punctuation correction telling why the correction was made.

4. Partner A watches and listens, checks, and praises.

5. Repeat starting at Step 1. (For the Capitalization and Punctuation Sentence Strip activity, a new sentence strip is chosen.)

Blacklines

Conventions Cards
Capital Letters
RallyCoach

Instructions: The worksheet may be cut down the middle before the activity to help students focus on fewer letters at a time.

1.	v	V	14.	p	P
2.	H	h	15.	F	f
3.	A	a	16.	u	U
4.	b	B	17.	G	g
5.	n	N	18.	c	C
6.	L	l	19.	t	T
7.	J	j	20.	M	m
8.	e	E	21.	W	w
9.	Q	q	22.	s	S
10.	i	I	23.	O	o
11.	D	d	24.	x	X
12.	R	r	25.	K	k
13.	z	Z	26.	Y	y

 Balanced Literacy • Kindergarten • Skidmore & Graber
Kagan Publishing • 1 (800) 933-2667 • www.KaganOnline.com

Capitalization and Punctuation Set #1

RallyCoach

Instructions: Make a copy for each pair of students. Cut sentence strips apart.

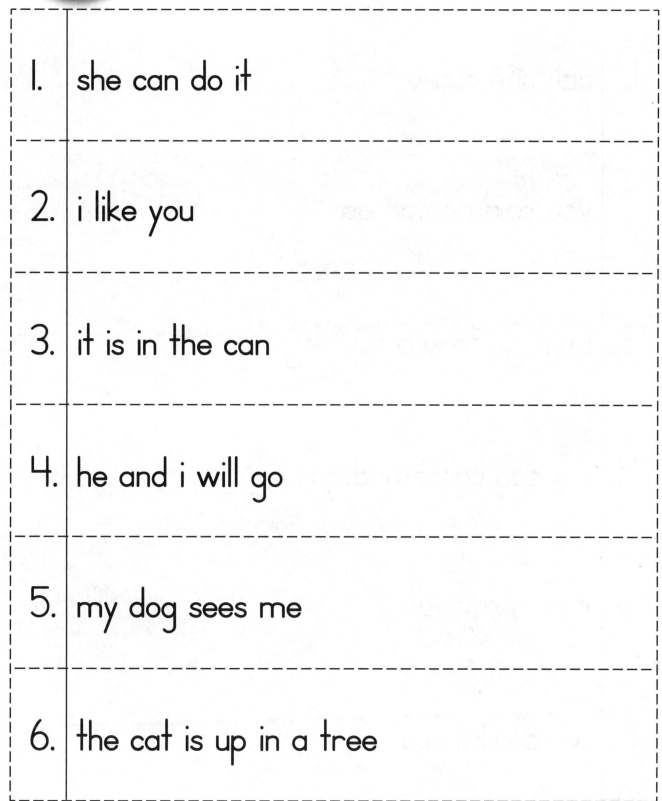

1. she can do it

2. i like you

3. it is in the can

4. he and i will go

5. my dog sees me

6. the cat is up in a tree

Capitalization and Punctuation
Set #2

RallyCoach

Instructions: Make a copy for each pair of students. Cut sentence strips apart.

1. | can she come

2. | you said he can go

3. | i will go to see my dog

4. | we can come and go

5. | it is in my van

6. | we do like you

 Balanced Literacy • Kindergarten • Skidmore & Graber
Kagan Publishing • 1 (800) 933-2667 • www.KaganOnline.com

Capitalization and Punctuation
Set #3

RallyCoach

Instructions: Make a copy for each pair of students. Cut sentence strips apart.

1. caN I go with you.

2. i liKe my Fish

3. i will go with moM and dad

4. can you siT with me?

5. I like red And Blue

6. I can Hop Up

Capitalization and Punctuation
Set #4

RallyCoach

Instructions: Make a copy for each pair of students. Cut sentence strips apart.

1. | look At Me

2. | i have a pet Dog

3. | You And i can sing

4. | The suN is hot

5. | my Dog is aT the vet.

6. | Frogs caN Jump

Blank Capitalization and Punctuation

RallyCoach

WRITING Blackline

Instructions: Teacher generates sentences. Make a copy for each pair of students. Cut sentence strips apart.

Conventions
Ending Punctuation
(pp. 476–479)

Teams play Showdown to practice correct ending punctuation.

The teacher is the Showdown Captain, rather than rotating the responsibility among the team.

Activity Steps

STRUCTURE
Showdown

1. The teacher is the Showdown Captain and makes one overhead transparency in place of Team cards. Every student receives a Student Set of cards.

2. One sentence strip is placed on the overhead at a time. Students hold their Student Set in their hands.

3. The teacher is the Showdown Captain for each round.

4. The Showdown Captain (teacher) places a sentence strip on the overhead and reads it aloud.

5. Working alone, students individually identify an answer (ending punctuation) from their card set."

6. When finished, students signal they are ready.

7. The Showdown Captain (teacher) calls, "Showdown!"

8. Students show their answers at the same time.

9. The Showdown Captain (teacher) leads checking.

10. If correct, the class celebrates. If not, the teacher or classmates coach, then celebrate.

11. The teacher continues as Showdown Captain for the next round.

Blacklines

Ending Punctuation (. ?) Set #1
Showdown (Teacher Set)

Instructions: Make a transparency for the teacher, who is Showdown Captain.

1. We went to the ballgame ☐

2. Do you have a pet snake ☐

3. Can you come over to my house ☐

4. I read a book at the library ☐

5. We have 20 kids in our class ☐

6. May I have a hot dog for lunch ☐

7. I love to eat pizza ☐

Ending Punctuation (. ?) Set #2

Showdown (Teacher Set)

Instructions: Make a transparency for the teacher, who is Showdown Captain.

1.	Mom made me a birthday cake ☐
2.	What will we do after school ☐
3.	We went to the store for milk ☐
4.	Will it rain today ☐
5.	It is time to go to bed ☐
6.	What is Dad cooking ☐
7.	He will walk to the park ☐

 Balanced Literacy • Kindergarten • Skidmore & Graber
Kagan Publishing • 1 (800) 933-2667 • www.KaganOnline.com

Ending Punctuation (. ?)
Showdown (Student Set)

Instructions: Copy and cut out a set of cards for each student. **Note:** There are cards for four students on the page.

Ending Punctuation (. ?) Student Set	Ending Punctuation (. ?) Student Set	Ending Punctuation (. ?) Student Set	Ending Punctuation (. ?) Student Set
.	?	.	?

Ending Punctuation (. ?) Student Set	Ending Punctuation (. ?) Student Set	Ending Punctuation (. ?) Student Set	Ending Punctuation (. ?) Student Set
.	?	.	?

Conventions
Capitalization and Punctuation
(pp. 480–487)

Students quiz a partner, get quizzed by a partner, and then trade cards to repeat the process with a new partner.

Setup

• *Card for each student (with a question on the front and the answer on the back)*

STRUCTURE
Quiz-Quiz-Trade

Activity Steps

1. Stand Up–Hand Up–Pair Up.
2. Partner A quizzes.
3. Partner B answers.
4. Partner A praises or coaches.
5. Switch roles.
6. Partners trade cards.
7. Repeat Steps 1–6 a number of times.

Question (Front)

Capitalization and Punctuation
Question: Is this sentence written correctly?
Yes or No

The frog is green

Answer (Back)

Capitalization and Punctuation
Answer:
Yes
The frog is green.

Blacklines

Capitalization and Punctuation
Quiz-Quiz-Trade

Instructions: Copy enough cards so each student has one card. Cut on dotted lines and fold in half. Students take turns sharing if the sentence is written correctly or not. They explain why or why not.

Capitalization and Punctuation

Question: Is this sentence written correctly?

Yes or No

Can you do it?

Capitalization and Punctuation

Answer:

Yes
Can you do it?

Capitalization and Punctuation

Question: Is this sentence written correctly?

Yes or No

i like you.

Capitalization and Punctuation

Answer:

No
i like you.

Capitalization and Punctuation

Question: Is this sentence written correctly?

Yes or No

My mom is at home

Capitalization and Punctuation

Answer:

No
My mom is at home_

Capitalization and Punctuation

Question: Is this sentence written correctly?

Yes or No

I see a red bird.

Capitalization and Punctuation

Answer:

Yes
I see a red bird.

Capitalization and Punctuation
Quiz-Quiz-Trade

Instructions: Copy enough cards so each student has one card. Cut on dotted lines and fold in half. Students take turns sharing if the sentence is written correctly or not. They explain why or why not.

Capitalization and Punctuation

Question: Is this sentence written correctly?

Yes or No

he is not mad.

Capitalization and Punctuation

Answer:

No

he is not mad.

Capitalization and Punctuation

Question: Is this sentence written correctly?

Yes or No

do you see me?

Capitalization and Punctuation

Answer:

No

do you see me?

Capitalization and Punctuation

Question: Is this sentence written correctly?

Yes or No

We can go

Capitalization and Punctuation

Answer:

No

We can go_

Capitalization and Punctuation

Question: Is this sentence written correctly?

Yes or No

the cat ran up the tree.

Capitalization and Punctuation

Answer:

No

the cat ran up the tree.

Capitalization and Punctuation

Quiz-Quiz-Trade

Instructions: Copy enough cards so each student has one card. Cut on dotted lines and fold in half. Students take turns sharing if the sentence is written correctly or not. They explain why or why not.

Capitalization and Punctuation	Capitalization and Punctuation
Question: Is this sentence written correctly? Yes or No She can go too	Answer: No She can go too_
Question: Is this sentence written correctly? Yes or No He sat on the bug	Answer: No He sat on the bug_
Question: Is this sentence written correctly? Yes or No i like dogs.	Answer: No i like dogs.
Question: Is this sentence written correctly? Yes or No can we play ball?	Answer: No can we play ball?

Capitalization and Punctuation
Quiz-Quiz-Trade

Instructions: Copy enough cards so each student has one card. Cut on dotted lines and fold in half. Students take turns sharing if the sentence is written correctly or not. They explain why or why not.

Capitalization and Punctuation Question: Is this sentence written correctly? Yes or No The frog is green.	**Capitalization and Punctuation** Answer: Yes The frog is green.
Capitalization and Punctuation Question: Is this sentence written correctly? Yes or No my hat is on the rug.	**Capitalization and Punctuation** Answer: No my hat is on the rug.
Capitalization and Punctuation Question: Is this sentence written correctly? Yes or No He likes to run fast	**Capitalization and Punctuation** Answer: No He likes to run fast_
Capitalization and Punctuation Question: Is this sentence written correctly? Yes or No Can you run fast?	**Capitalization and Punctuation** Answer: Yes Can you run fast?

Capitalization and Punctuation
Quiz-Quiz-Trade

Instructions: Copy enough cards so each student has one card. Cut on dotted lines and fold in half. Students take turns sharing if the sentence is written correctly or not. They explain why or why not.

Capitalization and Punctuation

Question: Is this sentence written correctly?
Yes or No

I like to play in the sand

Capitalization and Punctuation

Answer:

No

I like to play in the sand_

Capitalization and Punctuation

Question: Is this sentence written correctly?
Yes or No

The sun is hot.

Capitalization and Punctuation

Answer:

Yes

The sun is hot.

Capitalization and Punctuation

Question: Is this sentence written correctly?
Yes or No

We have a black van

Capitalization and Punctuation

Answer:

No

We have a black van_

Capitalization and Punctuation

Question: Is this sentence written correctly?
Yes or No

My cat sleeps on my lap.

Capitalization and Punctuation

Answer:

Yes

_My cat sleeps on my lap.

Capitalization and Punctuation
Quiz-Quiz-Trade

Instructions: Copy enough cards so each student has one card. Cut on dotted lines and fold in half. Students take turns sharing if the sentence is written correctly or not. They explain why or why not.

Capitalization and Punctuation

Question: Is this sentence written correctly?

Yes or No

i will not go with you.

Capitalization and Punctuation

Answer:

No

i will not go with you.

Capitalization and Punctuation

Question: Is this sentence written correctly?

Yes or No

I am up here.

Capitalization and Punctuation

Answer:

Yes

I am up here.

Capitalization and Punctuation

Question: Is this sentence written correctly?

Yes or No

Do you like gum?

Capitalization and Punctuation

Answer:

Yes

Do you like gum?

Capitalization and Punctuation

Question: Is this sentence written correctly?

Yes or No

the frog will jump
in the pond.

Capitalization and Punctuation

Answer:

No

the frog will jump
in the pond.

Capitalization and Punctuation

Quiz-Quiz-Trade

Instructions: Copy enough cards so each student has one card. Cut on dotted lines and fold in half. Students take turns sharing if the sentence is written correctly or not. They explain why or why not.

Capitalization and Punctuation

Question: Is this sentence written correctly?

Yes or No

We ran up the hill

Capitalization and Punctuation

Answer:

No

We ran up the hill_

Capitalization and Punctuation

Question: Is this sentence written correctly?

Yes or No

It is a hot day.

Capitalization and Punctuation

Answer:

Yes

<u>It</u> is a hot day<u>.</u>

Capitalization and Punctuation

Question: Is this sentence written correctly?

Yes or No

is this red?

Capitalization and Punctuation

Answer:

No

<u>is</u> this red?

Capitalization and Punctuation

Question: Is this sentence written correctly?

Yes or No

i am going to bed.

Capitalization and Punctuation

Answer:

No

<u>i</u> am going to bed.

Index of Structures for Balanced Literacy

Structure

CenterPiece

Students brainstorm ideas, always trading their paper with the centerpiece.

Setup

• *Five pieces of paper per teams of four, one per person and one in the center*

Steps

1 Teacher assigns a brainstorming topic.

2 Students generate items. They write one idea at a time and trade their paper with the one in the center.

3 Students continue brainstorming items, each time trading their paper with the centerpiece.

CenterPiece Activities and Blacklines

Find My Rule

Students induce a rule from examples provided by the teacher.

Steps

1. Teacher places one item in each area of the category frame.

2. Teacher asks, "What is my rule for placing items?" and provides think time.

3. Students RallyRobin with their shoulder partners to generate possible rules the teacher is using.

4. Teacher places two more objects in the category frame.

5. Teacher again says, "What is my rule?" and provides think time.

6. Students RallyRobin with their face partners to generate possible rules.

7. Teacher places more objects in the category frame, each time having teams discuss possible rules.

8. Teacher says, "Don't tell me your rule. Name an item that fits in each category," and calls a number. Students with that number stand to share their items. The teacher confirms correct answers.

9. When most students seem to know the rule, the teacher calls on one student to verbalize the rule for the class.

10. Teacher confirms the rule.

11. Teacher presents new items one at a time, each time calling for students to hold up fingers indicating the category for the item.

12. Teacher congratulates the class.

Find My Rule Activities and Blacklines

Find Someone Who

Students circulate through the classroom, forming and reforming pairs, trying to "find someone who" knows an answer, then they become "someone who knows."

Setup

• *The teacher prepares a worksheet or questions for students.*

Steps

1. Students mix in the class, keeping a hand raised until they find a partner that is not a teammate.

2. In pairs, Partner A asks a question from the worksheet; Partner B responds. Partner A records the answer on his or her own worksheet, and expresses appreciation.

3. Partner B checks and initials the answer.

4. Partner B asks a question. Partner A responds. Partner B records the answer on his or her own worksheet, and expresses appreciation.

5. Partner A checks and initials the answer.

6. Partners shake hands, part, and raise a hand as they search for a new partner.

7. Students repeat Steps 1–6 until their worksheets are complete.

8. When their worksheets are completed, students sit down; seated students may be approached by others as a resource.

9. In teams, students compare answers; if there is disagreement or uncertainty, they raise four hands to ask a team question.

Find Someone Who Activities and Blacklines

Listen-Sketch-Draft

Students sketch content chunk by chunk, create and compare summaries, and finally draft a statement of the main idea.

Steps

1. Students listen while teacher presents the first chunk of information.

2. Teacher stops presenting and calls for each student to sketch the most important details.

3. Students share sketches using:
   • RoundRobin
   • Timed Pair Share

4. Students draft a main idea statement, based on the information shared in Step 1. While students draft their main ideas, teacher circulates and monitors.

5. The process is repeated for the next chunk.

6. When all chunks have been presented, students draft a summary statement.

7. Students compare their summaries with a partner or teammates praising ideas.

Listen-Sketch-Draft Activity and Blacklines

Numbered Heads Together

Teammates put their "heads together" to reach consensus on the team's answer. Everyone keeps on their toes because their number may be called to share the team's answer.

Setup

• Teacher prepares questions or problems to ask teams.

Steps

1. Students number off.

2. Teacher poses a problem and gives think time. (Example: *"How are rainbows are formed? Think about your best answer."*)

3. Students privately write their answers.

4. Students stand up and "put their heads together, showing answers discussing, and teaching each other.

5. Students sit down when everyone knows the answer or has something to share.

6. Teacher calls a number. The student with that number simultaneously using:
   • AnswerBoard Share
   • Chalkboard Responses
   • Choral Practice
   • Response Cards
   • Finger Responses
   • Manipulatives

7. Classmates applaud students who responded.

Numbered Heads Together Activities and Blacklines

Poems for Two Voices

Partners create and present a poem they recite using one voice, the other voice, or both.

Setup

• The teacher prepares a poem with lines labeled A, B, or AB.

Steps

1. The teacher assigns each pair a poem topic.

2. Partners work together to write their poem.

3. Partners label each line of their poem, A, B, or AB, representing who will read each line.

4. Pairs rehearse their poems.

5. Pairs recite their poems to another pair or to the class.

Note: Students may progress through three stages:
1. Teacher provides poem and AB scripting.
2. Teacher provides poem, and students provide AB scripting.
3. Students create or select poem and script it.

Poems for Two Voices Activities and Blacklines

Quiz-Quiz-Trade

Students quiz a partner, get quizzed by a partner, and then trade cards to repeat the process with a new partner.

Setup

- *The teacher prepares a set of question cards for the class, or each student creates a question card.*

Steps

1. The teacher tells students to "*Stand up, put a hand up, and pair up.*"
2. Partner A **quizzes** B.
3. Partner B **answers**.
4. Partner A **praises** or **coaches**.
5. Partners **switch** roles.
6. Partners **trade** cards and thank each other.
7. **Repeat** Steps 1–6 a number of times.

Quiz-Quiz-Trade Activities and Blacklines

(continued on next page)

Quiz-Quiz-Trade (continued)

Students quiz a partner, get quizzed by a partner, and then trade cards to repeat the process with a new partner.

Quiz-Quiz-Trade Activities and Blacklines

Structure

RallyCoach

Partners take turns, one solving a problem while the other coaches.

Setup

- *Each pair needs one set of high-consensus problems and one pencil.*

Steps

Note: RallyCoach may be used with worksheet problems, oral problems provided by the teacher, or manipulatives.

1. Partner A solves the first problem.
2. Partner B watches and listens, checks, coaches if necessary, and praises.
3. Partner B solves the next problem.
4. Partner A watches and listens, checks, coaches if necessary, and praises.
5. Partners repeat steps 1–4, taking turns solving successive problems.

RallyCoach Activities and Blacklines

(continued on next page)

RallyCoach (continued)

Partners take turns, one solving a problem while the other coaches.

RallyCoach Activities and Blacklines

(continued on next page)

Structure

RallyCoach (continued)

Partners take turns, one solving a problem while the other coaches.

RallyCoach Activities and Blacklines

RallyRobin

In pairs, students take turns responding orally.

Steps

1. Teacher poses a problem to which there are multiple possible responses or solutions, and provides think time.

2. Students take turns stating responses or solutions.

Activities Using RoundRobin

Showdown

When the Showdown Captain calls, "Showdown!" teammates all display their own answers. Teammates either celebrate or tutor, and then celebrate.

Setup

• *Teams each have a set of question cards stacked facedown in the center of the table.*

Steps

1. The teacher selects one student on each team to be the Showdown Captain for the first round.

2. The Showdown Captain draws the top card, reads the question, and provides think time.

3. Working alone, all students, including the Showdown Captain, write their answers.

4. When finished, teammates signal they're ready.

5. The Showdown Captain calls, "Showdown."

6. Teammates show and discuss their answers.

7. The Showdown Captain leads the checking.

8. If correct, the team celebrates; if not, teammates tutor, then celebrate.

9. The person to the left of the Showdown Captain becomes the Showdown Captain for the next round.

> *Metacognitive resources are included in the Comprehension Resource Section on pages 10–23.*

Showdown Activities and Blacklines

(*continued on next page*)

Showdown (continued)

When the Showdown Captain calls, "Showdown!" teammates all display their own answers. Teammates either celebrate or tutor, and then celebrate.

Showdown Activities and Blacklines

Simultaneous RallyTable

In pairs, students each record an idea or answer on a separate sheet of paper, then switch papers to record each new idea or answer.

Setup

• One paper and one pencil per student

Steps

1. Teacher assigns either one or two topics, or one or two worksheets per pair.

2. If there are two topics, one student labels a paper with one topic while the other student labels the other paper with the other topic. If there is one topic, each student labels his or her paper with the same topic.

3. Each student records a response on her or his sheet.

4. Students exchange papers to record each new question or idea.
   • For lists, each student adds another item to the list.
   • For worksheets, each does the next problem.
   • For drawings, each adds something to the drawing they receive.

Simultaneous RallyTable Activities and Blacklines

StandUp-HandUp-PairUp

Students stand up, put their hands up, and quickly find a partner with whom to share or discuss.

Steps

1. Teacher says, "When I say go, you will stand up, hand up, and pair up!" Teacher pauses, then says, "Go!"

2. Students stand up and keep one hand high in the air until they find the closest partner who's not a teammate. Students do a "high five" and put their hands down.

3. Teacher may ask a question or give an assignment and provides think time.

4. Partners interact using:
   • RallyRobin
   • Timed Pair Share

   Hint: In some classes, it may be necessary to make sure students pair with the classmate they are closest to rather than running to a friend.

StandUp-Hand-Up-PairUp Activity and Blacklines

Structure

Team Line-Ups

Students line up within their teams.

Setup

• *Teacher may prepare Line-Up cards or manipulatives for each team.*

Steps

1. Teacher gives teammates a problem.
2. Within their teams, teammates line up in order of their answers.

Team Line-Ups Activity and Blacklines

Timed Pair Share

In pairs, students share with a partner for a predetermined time while the partner listens. Then partners switch roles.

Steps

1. The teacher announces a topic, states how long each student will share, and provides think time.

2. In pairs, Partner A shares; Partner B listens.

3. Partner B responds with a positive gambit.

4. Partners switch roles.

Hint: The teacher provides positive response gambits to use in Step 3:

Copycat response gambits
- *"Thanks for sharing!"*
- *"You are interesting to listen to!"*

Complete the sentence gambits
- *"One thing I learned listening to you was…."*
- *"I enjoyed listening to you because…."*
- *"Your most interesting idea was…."*

Timed Pair Share Activity and Blacklines

(continued on next page)

Timed Pair Share (continued)

In pairs, students share with a partner for a predetermined time while the partner listens. Then partners switch roles.

Timed Pair Share Activity and Blacklines

Notes